M000316020

Life
Markets

Founded in 1807, John Wiley & Sons is the oldest independent publishing company in the United States. With offices in North America, Europe, Australia, and Asia, Wiley is globally committed to developing and marketing print and electronic products and services for our customers' professional and personal knowledge and understanding.

The Wiley Finance series contains books written specifically for finance and investment professionals as well as sophisticated individual investors and their financial advisors. Book topics range from portfolio management to e-commerce, risk management, financial engineering, valuation, and financial instrument analysis, as well as much more.

For a list of available titles, visit our Web site at www.WileyFinance.com.

Life Markets

Trading Mortality and Longevity Risk with Life Settlements and Linked Securities

Edited by
VISHAAL B. BHUYAN

WILEY

John Wiley & Sons, Inc.

Copyright © 2009 by Vishaal B. Bhuyan. All rights reserved.

Published by John Wiley & Sons, Inc., Hoboken, New Jersey.
Published simultaneously in Canada.

No part of this publication may be reproduced, stored in a retrieval system, or transmitted in any form or by any means, electronic, mechanical, photocopying, recording, scanning, or otherwise, except as permitted under Section 107 or 108 of the 1976 United States Copyright Act, without either the prior written permission of the Publisher, or authorization through payment of the appropriate per-copy fee to the Copyright Clearance Center, Inc., 222 Rosewood Drive, Danvers, MA 01923, (978) 750-8400, fax (978) 750-4470, or on the web at www.copyright.com. Requests to the Publisher for permission should be addressed to the Permissions Department, John Wiley & Sons, Inc., 111 River Street, Hoboken, NJ 07030, (201) 748-6011, fax (201) 748-6008, or online at http://www.wiley.com/go/permissions.

Limit of Liability/Disclaimer of Warranty: While the publisher and author have used their best efforts in preparing this book, they make no representations or warranties with respect to the accuracy or completeness of the contents of this book and specifically disclaim any implied warranties of merchantability or fitness for a particular purpose. No warranty may be created or extended by sales representatives or written sales materials. The advice and strategies contained herein may not be suitable for your situation. You should consult with a professional where appropriate. Neither the publisher nor author shall be liable for any loss of profit or any other commercial damages, including but not limited to special, incidental, consequential, or other damages.

For general information on our other products and services or for technical support, please contact our Customer Care Department within the United States at (800) 762-2974, outside the United States at (317) 572-3993 or fax (317) 572-4002.

Wiley also publishes its books in a variety of electronic formats. Some content that appears in print may not be available in electronic books. For more information about Wiley products, visit our web site at www.wiley.com.

Library of Congress Cataloging-in-Publication Data:

Bhuyan, Vishaal B., 1983–
   Life markets : trading mortality and longevity risk with life settlements and linked securities / Vishaal B. Bhuyan.
        p. cm. – (Wiley finance series)
   Includes index.
   ISBN 978-0-470-41234-3 (cloth)
   1. Viatical settlements.   2. Life insurance.   I. Title.
   HG8819.B48 2009
   368.32–dc22

                                                            2009007402

Printed in the United States of America

10   9   8   7   6   5   4   3   2   1

To my family, especially my parents
"There are no rules in life, only consequences."
— Prashant B. Bhuyan

"Life insurance has become in our days one of the best recognized forms of investment and self-compelled savings."
Supreme Court Justice Oliver Wendell Homes in his 1911 opinion of the *Grigsby v. Russell* case

Contents

List of Contributors

Vishaal B. Bhuyan
Managing Partner
V.B. Bhuyan & Co.

Professor David Blake
Director
The Pension Institute
Desk Research by David Blake is
sponsored by Goldman Sachs,
Deutsche Bank, Royal Bank of
Scotland, and EFG International
Professor
Cass Business School
City University of London

Micah W. Bloomfield
Partner
Stroock & Stroock & Lavan

Matthew C. Browndorf, Esq.
Chief Investment Officer
Browndorf PEM, LLC

I. James Cavoli
CEO
Life Settlement Insights

Michael Fasano
President
Fasano Associates

Dr. Debbie Harrison
Research Associate
The Pension Institute

George J. Keiser
National Association of Insurance
Commissioners
House of Representatives R-North
Dakota

Joseph R. Mason Ph.D
Senior Fellow
The Wharton School

Emmanuel Modu
Managing Director
A.M. Best Co.

Antony R. Mott
Managing Director
Structured Insurance Products
ICAP Capital Markets

Nemo Perera
Managing Director
Risk Capital Partners

Jonathan T. Sadowsky
Managing Director of Finance /
Portfolio Manager
Browndorf PEM, LLC

Joseph Selvidio
Associate
Stroock & Stroock & Lavan LLP

Hal J. Singer Ph.D
President
Criterion Economics LLC

Charles A. Stone
Professor
Brooklyn College
CUNY
Department of Economics

Boris Ziser
Partner
Stroock & Stroock & Lavan LLP

Anne Zissu
Professor
Citytech
CUNY
Department of Business
The Polytechnic Institute of NYU
Department of Financial
  Engineering

Foreword

The great fact of the modern world is that people are living longer, and living better, almost everywhere. Medicine is better; diagnoses are better; health care is more available, despite the comments to the contrary by some on the left. The problem with this wonder is that as people live longer they are creating greater and greater problems for themselves and for governments as pension funds are simply not able to keep up with the extended lives of retirees. Living longer is wonderful; living longer in poverty is not.

Mr. Vishaal Bhuyan has written this excellent book that explains how we as investors can better prepare ourselves for our confusing and perhaps underfunded futures. Dealing with these problems is not for the faint of heart and might appear far too daunting for most writers and analysts, but Mr. Bhuyan has indeed dealt with them in a readily understandable and eminently readable fashion. Anyone with concerns about the investment future for themselves, their families, their friends, and the country should take the time to read this book . . . immediately.

DENNIS GARTMAN
Editor of *The Gartman Letter*

Preface

The idea that aging will have a profoundly negative impact on the global economy has been around for decades but has been dismissed or taken a back seat to other, seemingly more important problems. Unfortunately, all the years spent avoiding the aging and pension problem has served to magnify the issue.

In 2008, the number of deaths in Japan outnumbered the number of births 1.14 million to 1.09 million, respectively, and the population fell by 51,000 according to the Health Ministry. By 2050, both Japan and Russia will lose over 20 percent of their populations and 38 percent of Korea will be over 65, making it one of the oldest nations in the world. Since 2006, an astonishing 330 people have turned 60 every hour in the United States. Over 12 percent of the U.S. population and 16 percent of the U.K. population is 65 or older, compared to 5.2 percent in India and 8 percent in China, suggesting a major problem for the West.

Although longer living populations are a good thing, increased longevity can strain the economy, specifically retirement and health care programs. In the United States, Social Security and Medicare currently account for roughly 7 percent of the GDP, but within the next 25 to 30 years these programs will account for nearly 13 percent, essentially the majority of the entire federal budget. Proposals have been made to prevent these disasters, such as opening borders to immigrants to prop up the workforce, privatizing government programs, and increasing the retirement age from 65 to 71. These proposals, however, have failed to adequately address the matter and gain widespread acceptance. Plans have been made to extend the retirement age by 2 years in some countries over a 20-year period, but this is simply not enough. The retirement age should be at least 71 in order to adjust for dramatic increases in life expectancy over the past 100 years relative to a static 60- to 65- (in some places 55-) year-old retirement age, which has been in place since as far back as the nineteenth century.

Mass immigration will cause a number of national security problems and people are simply not fungible assets. Skill and education level must be comparable for immigrants to take on many of the skilled labor jobs the baby boomers will leave behind. Moreover, the sheer number of immigrants necessary to counteract the baby boomer phenomenon would be unthinkable.

It is not only an increase in life expectancy that is troublesome, but also the increasing uncertainty of life expectancies. For many pension funds this uncertainty creates a tremendous amount of unquantifiable risk, leaving them unprepared to address future obligations. Given that each additional year in life expectancy at age 65 adds roughly 3 percent to the present value of pension liabilities (according to the Pension Institute London), the cost of providing pensions in 2050 may be 18 percent higher than currently expected. Coupled with the current economic crisis, which has left major U.S. corporations with $400 billion in underfunded programs (from a $60 billion surplus at the end of 2007); longevity risk management should be of the utmost importance to pension fund managers.

The capital markets have developed a number of possible solutions (such as longevity bonds and swaps) to allow pension programs to hedge and manage this longevity risk and to allow large investors to capitalize on this extension in life expectancy. Although these longevity products are still in their nascent stages, given the magnitude of the market (according to Watson Wyatt's Global Pension Assets Study in 2007 there is roughly $23 trillion of longevity risk exposure among benefit pension funds) I am confident in the impact longevity derivatives will play in the coming years.

As pension funds continue to lose value over the next several years, greatly amplifying the current economic crisis, seniors will be left wondering how they will be able to fund their retirements. This unfortunate chain of events will give rise to "reverse equity transactions" such as life settlements and reverse mortgages. Although these types of transactions have been around for quite some time, in the coming years seniors will scramble to extract the remaining equity in their homes and sell their insurance policies to meet their daily cash obligations.

A life settlement is a transaction whereby a senior sells his insurance policy to an institutional investor for more than the cash surrender value but less than the coverage amount. The investor pays all subsequent premiums until the death benefit is collected. This gives investors revenue streams uncorrelated with other markets and allows consumers to receive a lump sum to pay off debt or simply provide financial stability. Life settlements also trade in pools on the tertiary market, allowing investors to capture substantial returns insulated from the broader economy. Many large investment banks and multistrategy hedge funds have already deployed billions of dollars in life settlements or linked products.

This book aims at providing a complete analysis of the life settlement market, while touching upon some of the derivatives available in the longevity risk market. Each chapter draws on industry experts, who have several years of experience in the life markets.

Acknowledgments

I would like to extend my deepest and most sincere gratitude to all of the contributing authors who have helped shape and build this new market, and who have been kind enough to share their knowledge with us all. I would also like to thank Pia for always encouraging me to think bigger, and Mark for giving me my start.

PART One

Life Settlement Basics

CHAPTER 1

A Brief History of Life Settlements

Vishaal B. Bhuyan
Managing Partner, V.B. Bhuyan & Co.

The legal and conceptual basis for a secondary market in life insurance originated from the U.S. Supreme Court case of *Grigsby v. Russell* (1911), which established that policy owners have the right to transfer an insurance policy in a manner similar to any other asset. Justice Oliver Wendell Holmes represented that life insurance contained all of the legal attributes of property such as real estate, stocks, and bonds, so was therefore "transferable without limitation" by the policy owner. Holmes stated, "Life insurance has become in our days one of the best recognized forms of investment and self-compelled saving." The case set forth the rights of a policy owner, allowing an owner to:

Name the policy beneficiary.

Borrow against the policy.

Sell the policy to another party.

Change the beneficiary designation of the policy.

The first form of the modern day life settlement market was the viatical settlement market of the 1980s, where men diagnosed with AIDS sold their life insurance policies to third party investors. A viatical settlement is defined as the sale of an insurance policy when the insured's life expectancy is less than two years. The majority of the population diagnosed with AIDS in the 1980s was homosexual, so most did not have wives or children to consider when making their financial plans. Moreover, these transactions allowed viators to generate cash for their medical expenses. At the time, the medical community understood very little about the virus, so life expectancies were typically very short once a patient was diagnosed. But as researches started to effectively prolong the lives of infected individuals, investors holding viatical settlements in their portfolios started to amass considerable losses. Moreover, the generally controversial nature of the investment curbed institutional interest in the market.

Although a small number of U.S. and European investors continued to participate in the viatical settlement market in the mid 1990s, due to favorable tax regulation (viatical settlements were not subject to income or capital gains tax), the market's rebirth occurred around 2000 when regulatory bodies began to establish industry standards to minimize fraud and encourage best practices. Moreover, the formation of the Life Insurance Settlement Association from the Viatical and Life Settlement Association of America in 2004, further helped to establish the modern day life settlement market and separate it from the controversial and speculative market of viatical settlements.

Today, life settlements are experiencing tremendous growth, exploding from a $3 billion market in 2003 to more than $15 billion in 2008 and are projected to grow to a whopping $160 billion market in the next several years, according to Conning & Co. Moreover, trade associations such as the Institutional Life Markets Association, which is composed of major financial institutions focusing on the regulation and development of life settlements and other life-linked financial products, helped to legitimize the industry.

The growth of the market can also be attributed to strong demographic shifts such as the aging baby boomers and instable financial markets, which are creating further incentives for seniors to part with their life insurance policies and attracting investment funds that wish to gain exposure to assets with a low correlation to other markets.

CHAPTER 2

Features of Life Insurance

Vishaal B. Bhuyan
Managing Partner, V.B. Bhuyan & Co., Inc.

This chapter explores only the most important features of life insurance contracts as they apply to the trading of life settlements. Life insurance and life settlements cannot be discussed without examining the topic of "beneficial interest," which is covered in depth in Chapter 19, but is also touched on briefly in this chapter. Overall, it is important to develop a strong understanding of retail life insurance before developing a strategy to invest in the secondary life market.

A life insurance policy is a legal contract between a policyholder (the owner of a policy) and an insurer (such as MetLife), whereby the insurer agrees to pay a death benefit (a lump sum of money) to the beneficiary or beneficiaries of the policy upon the death of the insured. The *insured* and the *policyholder* are not necessarily synonymous, although in most cases the insured and policyholder are the same person (see beneficial interest). As with all types of insurance, the policyholder, whether it be the insured or a third party investor, is required to pay monthly, quarterly, or annual premiums to keep the policy in force (active). The beneficiary of the policy is the individual(s) or entity that receives the death benefit once the insured has died. The beneficiary of the policy is designated by the owner of the policy at origination and may be anyone he wishes. The initial beneficiary of death benefit proceeds is required to have a *beneficial interest* in the contract.

Beneficial interest is defined as "the rights to receive distributions of interest or principle from a trust," but is used to determine whether the beneficiary of a policy will experience "loss" once the insured has died. Corporations and family members are said to have beneficial interest in the life of an insured. For example, it is commonplace for a wife to purchase a life policy on her husband, as she will most likely have an interest in his life. Moreover, a corporation may own a life policy on its partners to ensure the company has enough capital to purchase the partners' shares (if their families do not wish to hold an equity stake) if any of the partners meets an untimely demise. The corporation would pay the monthly premiums and would also be designated as the beneficiary of the death benefit at the origination of policy. In both of these scenarios the beneficiary of the policy has an interest in the insured's longevity. There must be beneficial interest when the policy is originated, but the beneficiary of the policy may be changed to an investor after the *contestable period*, unless the original contract contains an irrevocable beneficiary clause.

CONTESTABILITY PERIOD

The first few years that a life insurance policy is in force is known as the "contestability period." Although this period is typically two years there is a strong push from regulators to increase the period to five. During this period an insurance carrier can contest a death benefit if it suspects misrepresentation or fraud on the application or believes suicide to be the cause of death. Although in previous years a number of investors acquired policies during this two-year period due to large discounts in pricing, the overall trend in the market is to shy away from contestable policies (also known as "wet paper") due to regulatory risks. Investing in contestable policies is also known as STOLI/IOLI and will be discussed later in the book. It is important to note that the price of a traded life settlement increases dramatically after the contestability period is over.

Once a life insurance policy has passed the contestability period the insurer is not legally able to deny death benefits; however, if the insured is currently living, the carrier may rescind a policy at any time if it believes that the owner of the policy lacked insurable interest at the time of origination.

TYPES OF POLICIES

There are two primary types of life insurance contracts: permanent life insurance and term life insurance. Permanent insurance provides coverage for the insured until the policy matures and includes whole life, universal life, and variable universal life policies. Permanent insurance also contains a cash component, which builds up as premiums are paid into the policy. If a policyholder wishes to exit his policy at some point during the contract he is eligible to receive the cash value of the policy. Policyholders can access the cash value in their policies by either withdrawing or borrowing against them. Funds borrowed against the policy can either be repaid or deducted from the cash value or the death benefit of the policy. The way the policy's cash account is managed is what makes one type of permanent life insurance different from another. Term insurance typically offers lower premiums as it only provides coverage for a specified term such as 10 years. Term insurance is usually purchased by relatively younger customers so the comparative lapse ratios for term life are much higher, which enables carriers to offer coverage for low rates. See Exhibit 2.1.

Term life policies are typically not desirable for life settlement investors (unless the policy is convertible term) as there is a low probability that the insured expires during the coverage period. Variable universal life (VUL) policies may also be unattractive to secondary market participants as VUL contracts are regulated by the Securities and Exchange Commission requiring additional securities licenses; however, this varies among individual life settlement firms.

The following outline illustrates the various types of permanent life insurance most commonly found in the marketplace.

- **Whole Life** insurance covers an insured for the duration his life and offers both a death benefit and a savings component. Moreover, many carriers will pay dividends to policyholders for excess premiums.
- **Universal Life** insurance is a more flexible type of whole life insurance that provides a savings component, which generally accrues a guaranteed rate of interest. In addition, policy owners may borrow or withdraw funds from their savings accounts. Universal life policies also allow policy owners to adjust the death benefit and/or premium payments (within limits) to customize cash flow streams as necessary. For life settlement investors this is important as proper cash management and premium optimization results in higher returns.
- **Variable Life** insurance offers a variety of professionally managed investment options to customers in addition to a death benefit. Funds accumulated in the savings account may be used to invest in stocks, bonds, and money market mutual funds. Although there is some increased potential for upside (usually there is also a cap rate on returns), the policy is exposed to market risks. In variable life policies both the cash account and death benefit may decrease during times of market volatility, which may result in higher net premiums for the owner. Some policies, however, do guarantee a certain level of death benefit. Policy owners may also borrow against or withdraw the cash value, but this also may reduce the cash accounts and death benefits.
- **Variable Universal Life** insurance is a hybrid product that combines the characteristics of both variable and universal insurance such as the

EXHIBIT 2.1 Life Insurance Policy Features

	Insurance Type	Premium	Death Benefit	Cash Accumulation	Investment Choice	Regulatory Governance	Life Settlement
Term	Level Term Insurance	Relatively low, fixed	Fixed during the term, then zero	No	No	State	No
	Renewable Term Insurance	Relatively low, increasing	Fixed	No	No	State	No
	Decreasing Term Insurance	Relatively low, decreasing	Decreasing during the term, then zero	No	No	State	No
	Convertible Term Insurance	–	–	No	No	State	Yes
Permanent	Whole Life Insurance	Relatively high, fixed	Fixed minimum amount, some upside, guaranteed	Yes, guaranteed	No	State	Yes
	Universal Life Insurance	Relatively high, flexible	Variable	Yes	No	State	Yes
	Variable Life Insurance	Relatively high, fixed	Fluctuates with performance of the investment	Yes	Yes	SEC	Varies by investor
	Variable Universal Life Insurance	Relatively high, flexible	Fluctuates with performance of the investment	Yes	Yes	SEC	Varies by investor

Investing in variable universal life insurance policies (VUL) requires registration with the U.S. Securities and Exchange Commission. The internal rate of return in a VUL policy depends on the performance of the mutual fund to which the policy is linked. Typically there is a cap rate on the policy, which limits upside performance.

ability to alter premium payments and the death benefit and also have an investment component to the policy, which is subject to market exposure.

- **Convertible Term Life** insurance is a term policy which may be converted into a permanent policy without any additional medical information on the insured and without an increase in the premium amount if the insured's health has changed.

CHAPTER 3

What Is a Life Settlement?

Professor David Blake
Director, The Pensions Institute, Cass Business School

Dr. Debbie Harrison
Senior Visiting Fellow, The Pensions Institute[1]

Desk Research Sponsored By:
Deutsche Bank
EFG International
Goldman Sachs
The Royal Bank of Scotland

Whole life policies can be assigned, which means that the insured individual—or policyholder if this is a different individual or entity—can sell a policy and assign the interest in the death benefit to the purchaser. When a third party buys the rights to the benefits of a life insurance policy, the arrangement is known as a "life settlement" or "traded life policy" (TLP).

Under noncontestability provisions that govern U.S. life insurance, life insurers cannot usually contest the payment of death benefits after the end of the contestability period, provided premiums have been fully paid up to the date of the policyholder's death.

To understand how the secondary market works, it is important to appreciate why whole life policies are purchased in the first place and why they might be sold at a later date.

The most common reason for the original purchase is to secure life cover so that dependants (or businesses) receive a capital sum in the event of the policyholder's death. However, this need can be met through the purchase of term insurance, which is considered to be a simpler and, in many cases, cheaper product than whole life. So, why buy the more complex and expensive alternative? It might be because of customer preferences (the buy side), but it might also be due to insurance company and intermediary marketing (the sell side). From a behavioral perspective, whole life looks more attractive than term insurance to consumers who are not comfortable with buying pure insurance products—that is, policies that only pay out if a claim arises (in this case upon death). Motor and home insurance fall into this category, as does term insurance, which only pays out if the policyholder dies within the term covered. Whole life insurance might, therefore, be perceived as an easier sell because the investment element of the policy provides an additional cash value that can be used in various ways, while the insurance value will be paid on the insured's death, whenever this occurs. There is a further potential distortion due to the large sales commissions paid to life insurance agents on whole life and universal life, which are not available on term products.

Whole life policies are sold by policyholders for a range of reasons. Typically the policyholders' circumstances have changed so that they no longer need the life cover and would like to gain access to the embedded capital value rather than simply let the policy lapse. In a period of comparatively low interest rates, the growth of the investment element (linked to deposit and fixed-interest bond rates) might be limited, and this might provide an additional reason for a sale.

The Bernstein study, which reports the findings of the Hartford 2003 Consumer Survey, lists four main reasons for the purchase of life settlements.[2] Here we reproduce the headline percentages (that is, the percentage of policies purchased for the stated reason) and then for each we consider briefly why the purchaser might subsequently wish to sell.

1. **Income protection (79 percent):** This is by far the most common reason for purchase, with the objective of replacing the income of an individual who dies and who has financial dependants, for example, a working parent with children still in school. Once the dependants become independent financially, the insurance might be considered redundant and the sale of the policy might appeal if this would secure a capital sum and remove the need to continue paying monthly premiums, which in retirement, for example, might become unaffordable. Where ill health is an issue, the capital secured on surrender or on sale in the secondary market could help fund medical care and other needs.

2. **Estate planning (9 percent):** Estate planning refers to the use of the policy by individuals who would like to provide a lump sum on their death to

their beneficiaries, for example, to cover any tax bills that might arise on the value of their estate. Changes in family arrangements—for example, a divorce or the death of a dependant—might make the policy redundant as might a significant reduction in the estate's value. A change to estate tax legislation in the United States in the future could also reduce the need for this type of protection.

3. **Retirement planning (8 percent):** Retirement planning is likely to be a reason for purchase on the part of those who are seeking a combination of insurance and investment, with the ability to borrow against the cash value or to use it for drawdown purposes, where this is possible. Reasons for the sale might reflect age and also the desire to consolidate retirement financing vehicles.

4. **Business planning (4 percent):** This is the smallest component and refers to the purchase of policies by businesses that would suffer if an important employee or partner were to die. Key-man insurance pays the policyholder (the employer or partnership) upon the death of the named individual, which might otherwise destabilize the business in some way. It might also be used by a partnership to assist with succession planning, so that the remaining partners have sufficient capital to buy out the rights of the family of a deceased partner's share in the business. Such needs might change if an insured employee/partner leaves the business or a partnership dissolves, for example.

Of these four reasons for a policy sale, we suggest that the last is the least contentious from an ethical perspective, as the third-party nature of the arrangement avoids the potential for distress sales. However, the potential for market abuses still remains.

The Wharton report observes that, generally speaking, life policies are assignable, which means they can be taken over by a third party who purchases the rights to the benefits.[3] When a policy is genuinely no longer wanted, or the need for capital is more urgent than the need for life cover, the policyholder has three options: let the policy lapse, which occurs when premiums stop, in which case there is no return to the policyholder; sell back to the insurer and receive in return a surrender value; or sell in the secondary market in the hope of receiving a larger sum than the surrender value.

Surrender values tend to be based on normal health assumptions—indeed there might be complex regulatory issues for insurers that offer explicit health-dependent surrender values—and so for those with impaired lives, they are not generally attractive. The life settlement market focuses on senior impaired lives—that is policyholders over age 65, who have a reduced life expectancy. Opinion varies as to the length of life expectancy that investors consider acceptable: It can start as low as 3 years and is generally capped at between 15 and 20 years. The sale of a policy where the insured is expected to live less than two years is classed as a viatical settlement, and such policies are excluded from the life settlement market.

A.M. Best describes the secondary market in this way:

> *The life settlement market is an outgrowth of the viatical settlement market in which policies of the terminally ill—normally those insureds expected to die within two years—are bought and sold. In the life settlement market, however, insureds generally are 65 years or older, with medical impairments resulting in life expectancies of about 3 to 15 years. . . . The more severe the chronic illness of an insured, the lower the life expectancy and, hence, the higher the price paid for the life settlement.*[4]

As the Wharton report notes, the availability of a secondary market introduces liquidity to an otherwise illiquid market. It provides a potentially better deal for policyholders who want to sell (or are forced to sell) policies, and it also stimulates competition among insurers, who otherwise would be under no pressure to improve surrender values or to offer other arrangements, such as a loan against the policy, which would be repaid on the death of the policyholder:

> *If there is no external market for reselling policies, insurers have no incentive to adjust their surrender values for impaired policies to competitive levels because they wield monopsony power over the repurchase of "impaired" policies. Viatical and life settlement firms erode this monopsony power.*[5]

It could also be argued that the secondary market might have a beneficial effect on the primary market. When customers see that they are not locked in for life, they might be more willing to take out life insurance in the first place. In these two respects—greater competition and a more positive consumer attitude to life insurance—the secondary market would seem to offer, in principle, ethically sound consumer benefits, *provided* it is well regulated and customers fully understand the nature of the transactions in which they are involved.

Life settlement companies have sprung up over the past decade to buy unwanted policies in the hope of making an attractive return on the capital employed. They offer a larger capital sum to policyholders than the provider's surrender value, but still purchase policies at a deep discount on the face value.

Life settlement companies might purchase policies for their own investment purposes or with the objective of selling the acquired policies to third parties. In the latter case, they act as an intermediary between the seller (the policyholder) and the ultimate buyer (the end investor). The ultimate buyer could be an institutional investor, such as an investment bank, insurance company, hedge fund, or pension fund, or it could be a retail investor. While a wealthy private investor might buy direct, a typical retail investor would buy units in a pooled fund established by an asset manager or in a bond issued by an investment bank (a different type of pooled fund that usually has a fixed term—say, five or seven years). The asset manager or investment bank will have bought the underlying policies from a life settlement company and will need to hold cash in addition to the life settlements in order to maintain the premium payments and to pay investors who request a drawdown of cash, where this feature is offered. An investment bank bond might offer a target annual return over the term of the investment and might aim, but not guarantee, to return the investor's original capital at the end of the term.

When the original policyholder dies, the proceeds from the traded life policy accrue to the life settlement investor. The return on a traded policy can be calculated as follows: the difference between the total payout (policy face value) on the policyholder's death and the sum of the purchase price, maintenance costs, and operating costs. Maintenance and operating costs include the periodic premiums, which can be monthly, quarterly, semi-annual, or annual, paid between the date of purchase and date of death, plus any transactional and operational costs, including sales commission to intermediaries. Based on Bernstein's research, the estimated return on a life policy held for seven or eight years is likely to be in the region of 9 to 13 percent. The ultimate return to the investor might be higher or lower, depending on transaction costs and the time of death. A.M. Best's analysis shows that the typical transaction costs can be between 50 and 100 percent of the price paid to the policyholder. Therefore, where the settlement company pays a policyholder 15 percent of the face value, it might sell the policy to investors for 23 to 30 percent of face value. These figures vary significantly, depending on the individual's age, state of health, and the premiums required to maintain the policy.

Where the purchaser of policies constructs a fund for sale in the institutional or retail market, there will also be intermediaries (consultants, private client advisors, and sales representatives), who recommend these products to investors and who receive a fee or commission in return. Finally, there are the fund-rating agencies, which issue ratings for securities backed by life settlements based on a wide range of factors. However, we understand that, at the time of writing, there had been no issues of rated life settlement securities with longevity risk.

It can be seen that, although in its infancy, the life settlement market has already developed a comparatively complex infrastructure. Certain processes clearly are critical to the market's operation, but others are potentially unnecessary and add to the cost for the ultimate investor. While A.M. Best's research indicates that the transaction costs can add between 50 percent and 100 percent to the price the life settlement company pays the insured, in the future these costs might be reduced as a result of the development of auctions with platforms linking seller and buyer without the need for a fully intermediated purchase and resale. The newer synthetic transactions, which are linked to pools of (anonymous) older individuals, can also reduce such costs.

NOTES

1. This chapter is drawn from a Pensions Institute report, "And death shall have no dominion: Life settlements and the ethics of profiting from mortality," published in July 2008 (http://pensions-institute.org/DeathShallHaveNoDominion_Final_3July08.pdf).
2. Suneet Kamath and Timothy Sledge, "Life Insurance Long View: Life Settlements Need Not Be Unsettling" Bernstein Research Call, March 2005. Hereafter referred to as "Bernstein," www.bernsteinresearch.com.
3. Neil A. Doherty and Hal J. Singer, "The Benefits of a Secondary Market for Life Insurance Policies," Wharton School, October 2002 www.coventry.com/pdfs/wharton.pdf., hereafter referred to as "Wharton."
4. "Life Settlement Securitization," A. M. Best, March 2008 www.ambest.com/debt/lifesettlement.pdf.
5. Wharton, p. 1. "Monopsony" refers to a situation where there is only one purchaser of a good or service in a given market.

CHAPTER 4

Parties Involved in a Life Settlement

Vishaal B. Bhuyan
Managing Partner, V.B. Bhuyan & Co. Inc.

This chapter further examines the parties involved in a life settlement transaction. Exhibit 4.1 is shown from the perspective of an investor.

FINANCIAL ADVISORS

Due to the complexity of a life settlement, it is in the interest of a policyholder to consult with a financial advisor to decide whether a life settlement is an appropriate option. The following are various advisors a policyholder should seek out before entering into a life settlement transaction.

- Accountants, CPAs
- Attorneys
- Financial planners
- Insurance advisors
- Estate planners
- Certified senior advisors
- Charitable trust officers

PROVIDERS

A life settlement provider acts on behalf of institutional investors (pension funds, investment banks, hedge funds, etc.) to purchase life insurance

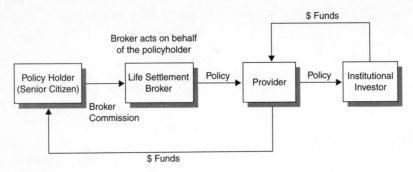

EXHIBIT 4.1 Life Settlement Transaction Micro View

policies from senior citizens (either through life settlement brokers or directly from seniors). Institutional investors may purchase life settlements through a number of providers, and providers may draw on a variety of investors for funds (see Exhibit 4.2). Provider firms are responsible for valuing individual life insurance policies and executing the paperwork necessary to

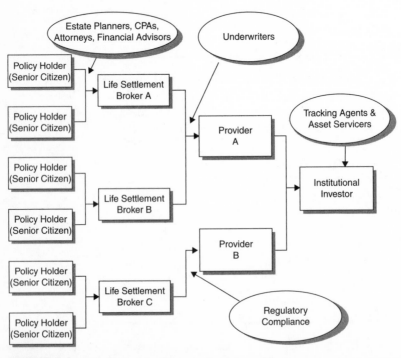

EXHIBIT 4.2 Life Settlement Transaction Macro View

transfer ownership of the policy and delivering funds to the original policy-holder. Providers are required to be licensed in the state in which a policy is originated so most major provider firms are licensed in the 41 states where life settlements are regulated. In order to adhere to strict regulation, most providers maintain in-house compliance departments. Because policyholders wish to sell their policies only to credible investors, working with a reputable provider firm is of the utmost importance. Well-established provider firms will strive to maintain the confidentiality of the insured and will be well versed in life settlement regulation and life settlement asset pricing. Of the states that regulate life settlements, most require that investors purchase and policyholders sell life settlements through a licensed provider.

Below is a list of major provider firms in the life settlement industry.

Abacus Settlements, LLC
708 Third Ave.
New York, NY 10017
www.abacussettlements.com

Peachtree Life Settlements
8301 Quantum Blvd, 2nd Floor
Boynton Beach, FL 33426
www.peachtreelifesettlements.com

Coventry
7111 Valley Green Road
Fort Washington, PA 19034
www.coventry.com

Legacy Benefits
350 5th Ave., Suite 4230
New York, NY 10018
www.legacybenefits.com

Life Settlement Solutions, Inc
9201 Spectrum Center Blvd Suite 105
San Diego, CA 92123
www.lss-corp.com

Q Capital Strategies
950 3rd Ave.
New York, NY 10022
www.qcapitalstrategies.com

Secondary Life Capital
1010 Wisconsin Ave., NW Suite 620
Washington, DC 20007
www.secondarylifecapital.com

The Lifeline Program
1979 Lakeside Pkwy 2nd Floor
Tucker, GA 30084
www.thelifeline.com

BROKERS

Life settlement brokers aim to receive the highest possible offer for a life insurance policy by submitting the case to multiple providers. It is the broker's
duty to seek out reputable provider firms who have access to stable funding,
meet regulatory requirements, and who respect the privacy of the clients.
Life settlement brokers act much like residential or commercial real estate
brokers; however, their commissions are relatively higher and the transaction consists of considerably more sensitive information, thus requiring the
highest level of ethical standards. Disclosure of broker commissions is currently the subject of much debate in the life settlement industry as many feel
these unreported commissions come at the expense of the seller. Typically,
settlement brokers should charge the seller 0.5 percent to 2 percent of the
face value of the life insurance policy.

Although the broker must solicit various bids on the policy, it is up to
the policyholder to decide which offer to accept. This decision is usually
made along with a financial advisor and is based on various aspects specific
to the seller.

Much like providers, brokers must be licensed in the state where the
policyholder resides; however, brokerage firms do not require the in-house
compliance, or call on capital that providers do.

INVESTORS

Life settlement investors, also known as *financing entities*, acquire life insurance policies for a speculative purpose. Investors acquire life insurance assets through a provider firm that executes the transaction on behalf of the policyholder, but ultimately the owner of the contract is the investor. Investors in some cases become licensed providers or acquire a provider or premium finance firm (covered in Chapter 8) to ensure a steady inflow of policies.

Life settlement investing is not meant for individual investors (unless through an indirect vehicle such as a mutual or hedge fund, or life settlement sector stock), and providers do not conduct transactions with any entity that is not a well capitalized and reputable institution. Aside from the obvious privacy issues, the liquidity and longevity risk associated with life settlements is too great for individual investors to bear. Life settlement investors must be qualified institutional buyers as defined in the federal Securities Act of 1933. A qualified institutional buyer (QIB) is defined under Regulation D, Rule 144A as:

> *As used in rule 144A, this shall mean any of the following entities, acting for its own account or the accounts of other qualified institutional buyers that in the aggregate owns and invests on a discretionary basis at least $100 million in securities of issuers that are not affiliated with the entity.*

QIB requirements ensure that buyers of life settlements are sophisticated investors and have the market knowledge, risk management expertise, and capital to not only maintain solvency during volatile periods, but also to protect the consumer from questionable market practices.

Institutional investors may design a myriad of trading strategies based on investment horizon, capitalization, and profit model. Most financing entities utilize their own proprietary modeling tools to price life settlement investments but use life expectancies calculated by major underwriting firms. These pricing tools also aid in developing an appropriate trading strategy that meets the firm's overall thesis.

UNDERWRITERS

Underwriters are medical risk assesors that provide life expectancy projections for market participants based on the medical records of the insured.

Underwriters employ a number of actuarial methodologies to determine the level of impairment of an insured: however some underwriting firms are more fundamentally "actuaries" than others. In a limited fashion, underwriters may be compared to rating agencies such as Moody's or Standard & Poor's. Life expectancies are used by investors to model all relevant cash flows of a policy, namely the duration of premium payments and time of expected death benefit.

There are a few major underwriting firms that are used by almost all providers and investors. In most cases, providers or investors will require that two of the three firms below are used when submitting a case:

AVS Underwriting
175 Town Park Drive
Suite 400
Kennesaw, GA 30144

21st Services
200 South 6th Street
Suite 350
Minneapolis, MN 55402
www.21stservices.com

Fasano Associates
1201 15th Street, N.W.
Suite 250
Washington, DC 20005
www.fasanoassociates.com

ISC Services
17755 U.S. Highway 19 North
Clearwater, FL 33764
Suite 100
www.iscservices.com

Global Life Underwriting
3655 Torrance Boulevard, 3rd Floor
Torrance, CA 90503
www.globallifeunderwriting.com

CHAPTER 5

Other Involved Parties

Vishaal B. Bhuyan
Managing Partner, V.B. Bhuyan & Co., Inc.

This chapter examines the role of other involved parties in a life settlement transaction.

ASSET SERVICERS

Once policies have been acquired by an investor, the policies must be maintained; this can either be done in house, through most providers or through the use of an asset servicing firm.

Asset servicing firms specialize in managing premium payments on behalf of the clients, tracking the insured and delivering up-to-date mortality status information, and processing death benefits when an insured individual dies. Servicers generate monthly reports for investors detailing their profit and loss, their total holdings, and verification of premium payments. Some firms also provide analytics for their clients and are able to assist with optimizing their portfolios and reducing premium payments by drawing upon policy cash values.

These firms track the insured by phone, e-mail, mail, and various database checks such as the Social Security database. Close contacts of the insured such as a brother or neighbor may also be used for tracking purposes.

Note: Life insurance carriers will void a life insurance policy if a premium payment is missed. In some cases given sufficient funds, premium payments may be deducted from the cash value of the policy.

The costs incurred for servicing life settlement investments through providers may be cumbersome and institutional investors may work with various providers so it is not always reasonable for its life settlement holdings to be serviced by several different provider firms. Due to both of these reasons many institutional employ third party servicing firms which may offer servicing solutions for considerably less and through one central access point.

More important than the cost of an asset servicing firm, is working with a servicer(s) that ensure the safety and proper management of a portfolio of life settlements. Although most asset servicing firms will cover any policy that has lapsed due to premium payment error (this rarely occurs among reputable firms) using a backup servicer and tracking agent can be beneficial. This may seem to contradict the statement above regarding investors using multiple provider firms, but there is a difference between using two independent servicing firms and multiple providers. Provider firms offer less flexibility and centralization than third-party servicers.

EXCHANGES

Electronic exchanges have been the recent trend in the life settlement market; however, these platforms face a number of challenges before becoming widely adopted by buyers and sellers. Both smaller exchange operators such as Global Insurance Exchange and Life Exchange, and major investment banks such as Cantor Life Markets (a division of Cantor Fitzgerald) and Institutional Life Services (the joint venture between Goldman Sachs and Genworth Financial) must overcome a number of regulatory and logistical issues. The complexity and uniqueness of each life settlement transaction makes conducting a trade electronically extremely difficult—for now. Moreover, many exchanges require policyholders (or the financial advisors acting on their behalf) to sign a binding agreement with the exchange if they wish to sell their policies through the platform. This results in decreased liquidity for an asset that is already extremely illiquid. This agreement states that policy sellers may not sell their life insurance policies to any party not listed with the exchange.

Despite the dilemmas, there is a strong need for a transparent marketplace for life settlements and linked securities. Such a hub would decrease the commission of third-party brokers, decrease the number of links in the value chain, increase liquidity, and create transparency in regards to transaction and price data, thus creating an overall more efficient and more attractive asset class.

CHAPTER 6

Underwriting

Michael Fasano
President, Fasano Associates

L ife settlement underwriting is best understood in contrast to life insurance underwriting.

Life insurance underwriting has developed from the extensive mortality experience of the life insurance and reinsurance companies. Excess mortality for most medical conditions has been analyzed and translated into "debits," which converts this additional mortality into a percentage of standard mortality. Thus, to use an arbitrarily simple example, if we expected 100 deaths per thousand from a healthy, standard population, and there was a condition that resulted in 50 extra deaths per thousand, we would assign 50 debits for that condition and conclude that a person with that condition would experience mortality that was 150 percent of standard mortality.

This debit methodology is typically implemented by lay underwriters who rely on underwriting debit manuals developed by the major reinsurance companies. Both medical records and paramedical examinations, including blood and urine samples, are used to identify significant medical risks. Also, underwriters check with the Medical Information Bureau (MIB), an insurance industry information cooperative, to identify undisclosed conditions that could have a bearing on mortality.

Over the years, the debit methodology has proven to be a reliable predictor of excess mortality for the life insurance market (see "Multiple Medical Impairment Study," published by the Center for Medico-Actuarial Statistics of MIB, Inc.). However, the life insurance debit methodology presents analytic challenges when applied to underwriting of life settlements. Five of the major challenges presented are as follows:

1. Life insurance underwriting is applied to a generally healthy, insurable population with relatively few impairments. The life settlement

population, on the other hand, often includes people with multiple and significant impairments.

2. Life insurance underwriting generally is applied to a young population, with an average age less than 45. In contrast, life settlement underwriting is focused on an older population, with an average age of over 75. Mortality in an older population increases at a significantly faster rate than in a younger population. This complicates the process of converting research-based statistics with excess deaths per thousand into a percentage increase in standard mortality.

3. Diseases often move at different speeds in older people than in a younger population, or they move at a rate that does not present the same risk to mortality.

4. Life insurance underwriting is geared to avoid quick claims. Therefore, whenever there is any uncertainty as to an impairment, the underwriter will either assume the worst and assign significant debits or postpone the file. Because the risk presented to the life settlement funder is that the insured will live longer, rather than shorter, than expected, the life settlement underwriter has to take a more realistic approach to uncertainty and will often assume a more favorable outcome than will the life insurance underwriter.

5. Life insurance underwriting does not require the same level of sophistication as life settlement underwriting. Typically, if a file reflects a severe or potentially severe impairment, such as congestive heart failure, the underwriter will decline the case—with no real analysis required. However, the life settlement underwriter has to put the disease in proper clinical context in order to estimate life expectancy: Was the heart failure caused by heart damage from a heart attack and therefore unlikely to be reversed; or was it caused by an arrhythmia that is reversible with the prospect that the heart failure, too, might resolve. These are important distinctions that can help determine the insured's prognosis and likely life expectancy. Only a highly trained medical professional should tackle these difficult analyses.

Life Settlement Underwriting Methodologies

There are two methodologies that work best for life settlement underwriting: (1) a modified debit methodology, and (2) research-based clinical judgment.

Modified Debit Methodology   The modified debit methodology starts with the debit methodology developed for life insurance underwriting and adjusts it to the life settlement demographic. The following are the most common adjustments:

Diseases that Move More Slowly There are certain diseases, such as prostate cancer, that move more slowly in an older population. Debits are reduced for these types of impairments.

Impairments that Don't Have Time to Become Life Threatening Certain impairments move at a speed that would ultimately become a life-threatening risk in a young person, but would not in an older person. An abdominal aortic aneurysm is one such condition. The aorta pumps blood out of the heart to the rest of the body. Often there will be a thinning of the aortic wall outside of the heart in the abdominal region that results in a ballooning of the aorta that we refer to as an abdominal aortic aneurysm. A 4-centimeter abdominal aortic aneurysm that presents in a 35-year-old would be a significant mortality risk. If unrepaired, it will likely expand to the point where it will rupture, which often will result in death. If repaired, there often are complications—such as stroke—that also can result in death. For this reason, a life underwriter will usually assign significant debits for this condition.

However, if an 80-year-old presents with a 4-centimeter abdominal aortic aneurysm, the life settlement underwriter will assign only a small number of debits, as the chance of that aneurysm expanding to the point of rupture in the older person's remaining life is quite small.

Diseases that Present Less Relative Risk because of Increasing Overall Mortality There are impairments that may present the same additional mortality when expressed as excess additional deaths per 1,000 of population. However, when this excess mortality is converted to debits, in other words, when it is expressed as a percentage of standard, or average, mortality, it converts into a lesser percentage, in that the average (standard) mortality for older people is much greater than for younger people. This is a mathematical adjustment: A fixed number of extra deaths per thousand of population will be a small percentage of the larger denominator that is standard mortality for an older population.

Research-Based Clinical Judgment There are certain impairments for which a debit methodology, even if modified, will be an unsatisfactory way to estimate life expectancy. Bearing in mind that the debit methodology was developed for healthy or relatively healthy people, it becomes a less precise analytic tool as the impairments become more severe. Metastasized cancers, Alzheimer's disease, and amyotrophic lateral sclerosis (ALS or Lou Gehrig's disease, as it is known) are examples of impairments with relatively short life expectancies for which significant research exists.

With research-based clinical judgments, we start with the research literature, which will establish median life expectancy and mortality curves that apply to the disease. The first step in the analysis is to identify the proper mortality curve, based on the risk profile of the insured. For example, for prostate cancer, there are at least four distinct mortality curves—ranging from a median life expectancy of 7 years for the worst risk profile to a greater than 70 percent survival rate after 15 years for the best risk profile. Given this wide a range of outcomes, it is critically important that prognostic variables be analyzed to put the insured in the proper cohort.

The second basic step in a research-based clinical judgment is to measure progression of the disease along the relevant mortality curve, as we know that diseases progress at different speeds in different people. For example, we know that people with Alzheimer's disease have a life expectancy of 9 to 10 years, on average, from onset of symptoms; but we also know that there can be significant differences in the rate of progression for this disease. So we will look at the relevant markers of progression. In the case of Alzheimer's we will analyze the results of mental status exams—both as to their absolute score and, as important, as to the rate of deterioration in scores; we will look for evidence of antisocial and/or psychotic behavior; and we will look for evidence of difficulties in performing activities of daily living. These markers will tell us how fast the disease is progressing to death.

Given the significant clinical experience required to analyze risk profiles and measure progression for research-based clinical judgment cases, it is important that the underwriter have extensive medical and analytic experience, such as would be possessed by a physician medical director.

MEASURING PERFORMANCE

An important element of life settlement underwriting is ongoing analysis of Actual to Expected performance, or accuracy. This information tells the funder how well the underwriter is doing his or her job, and it also helps the underwriter to improve performance. Actual to Expected analyses are best undertaken by independent actuarial firms. Typically, the actuary will derive the mortality distribution that is embedded in every life expectancy estimate made by the underwriter. The mortality distribution tells us what the pattern of deaths will be. For example, for a portfolio of 1,000 lives with average life expectancy of 10 years, the mortality distribution will tell us how many people are expected to die in the first year, the second year, and so on.

The actuary will aggregate the mortality distributions associated with each of the underwriter's predictions of life expectancy and will then compare actual deaths at various points in time with expected deaths as per the aggregate mortality distribution of the underwriter's predictions.

The closer the Actual to Expected ratio is to 100 percent, the better the underwriter is doing his or her job.

MORTALITY TABLES

A mortality table is a listing of the probabilities of death by age. These tables are compiled by various professional actuarial organizations in many countries and government agencies. These tables are distinguished by the source of the data from which probabilities were derived and the applications for which they were constructed.

Tables generated by government agencies from the data they collect are known as Population Mortality Tables. These tables are mainly used for demographic and Social Security applications and are rarely used in the life insurance market.

The main professional actuarial organization in the United States is the Society of Actuaries (SoA). It collects large amounts of data from the life insurance companies and periodically publishes many tables for various life insurance-related applications.

Similar organizations in other countries develop and publish mortality tables appropriate for their respective regions and applications.

Some commonly known mortality tables in the U.S. life insurance industry are:

- Experience tables, such as the Society of Actuaries 1975/80 mortality table, Society of Actuaries 1990/95 mortality table, and the 2001 Valuation Basic Table (also known as 2001 VBT), are used as basic life insurance pricing tables. (Recently, the 2001 VBT was updated with the 2008 Valuation Basic Tables, discussed later in this chapter.)

  2001 VBT mortality was originally intended for principle-based reserving but it has also gained popularity for various pricing applications. This table is the most commonly encountered basic mortality table in the life settlement market.

- Regulatory valuation tables such as the 1980 Commissioners' Standard Ordinary mortality table (also known as '80 CSO) and the more recent 2001 CSO are prescribed by the National Association of Insurance Commissioners as the standard for computing reserves required to be set up by the insurance companies. These tables have margins deemed sufficient to maintain the solvency of the regulated insurance companies.

- Group mortality tables. These tables are derived from the experience of various group insurance programs where insurance is issued to all eligible members of a group with little or no selection or underwriting. The amount of insurance is determined by a formula based on salary or level of responsibility of the insured employee or member of an organization. Such insurance generally terminates upon retirement or termination of employment or membership.

- Annuity mortality tables. These tables are derived from the experience of the buyers of life annuities, either individually or as participants in a pension plan. These are special purpose tables designed for the annuity or pension business with an emphasis on the long-term solvency of the issuers.

For this chapter, we will limit our discussion to the more recent life insurance mortality tables generally encountered in the life settlement market environment.

Most life insurance companies and practitioners in the life settlement market make some modifications and adjustments to the basic tables based on their own experience and interpretation of the trends in their respective markets.

SELECT AND ULTIMATE MORTALITY RATES

Tables that we will discuss will have *select* and *ultimate* classification of their contents.

The term select identifies the experience of insured lives that were selected for issuance of life insurance by initial underwriting. These insureds generally experience lower mortality for a number of years from the selection date. This mortality difference eventually wears off and the experience merges with the mainstream.

The number of years during which the mortality experience is noticeably lower is known as the select period.

- Select period for the SoA 1975/80 table is 15 years.
- Select period for the SoA 1990/95 table and for the 2001 VBT is 25 years.

It should be noted that the basic data for 2001 VBT was the same as that for the SoA 1990/95 table. This data was smoothed (the actuarial term is *graduated*) and blended at older ages with data from other sources. Some allowance was also made for general mortality improvements up to the year 2001. The final iteration was a smooth increasing mortality rate table meant for calculating principle-based reserves for life insurance policies.

The ultimate portion of the tables represents the experience of insured lives that were selected at some point of time but are now indistinguishable from others of the same age.

MALES, FEMALES, SMOKERS, NONSMOKERS

Mortality tables are further differentiated by sex and by smoking classification.

In some iterations of the same tables, the smoker/nonsmoker differences are ignored and source data is combined. These tables are known as composite or aggregate tables.

SAMPLE MORTALITY RATES

Mortality rates, from three recent life insurance tables, for a male insured, who was underwritten (selected) at age 70, are depicted in Exhibit 6.1 to illustrate the differences between various mortality tables.

These are composite rates with smokers and nonsmokers combined.

2008 VBT Mortality Table

In March 2008, the Society of Actuaries released the updated version of the 2001 VBT mortality table. This version is known as 2008 VBT. Additional data was provided by U.S. life insurance companies. Data related to older ages was provided by the U.S. Social Security Administration. Improvement in general mortality was projected to 2008 at the rate of 1 percent per annum for males up to age 80, dropping to 0.50 percent from age 81 to 90 and 0 percent thereafter. Rate of improvement for females was half as much.

The select period was modified from 25 years for all ages in 2001 VBT to 25 years but not beyond attained age 90. A minimum select period of 2 years was retained at ages 88 and older.

The highest mortality rate was limited to 0.450 as opposed to 1.000 in the previous tables.

The 2008 VBT mortality rates are generally lower than those from 2001 VBT resulting in an extension of life expectancy at most ages.

Exhibit 6.2 offers a comparison of mortality rates under the 2001 VBT and 2008 VBT.

LIFE EXPECTANCY

Estimate of life expectancy is perhaps the most important information for determining a price in a life settlement transaction. It is also the most commonly misunderstood one.

EXHIBIT 6.1 Sample Mortality Rates

Male	Duration	SoA 1975/80 15 year Select	SoA 1990/95 25 year Select	2001 VBT 25 year Select
70	0	0.0083	0.0065	0.0051
70	1	0.0126	0.0102	0.0089
70	2	0.0172	0.0137	0.0121
70	3	0.0224	0.0173	0.0147
70	4	0.0271	0.0201	0.0170
70	5	0.0300	0.0232	0.0220
70	6	0.0345	0.0270	0.0245
70	7	0.0386	0.0309	0.0290
70	8	0.0429	0.0339	0.0338
70	9	0.0470	0.0365	0.0407
70	10	0.0524	0.0429	0.0488
70	11	0.0584	0.0542	0.0580
70	12	0.0670	0.0690	0.0683
70	13	0.0786	0.0842	0.0799
70	14	0.0864	0.0964	0.0934
70	15	0.1267	0.1084	0.1035
70	16	0.1378	0.1209	0.1143
70	17	0.1498	0.1332	0.1260
70	18	0.1626	0.1453	0.1399
70	19	0.1759	0.1571	0.1563
70	20	0.1896	0.1703	0.1712
70	21	0.2037	0.1853	0.1860
70	22	0.2182	0.2033	0.2035
70	23	0.2332	0.2236	0.2204
70	24	0.2486	0.2434	0.2358
70	25	0.2644	0.2598	0.2509
70	30	0.3497	0.3261	0.3321
70	35	1.0000	0.5244	0.4393
70	40	1.0000	0.8849	0.5803
70	50	1.0000	1.0000	1.0000

Actuarially speaking, it is defined as:

$$ex \approx \left[\sum_{t=1}^{\infty} lx + t \right] / lx$$

ex is the life expectancy.
lx is the number of lives living at age x, and

t is the duration from age *x*. Range for *t* is 1 to infinity.
In words—life expectancy is the sum of all future probabilities of survival, starting at age *x*.

Another way to conceptualize it is that the life expectancy is a point in time (the median) when half of the lives in a large group of similar age and characteristics are expected to have expired. Strictly speaking, the actuarial life expectancy is a weighted average, and it will not necessarily be the same as the median life expectancy. But in most cases, the mean and median life expectancies will be close to each other.

EXHIBIT 6.2 Comparative Mortality Rates: 2001 versus 2008 Valuation Basic Tables

Duration	2001 VBT Nonsmoker Male 70	2008 VBT Nonsmoker Male 70	2001 VBT Nonsmoker Female 70	2008 VBT Nonsmoker Female 70
1	0.0045	0.0037	0.0034	0.0023
2	0.0079	0.0058	0.0053	0.0038
3	0.0108	0.0079	0.0060	0.0054
4	0.0133	0.0103	0.0072	0.0070
5	0.0155	0.0128	0.0090	0.0088
6	0.0202	0.0155	0.0114	0.0106
7	0.0225	0.0185	0.0144	0.0126
8	0.0269	0.0218	0.0180	0.0149
9	0.0315	0.0255	0.0223	0.0174
10	0.0382	0.0295	0.0272	0.0203
11	0.0460	0.0339	0.0327	0.0235
12	0.0549	0.0390	0.0389	0.0271
13	0.0650	0.0446	0.0458	0.0312
14	0.0765	0.0508	0.0521	0.0358
15	0.0898	0.0575	0.0570	0.0408
16	0.1000	0.0675	0.0629	0.0490
17	0.1110	0.0788	0.0693	0.0582
18	0.1229	0.0915	0.0763	0.0684
19	0.1370	0.1059	0.0840	0.0796
20	0.1537	0.1221	0.0923	0.0917
25	0.2338	0.2115	0.1477	0.1470
30	0.3129	0.3070	0.2360	0.2402
35	0.4154	0.4034	0.3680	0.3703
40	0.5489	0.4469	0.5415	0.4402
45	0.7238	0.4500	0.7237	0.4500
50	0.9499	0.4500	0.9378	0.4500

EXHIBIT 6.2 (*Continued*)

Life Expectancy: Male Nonsmokers – Standard Mortality

	2001 VBT Yrs	2008 VBT Yrs	Change Yrs
Age 65	19.7	21.6	1.9
Age 70	16.4	17.7	1.3
Age 75	13.5	14.1	0.6
Age 80	10.4	10.7	0.3
Age 85	7.4	7.4	0.0
Age 90	4.6	5.0	0.4

Life Expectancy: Female Nonsmokers – Standard Mortality

	2001 VBT Yrs	2008 VBT Yrs	Change Yrs
Age 65	22.3	24.0	1.7
Age 70	19.2	19.9	0.7
Age 75	15.8	16.1	0.3
Age 80	12.4	12.5	0.1
Age 85	9.3	8.9	−0.4
Age 90	6.7	6.3	−0.4

Following is a graphic representation of probability distribution for a group of 1,000 lives, all 70-year-old male nonsmokers with mortality level expectation of 100 percent of the standard 2001 VBT mortality. See Exhibit 6.3.

Life expectancy is computed to be 16.68 years.

Life expectancy (LE) providers (life underwriters) usually provide an estimate of life expectancy that is based on their review and analysis of the medical information submitted to them. Some would also provide a mortality ratio.

FUNDERS COMPUTATIONS

Funders take the information provided by the LE providers. They either use the LE or the mortality ratio and apply this to a mortality table of their choice.

They compute conditional probabilities of death and survival to estimate positive and negative cash flows in the future years. Using a discount rate of their choice, funders then discount these cash flows to the present time to compute the net offer price for a contract.

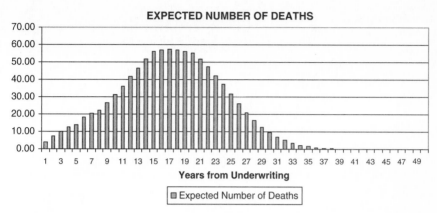

EXHIBIT 6.3 Expected Number of Deaths

If they choose to use LE as given then they solve for a mortality ratio to be applied to the mortality table that they have selected.

If they use the mortality ratio supplied by the LE provider, their model may produce a LE that is different from the one provided.

These differences arise due to the fact that either the mortality table used by the funders is different from the one implicit in the computations of the LE provider or the funder's view of the incidence of mortality is different from that of the LE provider.

Most funders will obtain LE estimates from more than one LE provider. They can then use one or a blend of the estimates obtained.

Differences in LE Estimates

Different LE providers will likely come up with different estimates based on their view and assessment of the same medical history file.

In selecting an LE provider, funders should discuss their objectives with underwriters and gain comfort with their experience, methodology, and performance history.

Choice of Mortality Tables   As we have seen, most standard mortality tables differ from each other.

Also keep in mind that these tables were developed for the life insurance industry and from the data submitted by life insurance providers.

Insurance companies have traditionally been interested in healthier, younger lives while the life settlement market focuses on predominantly older lives with some level of impairment.

Raw data is smoothed (graduated) to produce tables for specific purposes such as computation of life insurance premiums, cash values, reserves, and so forth. These considerations require mortality rates to increase smoothly between ages and durations.

There is also a view that healthier lives tend to voluntarily terminate their insurance early while unhealthy lives tend to retain their policies longer. Data at older ages may therefore become heavily weighted by less than standard lives.

High lapse rates in some forms of life insurance contracts result in there not being enough data at older ages to produce reliable rates.

Mortality is generally improving but the incidence of improvement varies by geographic areas, socioeconomic, and other factors. These factors are difficult to quantify with confidence.

At this time, there is no generally available mortality table that would be deemed most suitable for the life settlement market.

Level Mortality Ratios

Most pricing calculations are made assuming that the level of current mortality represented by the mortality ratio remains constant throughout life.

In reality, there is hardly a medical condition that remains the same indefinitely. It either improves or it gets worse.

Competent underwriters take that into account in estimating life expectancy.

Impact of Level vs. Varying Mortality Ratio   To illustrate the impact of level vs. varying mortality ratio assumptions on mortality distributions, let us consider the following hypothetical situation:

Underwriters review the file of a 70-year-old male nonsmoker and form the opinion that mortality level will start low but increase with duration, slowly at first and then rapidly in later years. They estimate the life expectancy to be 11.6 years.

The funder takes this LE estimate and solves for a level mortality ratio of 250 percent to reproduce the same LE.

They both use the standard 2001 VBT mortality table.

Probability distributions for the two assumptions are shown in Exhibit 6.4.

Probability distribution for the level mortality assumption anticipates more expected deaths in early years, fewer in the middle years, and more in the later years.

Present value of the death benefits computed based on the level assumption will be higher than the one computed based on increasing mortality

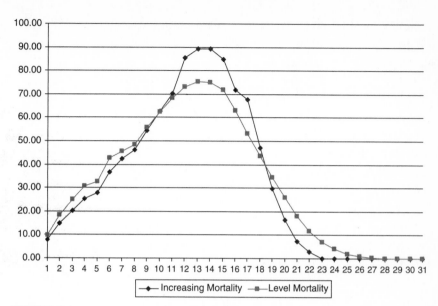

EXHIBIT 6.4   Comparative Probability Distributions

assumption, even though the LE is the same. This will have an impact on the projected rate of return.

RISK MANAGEMENT STRATEGIES

Unpredictability of the various risk factors inherent in a life settlement trans-action makes it a challenge to manage the risk more tightly. It is, however, manageable. As the industry matures and more data is accumulated, the risk management tools will also improve.

Funders could work more closely with their LE providers to provide more in-depth information about the risks they review.

A large, well-diversified portfolio offers improved spread of the risk.

Portfolios should be diversified for length of LEs and policy sizes as well as for major impairments. Concentration in only a few impairments leaves the portfolio vulnerable to improvement in treatments and discov-ery of new drugs—such as the drug protocols that exponentially reduced HIV/AIDS mortality. Stop-loss insurance products are being developed and, when available, these will significantly improve the risk management situa-tion by insulating the investor from the extreme instances where an insured outlives his or her life expectancy by a substantial margin.

CHAPTER 7

Life Insurance Policy Swaps

Vishaal B. Bhuyan
Managing Partner, V.B. Bhuyan & Co., Inc.

Swapping paid up life insurance policies for underperforming policies is another way investors can access the secondary life insurance market. Similar to traditional life settlements, the counterparties in these transactions are high net worth senior citizens. In the past, swap outs were conducted exclusively between policyholders and carriers and only viable for cash account policies. These swaps were based on the cash surrender value of the policy and were offered to policyholders as an alternative to surrendering the policy.

A major reason policyholders would swap their policies with an insurance carrier is to account for a drop in interest rates since origination. For example, a policyholder would swap a policy when the original contract illustrated premium payments based on a 9.00 percent interest earning account that projected the policy to be paid up after 12 years. However if rates dropped to 4.5 percent 6 years later the policy would require premiums to be paid for approximately twice the estimated time. By swapping out the contract the policyholder can significantly reduce his or her premium payments (but also the death benefit), which may have increased in duration due to a similar drop in rates.

In a swap, policyholders are also able to roll over their cash accounts into their new policies without having to pay income tax on any gains in the cash account as opposed to surrendering the policy and purchasing a new one.

Note: The death benefit of the new policy in a life insurance swap is less than the death benefit of the original policy.

Exhibit 7.1 is an illustration of the basic swap out transaction between a policyholder and insurance carrier.

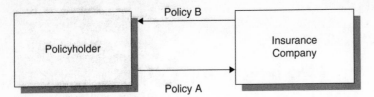

EXHIBIT 7.1   Life Insurance Policy Swap with Carrier

The following are other economic reasons why a policyholder would swap out an insurance policy with the insurance carrier:

- Policyholder wishes to reduce premium payments or discontinue premiums entirely.
- Change in interest rates.
- The insured's health has improved significantly.
- Policyholder wishes to increase the death benefit but not premium payments.
- Change in the policyholder's financial situation.
- Change in insurance pricing from the carrier.
- Policyholder does not want to surrender the policy, which would expose gains in the cash account to income taxes.

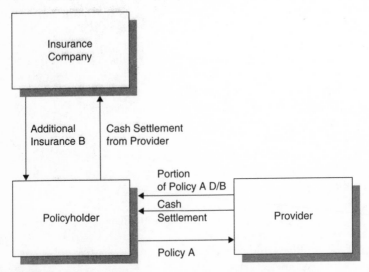

EXHIBIT 7.2   Life insurance Policy Swap with Provider

With the creation of the secondary market however, investors (via providers) have designed innovative swap products to meet the needs of their clients and provide additional flexibility to address shortcomings in carrier offered swap transactions. Providers understand that each client has different needs in terms of life insurance and estate planning. Some wealthy individuals wish to reduce premium payments but retain an equal amount of coverage. Exhibit 7.2 illustrates a life insurance swap out between a policyholder and a provider.

As opposed to swap outs with an insurance carrier, these transactions are not based on the cash surrender value of the policy but on the life expectancy of the insured. This results in greater value to the policyholder. In this scenario the policyholder retains a portion of the death benefit from the original policy (Policy A in Exhibit 7.2) in addition to a cash settlement from the provider. This cash settlement, which is less than the amount that would be received in a traditional life settlement, may be used to purchase additional life insurance (Additional Insurance B in Exhibit 7.2) in order for a client to maintain a desired level of coverage.

In provider-based swaps, clients do not pay income tax on any profits made in the cash value of the policy.

CHAPTER 8

Premium Financing

Vishaal B. Bhuyan
Managing Partner, V.B. Bhuyan & Co., Inc.

Premium financing is a financial transaction whereby a lender provides funding to a high net worth individual for the purpose of purchasing life insurance or simply financing the premiums of an existing policy.

Lenders in premium financing transactions are dedicated premium financing entities, investment banks, hedge funds, providers, or a combination of these. Premium financing has been widely used in commercial applications for varying types of business and property and casualty insurance, but it is now being used as a method of participating in the secondary life insurance market.

By financing the costs associated with purchasing life insurance, high net worth individuals are able to tap into their excess insurance capacity without a substantial cash outlay for premium payments. Premium financing is best used for estate planning purposes, and loans generally borrowed by an irrevocable life insurance trust (ILIT). Moreover, premium financing is most economically viable in periods of relatively low interest rates, as the interest on the loan must be less than the interest earned on the assets that would otherwise be liquidated to make premium payments on the desired life insurance policy.

Although there are variations of premium financing programs in the market, premium financing may be divided into three major types: full recourse, nonrecourse, and limited or partial recourse.

In the full recourse premium financing model loans are secured with collateral such as the cash value of the policy, government bonds, certificates of deposit, cash, nonfinanced life insurance policies with substantial cash values, or a letter of credit from a major bank. Lenders may require that borrowers overcollateralize their loans by as much as 50 percent and in these types of lending programs, the credit worthiness of the borrower is important.

In the nonrecourse premium financing model, the lender may not make any claims on assets held by the borrower other than the cash value and the death benefit of the policy in question. The risk in nonrecourse premium financing is life expectancy, not the credit worthiness of the borrower; however, because the loan is not secured by any assets other than the policy's value components, interest rates are generally higher than full recourse funding. Other types of nonrecourse premium financing available today allow policyholders to finance premiums of existing life insurance policies as opposed to financing the purchase of new policies. Nonrecourse premium financing programs have come under a great deal of scrutiny over the past few years however, as these programs may incentivize stranger-owned life insurance (STOLI) transactions. Nonrecourse programs are rapidly decreasing in availability.

Limited or partial recourse premium financing is a hybrid program, which uses various types of assets or a personal guarantee in addition to the policy's death benefit and cash value as collateral. This crossover allows funds to be lent at slightly lower rates than nonrecourse programs but with less risk to the lender. These programs also curb the level of STOLI transactions, which are otherwise a strong part of the premium financing market. Limited recourse is the most widely available program available.

In all types of premium financing the borrower is responsible for repayment of the principal and interest of the loan at a specified maturity date or the time of the payout of the life insurance policy. Interest may either be paid annually or accrued and paid at the maturity of the loan. Interest on the loan is either fixed or floating spread over a benchmark rate such as the London Interbank Offered Rate or prime rate.

In situations where lenders require that interest be paid annually, borrowers may benefit from purchasing a Single Premium Immediate Annuity (SPIA) to fund the interest payments of their financed life insurance policy. The cost of the SPIA may be funded from cash on hand or by selling an underperforming asset and using a 1035 exchange[1] to purchase the annuity. The importance of this strategy is to ensure that the borrower is sufficiently capitalized to make interest payments. A SPIA also acts as a hedge, as the purchaser of a SPIA benefits from rising interest rates, which can counteract the negative effect rising rates will have on a floating rate loan. Although accrued interest programs delay interest payments until the maturity of the loan, if interest rates rise substantially (assuming there is a floating interest rate on the loan) there may be a shortfall between the death benefit of the policy and the total loan amount. See Exhibits 8.1 and 8.2.

Although there are different types of loan programs for premium financing, lenders generally require that borrowers meet certain criteria. In most cases, the borrower must be purchasing a policy worth no less than

EXHIBIT 8.1 Premium Financing Programs

	Collateral in addition to policy	In case of default	Availability
Full Recourse	Bonds, CDs, Letter of Credit	Collateral withheld	Uncommon
Nonrecourse	None	Policy purchased by lender or sold on open market	Rapidly becoming uncommon
Limited Recourse	Personal guarantee or other assets	Policy sold on open market and/or collateral withheld	Most common and increasing in availability

This is a general summary and different lenders may have differing requirements and reactions to borrower default.

$1,000,000, have a net worth of over $5,000,000 and, depending on the loan program, a life expectancy of less than 20 years.

Many lenders also require that the insurance carrier that is writing the policy that is to be financed, approve the transaction. This is known as *carrier approved premium finance*, and it decreases the risk of the insurance carrier withholding the death benefit at the time of maturity, if the lender takes possession of the life insurance policy.

There are many different variations of carrier approved partial and full recourse premium financing programs in the market. The two major

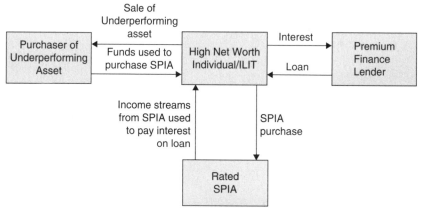

EXHIBIT 8.2 Premium Finance SPIA Structure

elements of a well structured program are well collateralized loans and, in the case of borrower default, the auction of the policy into the market (as opposed to the purchase of the policy by the lender).

In the nonrecourse, or limited recourse model, lenders may sell the policy of the borrower if the loan is defaulted on or there is insufficient collateral to match the loan. In nonrecourse programs many lenders lock up the borrowers so that they must sell their policies directly to the lender for less than their market value. Not only does this have a negative impact on the market but also raises regulatory and ethical issues. Not all programs work in this fashion, however. Well structured limited recourse programs will not use premium financing as a method of acquiring policies and if the lender is forced to sell a policy it may simply auction off the policy on the open market to recoup its losses. Both insurance carriers and regulators prefer this method.

From a lender's perspective, there are many different methods of conducting a premium financing business. It is important to remember, however, that the businesses that last in this market are ones that operate under the auspices of the regulators and insurance carriers. In these cases the insurance carrier is well aware the policy being written is being financed and may be sold on the secondary market if the lender feels there is insufficient collateralization or in the case of default.

Premium financing life insurance is a rapidly growing area in the banking and life settlement sectors. These loans provide uncorrelated returns for investors and, if the program is well structured, the risks are clear and relatively quantifiable (given accurate underwriting). Once some of the regulatory and underwriting hurdles of the life settlement industry are conquered, the premium financing business will flourish, especially in areas such as the securitization of premium finance loans. Insurance carriers, who are coming to accept the secondary insurance market and approve premium financing transactions, may increase the cost of insurance in order to hedge against any change in lapse ratios.

NOTE

1. 1035 exchange refers to the provision of the U.S. tax code which allows investors to transfer accumulated funds in one life insurance policy, endowment, or annuity policy to another without incurring a tax liability. Certain guidelines must be met to take advantage of the 1035 exchange provision. For example, an endowment qualifies for 1035 exchange status only if the maturity date of the replacement endowment is no later than the maturity date of the endowment being replaced.

Securitization

Life Settlement Securitization

Emmanuel Modu
Managing Director and Global Head of Structured Finance,
A.M. Best Company

A life settlement is an insurance policy sold by the owner—typically the insured or a trust—for an amount greater than the surrender value of the policy but lower than the face value of the policy. The purchaser of the life settlement becomes the new owner and beneficiary of the life insurance policy and is responsible for making future premium payments and collecting the death benefit of the insured. The list below offers some of the reasons to sell an insurance policy.

Reasons to Sell an Insurance Policy
- Premiums paid by the policyholder have become unaffordable and the policy is in danger of lapsing.
- Estate planning needs of the insured have changed significantly.
- Funds are needed for long-term health care.
- Beneficiary has changed because of death or divorce.
- Disposal of unneeded key man insurance or other business-owned insurance.
- Fund new annuities, life insurance or investments.
- Satisfy the need for cash in a forced liquidation due to bankruptcy or financial difficulties.
- Liquidate policies donated to not-for-profits.
- Dispose of policies that no longer are needed or wanted for a variety of other reasons.

The life settlement market is an outgrowth of the viatical settlement market, in which policies of the terminally ill—normally those insureds expected to die within 2 years—are bought and sold. In the life settlement market, however, insureds generally are 65 years or older, with medical impairments resulting in life expectancies of about 3 to 15 years.

Life settlements typically are sold through licensed providers by insurance brokers and agents. The price providers pay for the life settlements depends generally on the life expectancies estimated by medical examiners after evaluating the medical records of the insured, as well as policy-specific contract characteristics. The more severe the chronic illness of an insured, the lower the life expectancy and, hence, the higher the price paid for the life settlement.

Life settlement securitization has generated a lot of interest in the capital markets. Indeed, some financial institutions have been financing the accumulation of life settlement portfolios that they hope to securitize. The growth of life settlement securitization will depend on a number of factors:

- Increased clarity and standardization of the general methods for predicting life expectancies of insureds (including release of data on the performance of medical examiners).
- The transparency of the pricing of life settlements.
- The transparency of the fees earned by the various intermediaries in the transactions.
- The extent to which the life settlement industry provides safeguards regarding the identities, health conditions, and financial status of policyowners.
- Effective industry regulatory oversight and self-policing.
- The establishment of rating agency standards for assessing the credit risks associated with such transactions.
- The pace of the emergence of new initiatives supported by the life insurance industry to provide alternatives to the secondary market for life insurance policies.

This document outlines A.M. Best Co.'s considerations in rating securities backed by life settlements. The list below and Exhibit 9.1 describe and illustrate the parties involved in typical life settlement securitization transactions.

Parties Involved in Life Settlement Securitizations

The Issuer. The issuer normally is a bankruptcy-remote entity established for the sole purpose of purchasing life settlements, issuing securities collateralized by life settlements, and holding other assets for the sole purpose of servicing the interests of the noteholders.

The responsibility of the issuer is outlined in the indenture of the transaction.

The Providers. Providers are licensed entities that purchase insurance policies directly from sellers or licensed brokers or agents authorized to act for sellers. They are responsible for making sure that all transfer-related documentation and sale documentation packages conform to applicable state or federal statutes, laws, rules, and regulations relating to consumer protection and insurance and life settlement practices and procedures. Providers present policies to the issuer pursuant to an origination agreement.

Medical Examiners. Medical examiners provide comprehensive reviews of medical records and mortality profiles on the insureds looking to sell their insurance policies. The mortality profile provided by the medical examiners includes a summary of pertinent medical conditions as well as a determination of life expectancy. The issuer requires providers to engage the services of at least two independent medical examiners to evaluate the life expectancies of the insureds.

Adviser for Inconsistency. This adviser performs "inconsistency checks" verifying that medical records are consistent with the original insurance applications. Medical examiners sometimes can provide this service.

Collateral Manager. The collateral manager is responsible for choosing the policies that will be included in the transactions. This manager's specific responsibilities may include: confirming that the eligibility criteria for inclusion in a portfolio are satisfied; performing policy optimization to minimize premium payments and maximize death benefits; delivering the sales documentation package to the trustee; liquidating policies when necessary; determining which policies should lapse in the event of a liquidity crisis; and determining how much to reduce death benefits in order to reduce premium payments in a liquidity crisis.

Tracking Agent. The tracking agent is responsible for contacting the insureds or their representatives to verify the current life/death status of the insureds. The tracking agent normally uses methods similar to those developed for consumer loan servicing such as accessing databases for the insured's marital status, residence, and physicians' visits and matching Social Security numbers to individuals who have died. In addition, the tracking agent is responsible for obtaining copies of death certificates (and sometimes, filing the death claim with the insurance company) to facilitate the prompt collection of death benefits.

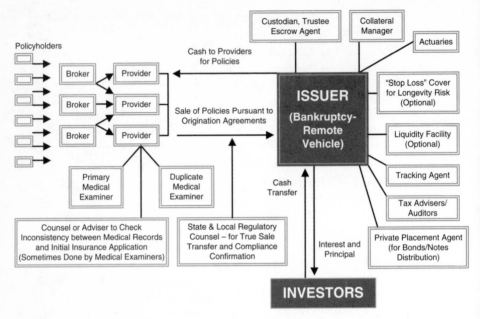

EXHIBIT 9.1 Parties Involved in Life Settlement Securitizations

Trustee. The trustee performs all the duties it is assigned in the transaction's indenture. In general, the trustee is responsible for holding the bonds/notes for the benefit of the noteholders; holding the security granted by the issuer over its assets; and for making payments and performing certain other obligations pursuant to the indenture. The trustee also holds all documents delivered to the issuer in connection with each life settlement. In addition, the trustee performs certain duties related to documenting life insurance policy acquisitions, fund transfers, and submission of claims for payment under life insurance policies on the instructions of the collateral manager.

Actuaries. Actuaries can play an important role by helping to determine the appropriate mortality tables for the transaction; assessing the reasonability of the mortality/survivorship schedule provided by medical examiners; performing an underwriting review of the medical examiners used in the transaction; and helping the issuer determine the liquidation value of life settlements.

Insurance Companies. The insurance companies that issued the life insurance policies in the transaction are critical, because they must be notified of the transfer of the policy's ownership, they can provide policy illustrations to help with policy optimization, and they are responsible for sending notices to the issuer about the policies and for sending the death benefits to the issuer.

Attorneys. Attorneys can help ensure that all documentation is complete and has been prepared in compliance with state insurance regulations, and that the integrity of the insurable interest doctrine is maintained. They also may provide comfort letters to verify the states in which providers are licensed, and they can help craft medical disclosure forms to comply with applicable privacy laws. In addition, attorneys ensure that the bankruptcy-remote entities from which the securities are issued have been created so as to protect the assets of such security holders.

Accountants/Auditors. Accountants can provide opinions about (1) the recognition of income and expenses in the bankruptcy-remote entity's country of domicile; (2) the tax implications, if any, of acquiring life settlements by the entity; (3) any special tax treatment/implications associated with the disposal of life settlements; and (4) identification of any tax withholding requirements that might be applicable to the entity. Auditors periodically provide opinions on the integrity of the balance sheet and income statement of the bankruptcy-remote entity.

A.M. BEST RATING POLICY

Analysis Based on a Newly Acquired Portfolio of Life Settlements

The acquisition of new life settlements for securitizations is fraught with uncertainties: the extent to which the seller of the insurance policies has established insurable interest in the lives of the insured; the price of the life settlements; the estimated life expectancies of the individuals who sell their insurance policies; the availability of an ample pool of policies to satisfy the requirement for the transaction; the extent to which the various intermediaries involved in facilitating the sale of insurance policies have adhered to legal and regulatory requirements; and other factors that can make building a suitable life settlement portfolio challenging. Due to these uncertainties, A.M. Best issues three types of evaluations for securities backed by life settlements: (1) a Preliminary Assessment, (2) an Indicative Rating and (3) a Long-Term Debt Rating (Debt Rating). These analyses represent increasing levels of certainty associated with the transaction, as further described in the following paragraphs.

Preliminary Assessment A Preliminary Assessment is issued to securities that are to be backed by a projected portfolio of life settlements that will be purchased over a specified period. Since the securities and the life settlement portfolio do not yet exist, the Preliminary Assessment is given only if the issuer (the bankruptcy-remote entity issuing the securities in the transaction) indicates to A.M. Best that it intends eventually to acquire a Debt Rating on securities backed by in-place life settlement collateral. To qualify for a Preliminary Assessment, all the major factors of the transaction must be specified, such as the:

- Providers of the life settlements.
- Policy accumulation period.
- Features of the securities contemplated for issuance.
- Features of each life settlement to be acquired for the transaction.
- Reserve amount and/or liquidity facility (if any).
- Stop-loss provisions (if any).
- The legal maturity of the transaction.
- The transaction's "waterfall."
- Overcollateralization or debt coverage triggers (if any) contemplated for the transaction.
- The term sheet for the transaction.
- Other significant parameters and requirements fully described in this methodology.

The Preliminary Assessment is valid only at the time of issue; it is not updated (unless the issuer explicitly requests an update); and it is communicated to the issuer via a private letter.

Indicative Rating An Indicative Rating, in the context of life settlement-backed securities, can only be sought by the issuer once it has purchased at least 80 percent of the life settlements targeted for the transaction. The Indicative Rating, which is a public rating, reflects the specific attributes of the purchased life settlements, as well as the life settlements targeted to fully ramp up the portfolio. Even though the transaction has not yet been fully completed, the Indicative Rating is given to the securities to give investors an indication of the current credit quality of the securities. A.M. Best requires a draft of the indenture or offering memorandum from the attorneys engaged by the issuer. In addition, all essential elements of the transaction must be in place, such as the:

- Providers of the life settlements.
- Tracking agent.

- Collateral manager.
- Features of the securities being issued.
- Features of the life settlements that have been acquired and projections of the features and timing of the life settlements to be acquired to complete the ramp-up.
- Formation of the bankruptcy-remote vehicle that will issue the securities.
- Two designated medical examiners.
- Underwriting review of the medical examiners and their operations.
- Actual and projected prices of life settlements.
- Actual and projected life expectancies.
- Actual and projected premiums of the policies.
- Reserve amount and/or liquidity facility (if any).
- The transaction's "waterfall."
- Stop-loss provisions (if any).
- Overcollateralization or debt coverage triggers (if any).
- All legal documents, at least in draft form.
- Other significant parameters and requirements as fully described in this methodology.

Long-Term Debt Rating (Debt Rating)   An issuer seeking a Debt Rating must have acquired 100 percent of the life settlements necessary for the transaction and met all the conditions outlined for the Indicative Rating. If an Indicative Rating was issued to the securities, that rating is replaced by a Debt Rating upon completion of the ramp-up and finalization of all legal documents. The Debt Rating is a public rating.

It is not necessary for the issuer to seek the Preliminary Assessment or an Indicative Rating before seeking a Debt Rating. For example, an issuer that already has accumulated or purchased a portfolio of life settlements could seek a Debt Rating without seeking either a Preliminary Assessment or an Indicative Rating before seeking a Debt Rating.

ANALYSES BASED ON AN EXISTING PORTFOLIO OF LIFE SETTLEMENTS

A.M. Best generally prefers to rate securities backed by new life settlements that have been purchased policy by policy over a period of about 12 to 18 months or less. In fact, this methodology focuses on such home-grown portfolios of life settlements. However, A.M. Best is aware that from time to time portfolios of life settlements are made available for sale by institutional investors or providers that wish to liquidate their holdings. Acquiring an existing portfolio eliminates the ramp-up period, which can be extensive for life settlement transactions, and may mitigate some of the other uncertainties associated with purchasing policies over time. Buyers of existing portfolios, however, run the risk of inheriting the legal and regulatory risks inherent in the manner in which the portfolios were originated.

A.M. Best, under certain situations, may make its decision on whether to rate securities collateralized by an existing portfolio based on various factors including (but not limited to): the original life settlement eligibility criteria; the medical examiners used and the availability of any and all life expectancy projections on the lives in the portfolio; when the medical examiner determined the life expectancies of the lives in the portfolio; the ease of the legal transfer of the portfolio to the issuer; the availability of the data needed for surveillance of the transaction (as described in the last section of this chapter); proven historical mortality experience of the portfolio; and the availability of legal opinions verifying adherence to insurable interest laws.

A.M. BEST'S ANALYTICAL APPROACH

Evaluating Life Settlement-Backed Securities

The A.M. Best Structured Finance Group is responsible for rating securities collateralized by life settlements. The mortality profiles of the insured, as provided by reputable medical examiners, are used in simulating the maturities in the entire life settlement portfolio. In addition, the probabilities of impairment of the insurance companies and the assumed recoveries are applied to the transaction. These factors, along with the price of each life settlement, the premium for each policy, and the projected increases in premium (if any) in the event the insureds live longer than expected are considered in arriving at the cash flows that will service the securities. The end result of A.M. Best's analysis is a determination of the default probability of the securities, which then is correlated to an idealized default probability matrix. This process, in conjunction with meeting various stress scenarios and qualitative considerations, helps establish the credit rating on the securities based on A.M. Best's credit market scale.

Rating Considerations and Requirements

Types of Policies Permitted/Conditions on Policies   Issuers of securities backed by life settlements can include life insurance policies most commonly found in life settlement transactions, such as: universal life, variable universal life, whole life, variable whole life, term life, joint survivorship, and group policies. A.M. Best also allows term policies that are convertible or exchangeable to permanent policies without a new medical evaluation and without a new contestability or suicide provision. The anticipated maximum increase in premiums at the time of conversion or exchange must be disclosed. Term polices that are neither convertible nor exchangeable are allowed in the transaction only if the term of the policy is at least 2.5 times the life expectancy of the insured. There is, however, a 10 percent limit on the number of lives covered by term policies in the pool and a 10 percent limit on the aggregate face value of the term policies in the pool. Because group policies are subject to the risk that the sponsoring employer, union, or association will become insolvent, A.M. Best allows only convertible group policies in the collateral pool.

The general rules related to the features of the insurance policies in life settlement securitizations are:

- Only policies issued by U.S. insurance companies on U.S. residents are allowed.
- Assignment of the policy to another party should not be restricted.
- Policies with decreasing death benefits are not allowed.
- Fractional shares of polices generally are not allowed.
- Confirmation is required that the policy is in force and is not within the grace period.
- No restrictions should exist on the payment of the full, current net death benefits in the event of the insured's death, except for nonpayment of the current premiums.
- Confirmation is required that nothing prevents the payment of insurance benefits in one lump sum.
- Verification is required that the policy is not encumbered by any other party.
- Verification is required that there is no outstanding debt on the policy.

Service Providers

Medical Examiners

Mortality Ratings and Life Expectancy Estimates   Medical examiners use a numerical rating system developed by reinsurers to determine how an individual's mortality differs from a standard risk. In general, standard risk is given a value of 100 percent, which represents a unit of risk. The system assigns debits and credits to a life where debits are factors that increase a person's mortality over a standard risk and credits are factors that decrease a person's mortality over a standard risk. For example, an individual might have coronary heart disease that may be assigned a debit of 150 percent, and if that person has had bypass surgery to manage the ailment, he or she may earn credits of 25 percent. When the debits and credits are summed, the person has a net debit balance of 125 percent. If a standard risk is considered to have a table rating of 100 percent, then this risk relative to standard will have a rating of 225 percent. This can be interpreted to mean that the probability that this individual will die is 125 percent higher than that of a standard risk—that is, 225 percent of a standard risk. It is important to recognize that one of the significant tasks a medical examiner has to undertake is to determine what constitutes a standard risk, given that the mortality rating is a relative measure of the probability of death, not an absolute measure. Authors Brackenridge, Croxson, and Mackenzie put it succinctly in the fifth edition of *Brackenridge's Medical Selection of Life Risks*:

> *The underwriting of substandard lives uses comparative mortality to judge substandard risks. Simply put, in order for a condition to be viewed as substandard, mortality observed among those people having the condition, must be greater than the mortality otherwise expected. And in order to know what mortality to expect, a reference mortality experience must be available.*

No matter the medical examiner, the standard risk class should represent a combination of risks that are substandard as well as risks that are above standard—not just risks of healthy individuals. To arrive at a life expectancy for most lives, the medical underwriter applies the mortality rating to its standard mortality, otherwise known as the "reference mortality experience" in the preceding passage. Because each medical underwriter uses its own mortality tables and has its own method of determining debits and credits to account for diseases, lifestyle, and mortality improvements, it is difficult to derive a mortality curve for an insured unless one knows the specific standard table used by that medical examiner. For this very reason, one who receives a mortality rating from a medical examiner for an insured also should get the corresponding standard mortality table that is used to derive the life expectancy; otherwise, the data set is incomplete for the purposes of analyzing mortality risk. The life settlement industry has surmised that most medical examiners currently use some version of the 2001 VBT as standard—a conclusion that is not entirely wrong. It should be noted that A.M. Best views favorably standard mortality tables that have been created with the help of qualified actuaries—especially those who are familiar with older age mortality patterns.

A medical examiner can provide some or all of the following information: 1) its standard mortality tables upon which debits and credits are applied; 2) a mortality rating (100% + net debits and credits) that the medical examiner applies to its base mortality table to derive the life expectancy for each insured; 3) a life expectancy estimate for each insured (including the joint life-expectancy estimates for second-to-die policies); 4) a mortality or survivorship schedule for each insured (given medical impairments); 5) the primary disease category for each insured, if one has been identified; and 6) a report that validates the historical accuracy of the medical examiners' life-expectancy projections (i.e. actual to expected results).

The primary disease is the impairment for which the most debits have been assigned and that accounts for 50 percent or more of the total debits. If no single impairment accounts for 50 percent or more of the total debits, then the disease category should be classified as "multiple." The categorization of diseases will help ensure the disease diversity required in the transaction. Medical examiners can categorize diseases using the groupings in Exhibit 9.2.

For investors, two of the most important factors in evaluating life settlements are longevity risk and the potential for medical examiners to systematically misestimate life expectancies. A.M. Best has observed that life

EXHIBIT 9.2 Disease Diversity

Disease or Category	Examples	Maximum Limits
Cardiovascular	Coronary Artery Disease, Arrhythmia, Other (e.g. Heart Valve Disease)	50%
Cerebrovascular	Stroke, Carotid Artery, Transient Ischemic Attack	20%
Dementia	Alzheimer's, Multi-Infarct	20%
Cancer	Lung, Prostate, Breast, Hematological, All Other Cancers	25%
Diabetes		10%
Respiratory Diseases	Emphysema, Asthma, Sleep Apnea, Chronic Obstructive Pulmonary Disease	20%
Neurological Disorders (Excluding Alzheimer)	Parkinson's, Lou Gehrig's Disease (ALS)	15%
Other	Renal Failure, Peripheral Vascular, etc.	20%
No Disease		100%
Multiple		40%
HIV/AIDS		0%

settlement portfolios accumulated about five years ago or so are beginning to show signs that maturities (deaths) are not keeping pace with the opinions given by medical examiners when the portfolios originally were formed. A.M. Best also has observed that since the last update of this methodology in September 2005, medical examiners have been issuing more conservative life expectancies for the lives they have evaluated. For example, in the earlier methodology, about 73 percent of the life expectancies issued were less than or equal to 144 months. Currently, the life expectancies issued less than or equal to 144 months have narrowed to about 51 percent. This may reflect more conservative methodologies by medical examiners and/or the possibility that medical examiners are determining life expectancies for healthier people than before.

Exhibit 9.3 shows the typical distribution of life expectancies for individuals aged 65 and older, as observed by A.M. Best over the past year. The table shows that A.M. Best expects 10.7 percent of all life expectancies issued were between 72 months and 96 months, and only 18.4 percent were less than or equal to 96 months. The table is important because it shows that the highly coveted low life expectancies sought by some investors in life settlements just are not plentiful.

To further illustrate why the supply of short life expectancies is limited, it is useful to observe the life expectancies of a 75-year-old, male nonsmoker—the typical profile of individuals likely to be in a pool of life settlements.

Exhibit 9.4 shows the life expectancy of 75-year-olds based on various mortality ratings applied to the 2001 VBT. A 100 percent mortality rating

EXHIBIT 9.3 Typical Distribution of Life Expectancies for Ages 65 and Over

Life Expectancy Range(Months)		Frequency Distribution	Cumulative Probability
	≤24	0.3%	0.3%
>24	≤48	1.8%	2.1%
>48	≤72	5.6%	7.7%
>72	≤96	10.7%	18.4%
>96	≤120	15.9%	34.3%
>120	≤144	16.7%	51.1%
>144	≤168	16.9%	67.9%
>168	≤192	14.5%	82.4%
>192	≤216	9.6%	92.0%
>216	≤240	5.0%	97.0%
>240	≤264	2.2%	99.2%
>288		0.8%	100.0%

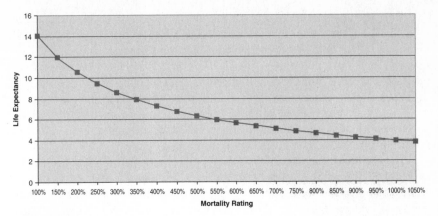

EXHIBIT 9.4 Life Expectancy as a Function of Mortality Rating (Based on a 75-Year-Old Male Non-Smoker)

applied to the 2001 VBT suggests that in the aggregate, the insureds being evaluated die based on the standard pattern established by the table. A 200 percent mortality rating suggests that the insureds die at twice the rate of the standard pattern established by the 2001 VBT, and so on. The mortality ratings, therefore, generally indicate the relative severity of diseases afflicting the insureds. As shown in Exhibit 9.4 a 75-year-old male nonsmoker has a normal (unimpaired) life expectancy (based on 100 percent mortality rating) of about 14 years. The mortality ratings generally issued by medical examiners for the impaired lives of this age, sex, and smoking status normally would range from 300 percent down to 150 percent, which translates to life expectancies between approximately 8.7 and 11.8 years. To achieve a life expectancy of about seven years or less for this type of individual, the mortality rating would need to be about 460 percent or more—rare mortality ratings for individuals with the profile under consideration.

While medical examiners, in general, have been issuing higher life expectancies than ever before, data evaluated by A.M. Best still show major differences in the life expectancies issued by various medical examiners on the same lives. A.M. Best compared life expectancies issued by three major medical examiners over the past year on the exact same 909 lives. The ages ranged from 75 to 79, and the male/female split was 66 percent/34 percent— the typical ages and gender distribution found in life settlement pools. After calculating the average life expectancies for each of the three medical examiners, the largest difference of average life expectancies issued by any two medical examiners was 24 months. The smallest difference was 8 months.

The differences in life expectancies generally mean that one would arrive at a different price for an insurance policy depending on what medical examiner is used in the price calculation—a lower life expectancy necessarily means a higher price for the policy. In a very competitive marketplace where policies are scarce, some industry intermediaries who buy policies on behalf of the ultimate investors may have an incentive to encourage the use of lower life expectancies for pricing purposes, because it gives them a better chance at winning the bidding contest for the policies and maintaining the internal rate of return (IRR) thresholds set by their clients.

The effect of life expectancy adverse development on a life settlement portfolio's IRR can be dramatic. Exhibit 9.5 shows the IRR of an actual portfolio of about 150 policies with premiums optimized to be equal to the cost of insurance. The IRR calculation incorporates just the cost of the portfolio purchase, the premium payments, and the death benefits. The exhibit shows the decrease in IRR as the life expectancy is increased from 3 months to 36 months. When the aggregate life expectancy is 24 months longer than is projected, the IRR goes from 12.4 percent to 6.5 percent—cutting the original IRR nearly in half. Of course, the relationship between life expectancies and IRRs will vary depending on a host of factors, such as the original portfolio life expectancy, the premium schedule, and the cost of the portfolio. However, the trend of a dramatically lower IRR as life expectancy increases by more than one year generally will be consistent across portfolios of life settlements.

EXHIBIT 9.5 Effect of Increase in Life Expectancy on IRR

Increase in Life Expectancy (Months)	Internal Rate of Return (%)
0	12.4
3	11.6
6	10.7
9	10.0
12	9.2
15	8.5
18	7.8
21	7.1
24	6.5
27	5.9
30	5.3
33	4.7
36	4.3

To mitigate the effect of systematic errors by medical examiners in the determination of life expectancies, A.M. Best generally requires that two independent medical examiners provide an evaluation of the health condition of the insureds in the collateral pool based on the medical records obtained from the primary physicians of the insureds. Of course, this is relevant only if the issuer is seeking an Indicative Rating or a Debt Rating as opposed to a Preliminary Assessment.

For the sake of clarity, A.M. Best primarily uses the mathematical definition of life expectancy, which is the weighted average time to maturity of the lives/cash flows in the life settlement pool.

A.M. Best's experience has shown that the mortality ratings typically assigned by reputable medical examiners rarely exceed 500 percent of their base mortality tables and that assigned mortality ratings generally decrease with age. A.M. Best recognizes that in cases where traditional underwriting is not applicable or in cases that merit extra mortality for a specified period of time ("flat extras"), the mortality rating could exceed the 500 percent threshold. However, A.M. Best does not believe that issuers can find enough supply to populate their life settlement portfolios with significant numbers of such policies unless the ramp-up period for the portfolio is several years. Therefore, A.M. Best imposes a mortality cap of 500 percent on all lives in the life settlement pool, unless the medical examiner that has issued the mortality ratings or the life expectancies in question shows precisely how it has applied net debits and credits to its standard mortality tables to arrive at its life expectancies, and a third medical examiner or a physician specialist is used to corroborate the mortality ratings or life expectancies.

Should an issuer decide not to seek a life expectancy from a medical examiner for an insured in a life settlement pool, A.M. Best will assume that the life expectancy is the same as that derived from a standard mortality table, such as the 2001 VBT (or any other table, such as the 2008 VBT, should that table be suitable for life settlements), and will stress the mortality rates for modeling purposes.

Underwriting Evaluation of Medical Examiners   If an issuer is seeking a Debt Rating, an independent actuarial firm or an independent consultant with demonstrated expertise in the life settlement market should be engaged to perform an audit/review of the processes and procedures medical examiners used to determine life expectancies. A.M. Best expects the issuer's representatives and/or the medical examiner to fully discuss the following regarding the medical examiner's underwriting practices:

- Underwriting methodology and philosophy.
- Physician/underwriter evaluator background and credentials.

- Standard mortality table(s) used to determine life expectancy estimates.
- Initial and ongoing training of staff.
- Self-auditing procedures (internal audits).
- Frequency of external/independent audits.
- The extent of the self-evaluation of the medical examiner's efficacy (that is, results of experience studies from internal database).
- Record keeping and process flow.
- Source materials such as reinsurance manuals and clinical studies for specific diseases.
- Extent and frequency of updates of source materials/reinsurance manual.
- Recent changes and reasons for changes in the methodology used by medical examiners.
- Comparative analyses of files selected by the actuarial firm or consultant reviewing medical examiner assessments; amount of files selected will depend on the number that the actuarial firm or consultant believes will help it form an informed opinion on the medical examiner's underwriting guidelines.

Among the questions that the issuer and the medical examiner should be prepared to answer are the following:

- What is the general nature of the adjustments made to the standard mortality table(s) used?
- Are flat extras used? If so, for what diseases?
- Are debits always additive? How are debits scaled back for comorbidity?
- Under what circumstances are mortality tables abandoned and other methods applied for estimating life expectancies?
- Are mortality improvements factored into the life-expectancy figures?
- When using mortality tables, is "age near" or "age last" the applicable age used for the analysis?
- What are the maximum and minimum ages for which a life expectancy will be provided?
- What are the maximum and minimum mortality ratings issued?
- What is the maximum age of medical records for an evaluation? (For example, if medical records are 15 months old, will a life expectancy still be issued?)
- When medical records have aged, are the life expectancies provided adjusted for the period between the time the records were created and the time of the medical examiner's evaluation?
- Is a survivorship schedule provided?
- Does the medical examiner provide joint life-expectancy calculations?

Policy Providers   The provider purchases insurance policies from a seller or a licensed broker or agent authorized to act for the seller. The purchases of life settlements are made through licensed providers approved by the collateral manager of the transaction. In the case of life settlement securitizations, the provider purchases policies for the issuer pursuant to an origination agreement between the issuer and the provider. A.M. Best requires that the purchase agreement comply with all applicable state insurance laws and regulations governing life settlement or viatical financing transactions between the issuer and the life settlement providers.

Issuers must identify the providers they intend to use for their transactions. A.M. Best's view on the providers will depend on the following considerations:

- The various states in which the providers are licensed to conduct business (in states where licensing is required).
- The partnerships between the providers and their network of policy suppliers and brokers.
- The providers' prior policy purchasing experience for institutional investors.
- The providers' historical policy acquisition pace.
- The providers' infrastructure and systems for handling the administrative tasks and regulatory compliance issues associated with life settlements.
- Any significant pending legal matters against the provider.
- Other factors that may give A.M. Best confidence in the transaction.

If a provider has any ongoing financial interest in the transaction aside from its capacity as the source of policies for the issuer, A.M. Best requires full disclosure of that relationship.

Note that A.M. Best maintains that a provider should not be the sole determinant of the policies that are to be purchased for the transaction. The provider certainly can present policies to the issuer's representative (such as the collateral manager for the transaction), but the issuer should be the ultimate arbiter as to what policies should be in the transaction's portfolio. One way to remove absolute discretion from the provider over which policies should be purchased for the transaction is for the issuer to give the provider a list of purchasing criteria; tell the provider which medical examiners will be used in the transaction; and have the collateral manager for the transaction put each life settlement through a designated pricing model, which determines rates of return for each policy.

One of the issues that has drawn the attention of life settlement market observers is the transaction cost paid by insureds to sell their insurance policies in the secondary market. The transaction cost consists of payments for providers, brokers, and insurance agents involved in the sale. A.M. Best's analysis indicates that the typical transaction cost can be as high as 50 percent to 100 percent of the price paid to the insured. Therefore, an insurance policy for which the insured is paid, for example, 15 percent of the face value ultimately may be sold to investors for 23 percent to 30 percent of face value. Although the money paid to the insured still may be higher than the value he or she would receive if the policy were surrendered to the insurance company that issued the policy, there is something to be said for the insured being aware of the various transaction costs associated with the policy he or she has sold in the secondary market. A.M. Best believes best practices in the area of life settlement transactions dictate that the seller of an in-force policy is fully aware of the various fees paid to intermediaries who facilitate the transaction.

Attorney Review of Insurable Interest, Licensing Requirements, and Sales Documentation Packages   One of the most fundamental concepts in life insurance is that of insurable interest. The insurable interest doctrine provides that in general, the beneficiary of an insurance policy must have (1) some relationship by blood or by law to the person being insured, or (2) must have an economic interest in having the life, health, or bodily safety of the individual insured continue. The insurable interest doctrine makes it possible, for example, for an individual to buy an insurance policy on his parents or business partner.

In the special case where a person procures a policy insuring his own life and pays the premiums for the policy, that person is said to have an unlimited insurable interest in his own life and, as such, may designate any person as the beneficiary of the policy. That beneficiary need not have any particular relationship to the insured. When the policy owner is not the insured, the beneficiary must be a person or an entity with insurable interest in the insured's life. A.M. Best requires that an attorney review each insurance policy to ensure that it conclusively passes the insurable interest test.

In general, after a provider makes a purchase offer to the seller of the insurance policy (normally, the insured), a sales documentation package is drafted. Through this documentation package, the issuer will contract to purchase from the seller all rights, titles, and interests in the life settlement policy. The sales documentation package must be complete and must follow all applicable state insurance laws and regulations.

A.M. Best requires that attorneys review the following items:

- The completeness of the sales documentation package (for each insured) for compliance with established regulations for life settlement acquisitions.

- The states in which each provider in the transaction is licensed to conduct business (for states that require such licenses) and the insurance regulations related to life settlements or viaticals for those states.
- Any outstanding, significant legal issues surrounding the provider.

Tracking Agent   The cash flow to the securities backed by life settlements depends on the payout of the death benefits that is, the maturity of the policies) by the insurers that have issued the policies in the collateral pool. Prompt collection of these death benefits requires the issuer to employ an independent tracking agent to track the lives covered by the insurance policies.

The specific roles of the tracking agent, which should be outlined in an agreement between the issuer and the tracking agent, are as follows:

- Preparing reports showing the insured's whereabouts, including address and date of last contact, to be provided to the issuer on at least a quarterly basis.
- Maintaining logs of the contacts with the insureds or other individuals, records of addresses and phone numbers of those contacts, and result of contacts.
- Preparing reports, if requested by the issuer, regarding the amount of funds needed to pay premiums prospectively.
- Filing all necessary documents with each insurance company, including premium waivers, policy conversions, death certificates, and documents necessary for the payment of death benefits.

A.M. Best will evaluate the tracking agents to be used in the transaction to determine whether they have experience in tracking large pools of lives and whether they have the technological resources to perform such functions. Issuers that feel they (or their providers) can track the insureds without employing a professional tracking agent must demonstrate to A.M. Best that they have experience in tracking lives, the software system set up to perform such tasks, and the ability to provide the information listed above.

Collateral Manager   A.M. Best expects the issuer to enter a collateral management agreement with a collateral manager or to demonstrate the ability to perform the duties of a collateral manager. Some of the duties of the collateral manager in life settlement securitizations include:

- Managing the selection and acquisition (through approved providers) of the life settlements.
- Optimizing the features of the insurance policies backing the life settlements.

- Determining the appropriate amount of the premium reserve.
- Determining whether to engage a stop-loss insurer or obtain a liquidity facility for the transaction.
- Investing cash balances in approved, high-quality, short-term instruments.
- Developing a liquidation plan for the life settlements.
- Determining the liquidation value of the life settlements.
- Updating mortality tables used in the transaction based on new information or new medical advances.
- Determining which policies should lapse in the event of a continued liquidity crisis.
- Performing other duties in the interest of the transaction's security holders.

Some of the factors that A.M. Best considers when evaluating a collateral manager are as follows:

- Experience in life settlement investments and portfolio optimization.
- Knowledge of insurance policy features or access to experienced consultants.
- Actuarial experience either on staff or through consultants.
- Staffing and resources necessary to support the collateral management activities.
- The quantitative skills to create financial models to select/manage a life settlement portfolio and to determine which policies to dispose of, lapse, or modify (if necessary).
- The systems and infrastructure necessary to carry out its duties.

Backup Service Providers Backup servicing agreements are important in life settlement transactions, because the industry is in its development stage and servicers usually are small, unrated organizations. A.M. Best recommends that issuers seek backup tracking agents and collateral managers (which presumably also perform policy administration and optimization).

A.M. Best recommends the use of an active backup tracking agent that will periodically (at least on a semiannual basis) receive information from the primary tracking agent on the lives it is tracking and on the latest contact it has made with the insured. The backup tracking agent should have the electronic systems in place to accept the data transmitted by the primary tracking agent and should be able to prepare reports on tracking activities as requested by A.M. Best.

The backup collateral manager should meet the same requirements described earlier in this chapter, and have the same expertise and experience any collateral manager should have.

Auditors   Public accountants play an important role in monitoring the activity of the bankruptcy-remote entity that issues the life settlement-backed securities. Accountants assist in the evaluation and identification of Generally Accepted Accounting Principles (GAAP) internal control and reporting-related issues. In addition, they perform specific, year-end audits to express an opinion on the consolidated financial statements of the bankruptcy-remote entity. A.M. Best requires the engagement of a certified public accounting firm to perform the following services:

- Perform audits of the books and records of the issuer (that is, the bankruptcy-remote entity).
- Issue a yearly report that expresses an opinion on the consolidated financial statements issued by the bankruptcy-remote entity.
- Review the internal controls over cash receipts and disbursements performed at the legal entity.
- Issue an opinion as to the GAAP consolidation requirements to the owners of the bankruptcy-remote entity.

Arrangers of the Transaction   The arrangers of the life settlement securitization transaction should define clearly their financial interest in the transaction. In addition, for arrangers that are not affiliates of large financial institutions, A.M. Best expects to be presented with their backgrounds, including their previous occupations and experience with life settlements.

Medical Records

Up-to-Date Medical Examiner Reports   As discussed earlier, all life settlements must be accompanied by two medical examiners' reports based on the most recent medical records on hand. The initial medical examiners' reports normally are completed within a few months of the insured's last medical visit with his physician. A.M. Best recommends that fresh medical examiners' reports be done if more than 12 months have elapsed between the first medical examiners' reports and the purchase of the policy for the pool. If the medical examiner's report on a life is "stale" (in other words, more than 12 months old), A.M. Best will apply a slightly higher stress on the mortality rating or life expectancy on the life in question in the stress scenarios described at the end of this chapter.

Obtaining up-to-date medical records on the insureds poses a potential problem, as federal and state confidentiality laws restrict long-term access to such records. The federal medical-record confidentiality law, the Health Insurance Portability and Accountability Act of 1996 (HIPAA), provides minimum federal standards for obtaining authorization to get an insured's medical records. State confidentiality laws, which sometimes can be more restrictive than HIPAA, also must be observed.

Medical Record Authorization Forms   In acquiring life settlement collateral for a securitization, it is up to the issuer to ensure that the medical records authorization forms signed by insureds are broad enough to allow for continued access (by the issuer) to up-to-date medical records over at least a 12-month period or over the longest period allowed by applicable laws. This means that the issuer would have to ensure that the medical authorization forms comply with HIPAA's privacy requirements. Alternatively, the issuer may have to explore other methods of receiving health records, such as using limited health care powers of attorney or providing incentives to the insureds for providing updated medical records.

A.M. Best recommends that issuers consult legal counsel for advice on any methods they choose to use to ensure that medical records can be obtained over the life of the portfolio in accordance with HIPAA's requirements in the event that the life settlement pool has to be liquidated. As a practical matter, it is unlikely that a buyer of a life settlement will have continual access to the medical records of the insured once the insured has been paid for his policy, even if the buyer has a limited health care power of attorney. First, as time elapses, the insured may move and engage the services of a new physician, who may not be willing to comply with the request for medical records. Second, the insured has no incentive to provide medical records to the buyer of his insurance policy, and it may not be practical for such a buyer to enforce the right to get the records through legal action, even if there is an enforceable limited health care power of attorney.

Consistency Checks   A.M. Best recommends that each policy be checked for consistency between the original insurance application and the medical records. This consistency check often can be performed by medical examiners or others who are familiar with the review of medical records. A.M. Best may engage outside consultants to perform consistency checks.

Policy In-Force Period/Proper Transfer of the Policy   Any policy contemplated for the collateral is required to have been in force for at least 24 months before being purchased by the issuer. Converted policies are considered new policies if new contestability or suicide conditions are imposed on the policies. It is the issuer's responsibility to ensure that its providers keep track of the dates on which policies were acquired by the insureds.

In addition, there should be some redundant checks and balances to ensure the proper transfer of policies to the bankruptcy-remote vehicle and to ensure that the policy will be unencumbered by challenges from relatives, former spouses, and others. Attorneys are best qualified to give an opinion on whether policy transfers have followed the proper protocols.

Diversity

Disease/Insurance Company   Diversity is an important factor in determining the composition of the collateral pool for life settlement transactions. In general, correlation among insureds in a life settlement portfolio occurs when a cure is discovered for a disease suffered by two or more insureds, because their life expectancies are increased simultaneously. Therefore, A.M. Best is unlikely to rate transactions based on only one specific disease, such as Alzheimer's or diabetes, without applying severe stresses on the transactions. The lives in such transactions are susceptible to cures that can make such lives highly correlated and that can increase the aggregate life expectancy of the insureds.

While life settlement portfolios are inherently diverse, based on the statistical distribution of disease categories as determined by the medical examiners, A.M. Best nevertheless recommends that issuers observe the maximum limits shown in Exhibit 9.2 on the broad disease categories in the collateral pool. The categorization of diseases is determined by the assignment of debits.

Diversity of insurance companies also is important in life settlement transactions. A.M. Best requires that the aggregate face value of the policies issued by any one insurance company not exceed 15 percent.

Policy Count, Policy Size   The number of lives in a portfolio of life settlements can help dampen the volatility of the cash flows produced by A.M. Best's stochastic life settlement model, which is discussed later in this chapter. Exhibit 9.6 shows the effect of the number of lives on the economic value of a portfolio of 100, 200, 300, and 400 lives—all with a portfolio life expectancy of 9.6 years. The cash flows (premium, death benefits, and expenses) were discounted at 12 percent. The exhibit shows that the expected economic value of each portfolio, expressed as the percentage of total death benefits of each portfolio, was about 19 percent. The standard deviations of the portfolios' economic values, expressed as a percentage of portfolio death benefits, were as follows: 3.8 percent for 100 lives, 2.7 percent for 200 lives, 2.2 percent for 300 lives, and 1.9 percent for 400 lives. Naturally, the more

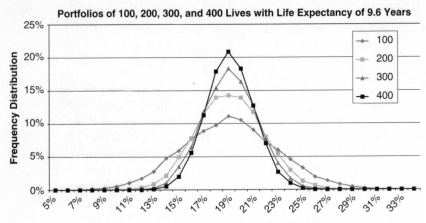

EXHIBIT 9.6   Distribution of Portfolio Economic Value

lives in the pool, the narrower the standard deviation of the portfolio's economic value, but the desire to have a large portfolio must be balanced with (1) the marginal benefit (in terms of narrowing the dispersion of economic values) gained by adding more lives to the portfolio, and (2) the fact that it can take a long time to accumulate a sizable portfolio of life settlements. For these reasons, A.M. Best recommends that the collateral pool consist of at least 300 lives. If fewer lives are included in the life settlement portfolio, A.M. Best will apply additional stress scenarios in evaluating the credit quality of the securities in the transaction. Please note that a flawed approach by the medical examiners in either how they have constructed their standard mortality tables or how they determine and apply net debits and credits to these tables will not be ameliorated simply by having a large number of lives in a life settlement pool. Such systematic errors will simply be duplicated across a larger portfolio.

No one life should comprise more than 3.33 percent of the face value of the entire collateral pool. Inclusion of "jumbo" policies ($10 million or more in face value) is considered on a case-by-case basis and is likely to be allowed if a third medical examiner issues a life-expectancy projection and/or the life expectancy is stressed further for modeling purposes.

Longevity Risk Mitigation   Longevity risk is the risk that the insured lives longer than was reasonably predicted by medical examiners. The longer the insured lives, the more premiums the owner of the life settlement will have to pay and the further in the future the death benefits will be realized. Longevity risk typically can be managed by stop-loss insurance that allows the issuer to put the insurance policies to an insurer at a price equal to the face value of the policies if the insureds live a fixed number of years beyond the predicted life expectancy. Stop-loss insurance also can be structured to cover an entire portfolio by giving the issuer the option to put the entire portfolio to the insurer at a specific date for a specific price. The stop-loss insurer must be a rated entity. In addition, A.M. Best will review the contract that covers the stop-loss provisions to ensure that it is indeed an unconditional obligation to pay claims during the life of the transaction. At this writing, A.M. Best is not aware of any rated insurer or reinsurer that specializes in issuing life settlement stop-loss insurance. While A.M. Best does not require stop-loss insurance, such contingency insurance may enhance the transaction, depending on the cost to the issuer, although it comes with the additional credit risk of the insurer.

Estimating Portfolio Residual Value A.M. Best's analytical model for life settlement securitization generally shows that an issuer of securities with legal maturities less than 20 years likely will depend heavily on the residual value of the portfolio of life settlements at maturity to meet its financial obligations to noteholders. Therefore, a comprehensive model for evaluating the credit risk of the securities has to use conservative assumptions about liquidation timing and liquidation prices if all the life settlements have not matured before the legal maturity date of the securities. To estimate the residual value of an aged life settlement portfolio, A. M. Best does not rely on the original estimates of mortality ratings and life expectancies issued by medical examiners, as those estimates probably would be about 10 years old or more by the time the liquidation of the portfolio would take place, if necessary. Instead, A.M. Best currently applies a mortality table such as the standard 2001 VBT (unadjusted for impaired lives); the applicable premium schedule for the policies (until the insureds are 100 years old); and various assumed discount rates to estimate the economic value of the remaining life settlements in the portfolio. Then, A.M. Best further haircuts this value to reflect the inefficiencies and extreme illiquidity of the life settlement market.

Liquidation Prospects/Liquidity Risk Mitigation While the liquidation value of a life settlement portfolio is important at the end of the transaction, it also is important during the life of the transaction if it becomes necessary to sell policies to meet the transaction's cash flow needs. A.M. Best's life settlement model assumes that liquidation is not a viable option to meet liquidity needs during the term of the transaction because of: (1) the uncertainties surrounding the liquidation value of an individual life settlement;

(2) the extensive amount of time and effort it might take to actually sell a life settlement; and (3) the dramatic effect excessive sales of life settlements would have on the transaction's future cash flows. In short, A.M. Best takes a dim view of any transaction that relies on the liquidation value of policies to meet short-term cash needs.

A transaction's liquidity risk may be greater in its early years, especially since empirical evidence from various life settlement portfolios suggests that few deaths occur in the early years of the life settlement pools underwritten thus far. A common method of mitigating liquidity risk is to have adequate cash in a reserve fund to meet short-term cash flow needs. The disadvantage of this method is that a large amount of cash in reserve reduces the amount of life settlements the issuer can buy for the transaction.

Another way to mitigate liquidity risk is with a liquidity facility from a rated financial institution. The liquidity facility can be used to pay premiums on the policies and/or interest to the noteholders. The financial institution offering the liquidity facility typically would place a lien on the life settlements in the transaction, and the repayment of the funds borrowed by the transaction usually is at the top of the transaction's "priority of payment" list or "waterfall." Maintaining and using a liquidity facility is beneficial if it is not expensive and the floating-rate costs are swapped to fixed costs. A.M. Best recommends that the liquidity facility be in place for a term equal to at least 125 percent of the life expectancy, LE_{final}, derived from the Final Mortality Matrix as described later in this chapter. The revolving credit line for such a facility should be determined through the modeling of the transaction to ensure timely payment of premiums and/or interest and principal.

Life Settlement Pricing The life settlement market still is developing, and there is no guarantee that any one policy provider or service provider will be in existence at the time the issuer is ready to acquire the policies or has completed its policy acquisition program. Therefore, A.M. Best will not consider the bargaining power of the issuer to achieve better prices on policies or services when evaluating the transaction for a Preliminary Assessment or an Indicative Rating. A.M. Best requires that all prices of policies and services reflect the prices prevalent in the market at the time of the evaluation of the transaction, not just prices promised by a provider and not theoretical prices developed from a model. As discussed in an earlier section, an issuer who has entered a financial arrangement with a provider (aside from the agreement for purchasing policies through the provider) must disclose the full nature of such an agreement. For the sake of clarity, the price that A.M. Best recognizes in life settlement transactions is the price that includes the fees paid to all the intermediaries involved in the transactions, such as fees paid to brokers, providers, and so forth.

Life Settlement Acquisition Schedule   The pace of portfolio acquisition depends on the availability of policies that meet the purchase criteria of the issuer. The data in Exhibit 9.3 show that about 8 percent of the individuals offering their insurance policies for sale have life expectancies of six years or less as determined by medical examiners. This indicates that the supply of short life expectancies is limited, and thus the ramp-up period could be extremely long for any transaction that seeks collateral with short life expectancies, and the prices for such life settlements probably will be higher than standard pricing models will predict. The duration of the purchase period is particularly important because if this ramp-up period were prolonged, the transaction would experience "negative carry" since the issuer could not deploy capital quickly enough to earn higher returns than the borrowing cost.

If the issuer seeks an Indicative Rating and has not purchased all the policies required for the transaction, A.M. Best expects the purchase to be completed within six months of the issuance of the Indicative Rating. A.M. Best requires that the issuer provide an acquisition schedule that outlines the number of life settlements it realistically expects to purchase each month by life expectancy categories. The issuer also must demonstrate that its providers have the ability to supply a sufficient number of life settlements for the transaction in the time frame required.

Exhibit 9.7 summarizes the general data requirements for a representative portfolio of life settlements pursuant to obtaining a Preliminary Assessment, an Indicative Rating, and a Debt Rating.

Policy Optimization   Issuers may choose to optimize premiums on certain types of insurance policies (such as universal life and variable universal life policies) by using the cash values in the policies to reduce premium payments or simply by reducing premium payments to the minimum levels necessary for keeping the policies in force. A.M. Best must be informed if the premiums on the representative policies upon which the rating is based have been altered in any way. Specifically, A.M. Best requests a monthly premium payment illustration showing premiums until the insured reaches age 100 or until the age at which the beneficiary is entitled to death benefits.

If the collateral manager uses commercially available software to determine premium payments under various optimization schemes, A.M. Best requires a demonstration of such software and wants comparisons between the software's output and some illustrations produced by the insurance companies that have issued the policies. If the collateral manager has developed

EXHIBIT 9.7   General Data Requirements for Life Settlements

	Representative Portfolio of New Life Settlements (For Preliminary Assessment)	Actual & Representative Portfolio of New Life Settlements (For Indicative Rating or Debt Rating)
Age	✓	✓
Sex	✓	✓
Smoking Status	✓	✓
Annual Premium	✓	✓
Disease Classification		✓
Name of Insurance Companies		✓
Rating of Insurance Companies		✓
Face Value of Policy	✓	✓
Assumed/Actual Life Expectancies	✓	✓
Mortality Rating		✓
Mortality/Survivorship Schedule		✓
Yearly Premium	✓	✓
Assumed/Actual Price of Life Settlements	✓	✓
Assumed Policy Accumulation Period		✓
Unique Identification for Insured		✓
Unique Identification for Policy		✓

its own software program for optimizing the policies, A.M. Best wants verification that the software can duplicate the results of some of the illustrations produced by the insurance companies. By doing so, A.M. Best is assured that the in-house software is able to produce accurate results.

As part of the optimization process, A.M. Best expects the collateral manager to consider scenarios under which charges that are realistically adjustable are increased to their maximum levels to observe the effect on the policies in terms of premium payments. A.M. Best may randomly sample the life settlements to observe the assumptions about the cost of insurance and expenses determined by the issuer.

Portfolio Liquidation Plan If the legal maturity of the securities is less than 20 years, A.M. Best requires a formal plan outlined in the legal document of the transaction for the liquidation of the portfolio to pay off the securities. Since the time needed to liquidate a portfolio of life settlements is difficult to determine, A.M. Best expects liquidation of the life settlement portfolio to begin at least two years before the maturity date of the securities, after considering the life settlements that are likely to mature in that two-year period. The liquidation value calculation should be determined with a mortality table, such as the standard 2001 VBT (unadjusted for impaired lives), and with stresses applied to this table as an extra measure of conservatism.

It is important to note that if the premiums on the policies have been optimized, the liquidation value of the life settlements at the end of the transaction could be affected adversely. The reasons for such an effect are as follows: (1) since premiums accelerate naturally with the cost of insurance, premiums can be extremely high at the time the portfolio would be liquidated; (2) A.M. Best applies a standard mortality table to life settlements to calculate the liquidation value of the portfolio; and (3) A.M. Best further stresses such calculated liquidation values to take into consideration the inefficiencies in the life settlement market.

Management Expertise A qualitative aspect of A.M. Best's analysis is the assessment of the issuer's expertise in life settlements and structured securities. A small number of participants comprise the life settlement industry. Its participants have developed reputations in various areas, such as the ability to source policies, integrity in soliciting objective life expectancies, and other matters related to the efficient execution of life settlement transactions. A.M. Best expects the issuer (or its representatives) to demonstrate a high degree of knowledge about policy providers, tracking agents, medical examiners, and other significant service providers associated with the transaction. In addition, A.M. Best should be informed of any significant legal actions or complaints against any service provider that may be involved in the transaction.

Documentation

Tax Opinion Since life settlement collateral is a new asset class for securitizations, it is important that issuers understand its tax implications. Specifically, A.M. Best expects the issuer to engage tax advisers to provide an opinion regarding the recognition or amortization of expenses such as premium and administrative expenses in a bankruptcy-remote vehicle in the vehicle's country of domicile. Any requirements for tax withholdings also should be determined by tax advisers.

General Legal Review/Tax Opinion/Documentation   The following are some of the other required general opinions, conditions, and verifications for setting up a transaction collateralized by life settlements:

- Unqualified legal opinion indicating that the transfer of life settlements from the seller to the issuer constitutes a true or absolute sale, not a pledge of collateral.
- Legal opinion stating that if the transferor becomes insolvent, neither the issuer nor its assets or liabilities would be substantively consolidated with the transferor.
- Unqualified legal opinion that the issuer will satisfy special-purpose, bankruptcy-remote criteria such as:
  - Issuer's business must be restricted to the purchase of the life settlements and the issuance of the rated debt.
  - Issuer may not incur any additional debt unless the additional debt is subordinated fully to the rated debt and the subordination is explicitly stated in the legal documents.
  - Additional debt will not impair the rating of the rated debt.
  - Issuer should have a separate corporate existence with independent officers and directors, separate books and records, and appropriate meetings of the board of directors to authorize corporate action.
  - Issuer shall not engage in any dissolution, liquidation, consolidation, merger, or asset sale (other than as provided in the relevant transaction documents) or amendment of its organizational documents so long as the rated securities are outstanding.
  - All of the issuer's assets, such as the life settlements, the various proceeds accounts, the escrow accounts and all other assets that generate income for the structure, should be pledged to secure the issuer's debt.
  - Tax opinion to the effect that the issuer would not be subject to federal, state, or local taxes.
  - If taxes are to be paid on the cash flow of the issuer, a tax opinion on the capitalization of certain expenses, including premium payments and fundraising costs.
  - Written agreements with all service providers, such as tracking agent, providers, and collateral managers.
- Normal documentation associated with private placements such as: offering memorandum, trust indenture, trustee agreements, and so forth.
- Report on each policy detailing any contradictions between the original insurance application and the medical records of the insured.
- Disclosure of any agreements (written or unwritten) between the issuer and any other parties that outline the distribution of the residuals in the transactions after the rated debt has been fully redeemed.
- Anti-money-laundering provisions in the legal documents.

Evaluating the Credit Risk of the Securities

Mortality Profile of the Life Settlements   Rating securities backed by life settlements is more difficult than rating standard collateralized debt obligation securities backed by corporate bonds. For one thing, there are many more parameters—from an analytical perspective—that can greatly affect the cash flow of a life settlement portfolio, such as: the age of the individuals behind the life settlements; their life expectancies (and the statistical distribution around the life expectancies); gender; smoking status; the premium payments; the credit risk of the insurance companies that issued the polices; and regulatory issues that surround the collateral in such transactions. By contrast, corporate bonds often are rated individually, and their maturity dates generally are known with certainty. Therefore, credit risk is the primary risk when rating securities backed by such bonds. The ratings of life settlement-backed securities are determined primarily by mortality risk, which is more difficult to quantify because of the various factors mentioned earlier. For example, two individuals can have the same life expectancy but different yearly probabilities of death because of differences in age, gender, or lifestyle.

As discussed earlier, it is important that a medical examiner provide: (1) its standard mortality tables upon which debits and credits are applied; (2) a mortality rating that the medical examiner applies to its base mortality table to derive the life expectancy for each insured; (3) a life expectancy estimate for each insured (including the joint life expectancy estimates for second-to-die policies); (4) a mortality or survivorship schedule for each insured (given medical impairments); (5) the primary disease category for each insured, if one has been identified; and (6) any reports that validate the historical accuracy of the medical examiners' life-expectancy projections.

If a medical examiner provides its standard mortality tables, the mortality ratings for the insureds in a life settlement pool, and its methodology for applying the mortality ratings to the tables, A.M. Best is willing to review and, perhaps, use the mortality tables for its analyses as long as they have been constructed with the help of a reputable, independent actuarial firm that provides a report on the methodology used for constructing the tables.

A.M. Best is aware, however, that some medical examiners consider their standard mortality tables to be proprietary, and thus only provide life expectancies and mortality ratings. In these cases, A.M. Best will assume each medical examiner's standard table is currently the 2001 VBT and solve for the mortality ratings that will yield such life expectancies and then apply those mortality ratings to the 2001 VBT. Please note that if A.M. Best derives mortality ratings that are much higher than the mortality ratings issued by the medical examiner, A.M. Best will conclude that the medical examiner's standard mortality tables are different from the VBT 2001 tables. In such cases, A.M. Best may apply more punitive stresses on the transaction. The resulting mortality profiles for insureds in a life settlement pool are used in the stochastic cash flow modeling. If, in the future, medical examiners base their standard table on another mortality table such as the 2008 VBT, A.M. Best will apply that table in its analysis if it deems that table to be suitable for life settlement transactions.

Insurance Company Impairment Risk   The risk of insurance company impairments is an additional factor to be considered in assessing the credit risk of securities backed by life settlements. A.M. Best designates an insurance company as financially impaired upon the first official state action taken by an insurance department on that company. Such state actions include involuntary liquidation, supervision, rehabilitation, receivership, conservatorship, a cease-and-desist order, suspension, license revocation, administrative order, and any other action that restricts a company's freedom to conduct its insurance business as normal. A.M. Best maintains ratings on an overwhelming majority of U.S. insurance companies, so it is highly likely that there are A.M. Best ratings on all the insurance companies in the life settlement pool. A.M. Best requires that the insurance company candidates for inclusion in the transaction pool have Financial Strength Ratings (FSRs) of "B+" or higher.

A.M. Best's approach to evaluating the credit risk in life settlement transactions begins with a determination of the impairment rate of each insurance company in the collateral pool. A.M. Best has developed a proprietary impairment rate table based upon its proprietary database of more than 5,000 domestic insurance companies it has rated over the past 30 years. This data set, combined with approximately 680 incidents of impairments, forms the basis for the most comprehensive impairment statistics in the insurance industry. As a result, A.M. Best has calculated long-term, cumulative average impairment rates that can be applied to structured transactions such as life settlement securitization transactions. Please see the latest methodology report "Best's Impairment Rate and Rating Transition Study," at www.ambest.com/ratings/methodology for a discussion on insurance company impairments. The latest available cumulative impairment rate table at the time of this writing is shown in Exhibit 9.8.

Recoveries of Death Benefits after Insurer Impairments   Insurance company impairments may result in the diminution of death benefits. In general, guaranty funds cover nearly all death benefits in the event of an insurance company's impairment, up to a limit of about $300,000 in many states. However, this $300,000 payment limit is probably smaller than the face values of the policies in most life settlement transactions, which generally

EXHIBIT 9.8 Best's Cumulative Average Impairment Rates

Years	A++/A+	A/A–	B++/B+	B/B–	C++/C+	C/C–	D
1	0.06%	0.20%	0.75%	2.09%	3.44%	6.08%	7.38%
2	0.20%	0.61%	1.80%	4.30%	5.73%	9.54%	12.42%
3	0.36%	1.14%	2.89%	6.38%	8.55%	12.08%	17.23%
4	0.53%	1.68%	4.24%	8.24%	11.29%	14.64%	21.50%
5	0.70%	2.30%	5.66%	10.21%	13.64%	17.28%	25.62%
6	0.94%	2.96%	6.88%	12.31%	15.93%	21.00%	29.71%
7	1.19%	3.61%	8.16%	14.27%	18.07%	24.10%	33.12%
8	1.46%	4.34%	9.19%	15.99%	20.85%	27.48%	36.00%
9	1.80%	5.00%	9.99%	17.73%	23.07%	30.04%	38.51%
10	2.15%	5.65%	10.90%	19.38%	24.73%	32.09%	40.87%
11	2.50%	6.33%	11.78%	21.05%	26.08%	34.67%	43.28%
12	2.95%	6.93%	12.72%	22.64%	26.98%	36.71%	45.23%
13	3.45%	7.50%	13.65%	24.13%	27.83%	38.17%	46.92%
14	3.95%	7.97%	14.57%	25.38%	29.12%	39.74%	48.22%
15	4.31%	8.42%	15.19%	26.57%	29.95%	41.42%	49.48%

Table is from the methodology document titled *Best's Impairment Rate and Rating Transition Study—1977 to 2006*, published on February 26, 2007.

range from $1 million to $2 million. The unpaid death benefits are paid out of the estate of the insolvent insurance company if the company goes into liquidation. While the anecdotal evidence is that policyholders rarely lose money in life insurance company insolvencies, a rigorous life settlement model must include the possibility of losing money should such events occur. In addition, no one can be certain that as more life settlement transactions and securitizations are consummated, legislators won't impose restrictions on payments to the bankruptcy-remote vehicles that own life settlements in the event of insurance company impairments. A.M. Best assumes the recovery rates in Exhibit 9.9 for the proceeds of impaired insurance companies. The recoveries are assumed to be achievable in three months.

EXHIBIT 9.9 Assumed Recoveries after Insurance Company Impairments

Policy Face Value	% Recovery
$300,000	100%
$1,000,000	86%
>$2,000,000	80%

Life Settlement Liquidation Value during Impairment   If there are life settlements that have not yet matured at a transaction's legal maturity, the issuer would have to liquidate policies and use the proceeds to pay any outstanding obligations to security holders. A.M. Best assumes no liquidation value for life settlements issued by insurance companies that have FSRs below "B+" (that is, ratings at "B" and below) and that have not matured by the end of the transaction. This is particularly important for transactions in which the legal maturity of the securities issued by a bankruptcy-remote vehicle is shorter than the maturity of the last life settlements in the transaction.

Exhibit 9.10, Best's One-Year Rating Transition Matrix, shows the movement of ratings over a one-year period. Such a matrix can be helpful in estimating the probability of company ratings moving below "B+." For example, the exhibit shows that a company originally rated in the "A/A−" (Excellent) category has a probability of 1.08 percent of being downgraded below "B+" over a one-year period. A.M. Best applies the appropriate transition matrix (after applying some simplifying assumptions and using matrix multiplication) to its analysis, depending on the legal term of the transaction being evaluated.

Cash-Flow Model/Use of Debt Default Table   A.M. Best has developed its own proprietary Monte Carlo simulation model for evaluating life settlement transactions, but the company expects to receive a copy of a model created by the issuer (or its representatives) that takes into consideration prices and face values of the life settlements, the statistical distribution of deaths, insurance company impairments, recoveries associated with such impairments, premiums, liquidation value, payments on the securities collateralized by the life settlements, and other significant modeling parameters. A.M. Best will model the transaction and compare its results with the output from the issuer's model.

Determining the Final Mortality Matrix   To model the transaction, A.M. Best first determines the Final Mortality Matrix, which is the mortality matrix used for the Monte Carlo simulation. This matrix is derived from the information provided by medical examiners, with modifications as determined by A.M. Best. The modifications are to compensate for the possibility that a) medical examiners are systematically misestimating life expectancies, and b) the individuals selling their policies are healthier than the insured population experience employed in creating standard mortality tables that are used for evaluating life settlement transactions.

EXHIBIT 9.10 Best's One-Year Rating Transition Matrix

	Rating One Year Later							
	A++/A+	A/A−	B++/B+	B/B−	C++/C+	C/C−	D	Impaired
A++/A+	92.62%	6.90%	0.39%	0.03%	0.00%	0.00%	0.00%	0.06%
A/A−	4.19%	91.15%	3.58%	0.61%	0.10%	0.06%	0.12%	0.20%
B++/B+	0.36%	10.93%	81.03%	5.51%	0.63%	0.31%	0.48%	0.75%
B/B−	0.27%	1.03%	15.12%	75.35%	3.96%	0.98%	1.21%	2.09%
C++/C+	0.23%	0.58%	1.86%	18.18%	67.07%	5.30%	3.32%	3.44%
C/C−	0.00%	0.63%	0.25%	4.43%	15.19%	65.44%	7.97%	6.08%
D	0.10%	0.55%	1.05%	3.06%	3.11%	3.56%	81.18%	7.38%

	Rating One Year Later	
	Secure	Vulnerable
Secure	98.03%	1.97%
Vulnerable	9.92%	90.08%

If the medical examiners only provide life expectancies and mortality ratings, then the following procedures will determine the Final Mortality Matrix:

1. Given a portfolio of life settlements, get the Standard Mortality Matrix for the pool given the age, gender, and smoking status for each life. The Standard Mortality Matrix currently is assumed to be taken from the 2001 VBT. The 2008 VBT may be used sometime in the future.
2. Given the Standard Mortality Matrix and the death benefit for each life in the life settlement pool, derive the weighted average time to maturity for the pool. This will be considered the base life expectancy for a cohort of standard risks, $LE_{standard}$.
3. Given the life expectancy for each life in the Standard Mortality Matrix, derive the mortality multiplier for each life, MM_i (where i ranges from 1 to the total number of lives in the portfolio).
4. Multiply each life in the Standard Mortality Matrix by its corresponding mortality multiplier, MM_i derived in Step 3. The new mortality matrix will be called the Impaired Mortality Matrix.
5. Given the Impaired Mortality Matrix and the face value for each life in the pool, derive the weighted average time to maturity for the pool. This will be considered the base life expectancy for a cohort of impaired lives, $LE_{impaired}$.
6. If $LE_{impaired} \geq 80\% \times LE_{standard}$, stop and use the Impaired Mortality Matrix derived in Step 4 as the Intermediate Mortality Matrix and go to Step 8.
7. If $LE_{impaired} \leq 80\% \times LE_{standard}$, multiply the mortality profile for each life in the Impaired Mortality Matrix by a constant factor (less than 1), Factor, such that $LE_{impaired} = 80\% \times LE_{standard}$. We will call the portfolio the Intermediate Mortality Matrix, and the LE that equates to 80 percent of $LE_{standard}$ will be called $LE_{intermediate}$.
8. Derive the Final Mortality Matrix by multiplying the Intermediate Mortality Matrix by an adjustment factor for each life, $Adjustment_i$, which is calculated as follows:
   - If Death Benefit is less than or equal to $2 million, $Adjustment_i = 100\%$
   - If Death Benefit is greater than or equal to $7 million, $Adjustment_i = 80\%$
   - If Death Benefit is between $2 million and $7 million, $Adjustment_i = (-4\% \times \text{Death Benefits in Millions}) + 108\%$
9. Calculate the life expectancy, LE_{final}, of the Final Mortality Matrix.

The procedures above are performed with data provided by each medical examiner. The Final Mortality Matrix chosen for the analysis will be the matrix that yields the highest portfolio life expectancy. The Final Mortality Matrix will be used in running the base Monte Carlo simulation for determining the base default probability of the securities. An example of how the Final Mortality Matrix is derived is shown in the appendix for a small portfolio of 20 life settlements.

If the medical examiner provides its standard mortality tables, mortality ratings, and life expectances (and assuming that A.M. Best decides to use the standard mortality tables for its analyses), then the Final Mortality Matrix is derived as follows:

1. Given a portfolio of life settlements, get the Standard Mortality Matrix from the medical examiner for the pool given the age, gender, and smoking status for each life.
2. Given the Standard Mortality Matrix and the death benefit for each life in the life settlement pool, derive the weighted average time to maturity for the pool. This will be considered the base life expectancy for a cohort of standard risks, $LE_{standard}$.
3. Multiply each life in the Standard Mortality Matrix by its corresponding mortality multiplier, MM_i, given by the medical examiner according to the methodology employed by the medical examiner. The new mortality matrix will be called the Impaired Mortality Matrix.
4. Given the Impaired Mortality Matrix and the face value for each life in the pool, derive the weighted average time to maturity for the pool. This will be considered the base life expectancy for a cohort of impaired lives, $LE_{impaired}$.
5. If $LE_{impaired} \geq 80\% \times LE_{standard}$, stop and use the Impaired Mortality Matrix derived in Step 3 as the Intermediate Mortality Matrix and go to Step 7.
6. If $LE_{impaired} \leq 80\% \times LE_{standard}$, multiply the mortality profile for each life in the Impaired Mortality Matrix by a constant factor (less than 1), Factor, such that $LE_{impaired}$ equals 80% of $LE_{standard}$. We will call the portfolio the Intermediate Mortality Matrix, and the LE that equates to 80% of $LE_{standard}$ will be called $LE_{intermediate}$.
7. Derive the Final Mortality Matrix by multiplying the Intermediate Mortality Matrix by an adjustment factor for each life, $Adjustment_i$, which is calculated as follows:
   - If Death Benefit is less than or equal to $2 million, $Adjustment_i = 100\%$
   - If Death Benefit is greater than or equal to $7 million, $Adjustment_i = 80\%$
   - If Death Benefit is between $2 million and $7 million, $Adjustment_i = (-4\% \times \text{Death Benefits in Millions}) + 108\%$
8. Calculate the life expectancy, LE_{final}, of the Final Mortality Matrix.

As before, the procedures above are performed with data provided by each medical examiner. The Final Mortality Matrix chosen for the analysis will be the matrix that yields the highest portfolio life expectancy. Once again, the Final Mortality Matrix will be used in running the base Monte Carlo simulation for determining the default probability of the securities.

Modeling Basics   At its most basic level, A.M. Best's model generates cash flows for every policy after considering the appropriate mortality table, the premiums and the death benefit. As an example, assume that a 75-year-old male insured has a 1.6 percent probability of dying by age 76, a 2.0 percent probability of dying by age 77 (if he survives age 76) and a 2.7 percent probability of dying by age 78 (if he survives age 77).

In the simulation process, for the first year when the probability of the insured dying is 1.6 percent, A.M. Best draws a random number between 0 percent and 100 percent. If that random number is less than or equal to 1.6 percent, the insured is assumed dead, premium payments on the life are stopped (after the first year), and the death benefit is collected. If that random number is greater than 1.6 percent, the insured is assumed to be alive, the insured survives to the second year, and premium payments continue. In the second year, where the probability of the insured dying is 2.0 percent, a random number is drawn once again and either the person lives (that is, the random number is above 2.0 percent) or dies (the random number is less than or equal to 2 percent). In the third year, where the probability of the insured dying is 2.7 percent, a random number is drawn once again and either the person lives (that is, the random number is above 2.7 percent) or dies (the random number is less than or equal to 2.7 percent). Exhibit 9.11 shows the possible pattern of death or survival over a three-year period for this example.

The analysis is the same for a portfolio of several hundred policies that may mature in 20 or 30 years. For each trial in the simulation, the model aggregates the cash flows (death benefits, premium payments, and so forth) for a portfolio of life settlements and makes payments as prescribed by the transaction's waterfall. When payments are not made in full because of a cash flow shortage, the model records a default. The ultimate output of A.M. Best's cash flow model is the default rate—the total number of defaults for all trials divided by the number of trials. This default rate then is tied to Best's Idealized Default Matrix (Exhibit 9.12), which shows the default rates associated with debt ratings. The credit quality of the securities is based on the long-term credit rating scale, not the FSR scale.

Please note that the simplified example above ignores insurance company defaults, correlation of lives, and other modeling parameters that are considered in the model.

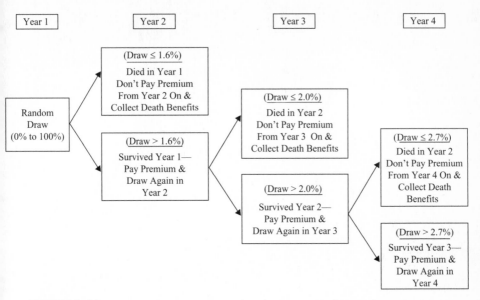

EXHIBIT 9.11 Paths of Death or Survival in the Monte Carlo Simulation

Stresses As discussed earlier, life settlement securitizations are more difficult to evaluate than a typical collateralized debt obligation because of the various risks, including longevity risk and regulatory risks, that must be considered. Some of the items A.M. Best stresses include the following:

1. The Final Mortality Matrix (including stresses in the first three years of the transaction when there typically are very few deaths).
2. Mortality improvements.
3. Premium payments.
4. The correlation of lives (based on cure discoveries).
5. The time between death of the insureds and the collection of the death benefits.
6. The cost of tracking the insureds (if a new tracking agent must be hired).
7. Interest rates for unhedged floating-rate funding.
8. Insurance company impairments and recoveries.
9. The ratings of liquidity providers.
10. The ratings of any companies providing longevity cover, if any.
11. The liquidation value of the remaining life settlement collateral (if any) at the end of the transaction.

EXHIBIT 9.12 Best's Idealized Default Matrix

	AAA	AA+	AA	AA−	A+	A	A−	BBB+	BBB	BBB−	BB+	BB	BB−
1	0.03%	0.03%	0.04%	0.05%	0.06%	0.11%	0.16%	0.21%	0.23%	0.27%	0.67%	1.20%	2.30%
2	0.08%	0.11%	0.13%	0.23%	0.32%	0.44%	0.56%	0.67%	0.74%	0.89%	1.96%	3.26%	5.28%
3	0.14%	0.20%	0.26%	0.42%	0.58%	0.76%	0.95%	1.13%	1.25%	1.51%	3.18%	5.23%	8.10%
4	0.22%	0.31%	0.41%	0.62%	0.84%	1.08%	1.33%	1.58%	1.76%	2.13%	4.35%	7.11%	10.78%
5	0.31%	0.45%	0.58%	0.84%	1.10%	1.41%	1.71%	2.02%	2.25%	2.75%	5.46%	8.91%	13.31%
6	0.42%	0.60%	0.79%	1.08%	1.37%	1.73%	2.09%	2.46%	2.74%	3.37%	6.51%	10.63%	15.71%
7	0.53%	0.77%	1.01%	1.33%	1.64%	2.06%	2.47%	2.88%	3.21%	3.98%	7.51%	12.26%	17.96%
8	0.66%	0.96%	1.25%	1.58%	1.92%	2.38%	2.84%	3.31%	3.68%	4.58%	8.45%	13.81%	20.09%
9	0.79%	1.15%	1.51%	1.85%	2.20%	2.70%	3.21%	3.72%	4.13%	5.18%	9.34%	15.28%	22.08%
10	0.94%	1.36%	1.79%	2.13%	2.48%	3.03%	3.58%	4.13%	4.58%	5.76%	10.18%	16.67%	23.95%
11	1.09%	1.58%	2.08%	2.42%	2.76%	3.35%	3.94%	4.53%	5.01%	6.33%	10.96%	17.98%	25.70%
12	1.24%	1.81%	2.38%	2.72%	3.05%	3.68%	4.30%	4.92%	5.43%	6.88%	11.69%	19.21%	27.34%
13	1.40%	2.05%	2.69%	3.02%	3.35%	4.00%	4.65%	5.31%	5.84%	7.42%	12.36%	20.36%	28.86%
14	1.57%	2.29%	3.01%	3.33%	3.64%	4.32%	5.01%	5.69%	6.25%	7.93%	12.99%	21.44%	30.28%
15	1.73%	2.53%	3.34%	3.64%	3.94%	4.65%	5.36%	6.06%	6.64%	8.43%	13.57%	22.43%	31.59%

Table is taken from the methodology report "A.M. Best's Idealized Default Matrix," published December 5, 2007.

Qualitative Issues In rating securities collateralized by life settlements, A.M. Best also considers some of the issues that may not be directly quantifiable but could have a significant impact on the rating of the transaction. Some of the issues A.M. Best considers in the analyses include, but are not limited to, the following:

1. The infrastructure set up by the collateral manager to manage the transaction.
2. The track record of the medical examiners as shown by actual to expected ratios certified by reputable actuarial firms.
3. Whether the issuer (or its representative) has hired actuaries to help it understand mortality profiles on impaired lives of the elderly.
4. How long the designated medical examiners in the transaction have been providing life expectancies to independent third parties.
5. Whether the issuer has performed a consistency check on the policies to ensure that the underwriting of the original insurance policy was done with accurate information.
6. The extent to which attorneys have reviewed the sales documentation packages for each life settlement in the portfolio and are satisfied that the sellers have insurable interest in the lives of the insureds.
7. The experience of the issuer or arranger with life settlement transactions—A.M. Best feels that total reliance on consultants (especially if their involvement is only at the beginning of the transaction) leaves the issuer vulnerable when decisions have to be made regarding policy management as the transaction ages.
8. The existence of designated backups for significant service providers, such as collateral managers and tracking agents.
9. The extent to which the sellers of the policies know all the fees paid to all intermediaries in the transaction.
10. The existence of a well-defined liquidation plan (for transactions with legal maturities of fewer than 20 years) that must be carried out by the collateral manager.
11. The ability and willingness of the issuer to provide the surveillance data on a timely basis for monitoring the transaction, including auditing information.
12. The capacity of the provider to originate policies at the pace assumed by the issuer.
13. The extent to which a purchased portfolio meets the requirements and recommendations outlined for newly originated policies in this methodology.

Surveillance Requirements for Transactions

There are no surveillance requirements for securities with Preliminary Assessments, because such evaluations are performed based on the projected portfolios and information provided to A.M. Best at the time of the evaluation. The Preliminary Assessment is not updated even when market conditions such as the available life expectances and prices change.

Unlike the Preliminary Assessments, the Indicative Ratings and Debt Ratings are public ratings on real securities and, as a result, may be revised as the ramp-up is completed or as the transaction matures. To monitor securities with Indicative Ratings or Debt Ratings, A.M. Best requires the following information about each insurance policy at the inception of the transaction:

- A unique identification number for each policy.
- A unique identification number for each life.
- The insurance company that issued the policy.
- Rating of the insurance company at the time of policy's purchase.
- Classification of the types of policies in the following categories: universal life, whole life, variable life, variable universal life, survivorship universal life and term.
- In-force date of the policy.
- Policy expiration date, if applicable.
- Policy face value.
- Date the policy first was sold into the secondary market.
- Date the policy was acquired for the transaction.
- Price of the policy.
- Medical examiners used.
- Insured's date of birth.
- Any and all life expectancies estimated by medical examiners.
- Date of each life expectancy evaluation.
- Date of the latest medical records used for the life expectancy evaluations.
- An indication of policies that required a third medical examiner.
- The monthly premium payments to age 100.
- Name of tracking agent.
- Primary disease category identified by medical examiners, if any.
- State where insured lived at the time the sale documentation package was executed.
- Name of policy provider and states where the provider is licensed.

After the transaction has been up and running, A.M. Best would like immediate notification of:

- The date of death of any insured as shown on the death certificate.
- The date the death was reported to the issuer or discovered by the issuer.
- The date the death benefit was collected.
- The liquidation price of the policy (if policy is sold).
- The cumulative premium payment for each deceased insured.
- Any changes in premium payments, death benefits, crediting rates, expense charges, borrowings against policies or other features that could affect the net cash flow of the life settlement.
- Any planned changes in the calculation methodologies by the insurers issuing the policies in the pool that can affect premium payments, death benefits, crediting rates, expense charges, or other features that could affect the net cash flow of the life settlement.
- Any lapse notification to the insurer.

On a quarterly basis, A.M. Best would like the following information for any insured:

- Cumulative death benefits received.
- Cumulative dividends received on each policy.
- Cumulative premium payment for each policy.
- The policies that had a change in premium or net death benefits.
- Policies with debt.

Every six months, A.M. Best expects a projection of the maturities in the life settlement portfolios from that point to the end of the transaction. If the projected maturities result in a shortfall of the cash flow necessary to pay the premiums or any principal or interest due on the securities, A.M. Best expects to see a plan from the issuer for averting a liquidity crisis. A.M. Best also will periodically request information from the backup tracking agent to make sure it has up-to-date records of the insureds being tracked.

PART

Three

Analytics and Pricing

CHAPTER 10

Life Settlement Pricing

I. James Cavoli
CEO, Life Settlement Insights

In any investment scenario, serious consideration must be given to a method for rationally determining what price should be offered to initiate a transaction. But with a life settlement contract, given that the ultimate cash payout for the policy buyer is already defined via the net death benefit, the importance of establishing the right price is elevated. Because there is no further upside beyond that which was already defined (unlike equities, or bonds that might sell above face value prior to maturity), it can be stated that this is clearly a transaction where profits are made on the way in rather than on the way out.

In the modern life settlement market, the dominant auction-style procurement process in which most funding entities or their designates participate ensures that buyers do not overpay for a given policy—but that is relative to other competitors and with respect to the laws of orderly markets. The forward auction process gives no consideration to the specific requirements and expected return of a particular buyer.

This chapter will explain the mechanics of developing a coherent pricing strategy pertaining to an investment in a life settlement contract. An explanation of the key drivers of a policy valuation is followed by a review of discounted cash flow analysis. The three most widely implemented life settlement pricing models—deterministic, probabilistic, and stochastic—are each then explained.

KEY DRIVERS OF POLICY VALUES

Prevailing market conditions and the particular funding entity's pricing model ultimately impact what is and is not purchased. But prior to the application of any specific pricing methodology, certain criteria relating to the policy and to the insured must be met to determine if there is a reasonable chance that a policy would be attractive to institutional buyers.

Insured's Age and Life Expectancy

Most policy buyers prefer to acquire policies from insureds aged 70 and over for men and 75 and over for women. That said, the insured's life expectancy (LE) is perhaps the most important element in determining the value of a life settlement. Life expectancy companies derive an estimate with consideration to age, overall health, family history, lifestyle habits, and other factors.

Life expectancy is significant because it sets the time frame for the duration of the life settlement investment. Longer LEs mean that more premium payments must be made to acquire the eventual death benefit, and because the death benefit lies further in the future, it would be assigned a lower present value. Shorter LEs result in the opposite: fewer premium payments, a shorter duration to the receipt of death benefit, and therefore higher policy valuations.

Most potential settlement buyers will only accept LEs that are considered current, meaning those generated in the last 90 to 180 days. Older life expectancy reports are not useful because of possible changes in the insured's health, and because of the ongoing improvements constantly being introduced by medical underwriters to their models.

In fact, buyers should insist that all policy and health information should be as current and complete as possible, allowing for the most accurate estimates of a policy's value.

Policy Type

Universal life policies (UL) are the most desirable to a life settlement buyer. ULs are attractive because they are easily broken down into their component parts: policy fees, cost of insurance, and excess cash. Most pricing models include these components when calculating minimum payment obligations required to keep the policy in force.

Term policies, if they are eligible to be converted to universal life policies, are often good settlement candidates for the reasons already mentioned.

Nonconvertible term policies are sometimes purchased if the insured has an unusually short life expectancy, but this exposes the investor to the risk that the policy could expire and leave the investor with no chance to receive the death benefit.

Joint survivorship policies can often be sold when one insured is already deceased or when one insured has suffered a significant decline in health.

Joint policies are attractive because they are sold at a lower "joint mortality" rate. When the health of one insured declines, the arbitrage between the policy's pricing and the actual market value becomes more pronounced.

Whole life policies are generally not good settlement candidates due to the "black box" nature of their cost structures. These policies are much more difficult to deconstruct into their component costs and therefore are more difficult to understand and properly evaluate. Many investors will not consider them at all.

Insurance Company Ratings

Most institutional life settlement funding entities require that the under-writing company have at least a B+ rating. Higher ratings equate to better counterparty risk for investors. Since a buyer may have to wait for years for a return on the investment, the financial stability of an issuer is very important. Strong reserves, adequate pricing, and a history of solid performance should be demonstrated by a carrier before its policies are considered for purchase.

Cash Values

Lower cash value can either hurt or help a policy's value. A substantial balance in the policy's investment account can be used to fund premium obligations, thus lowering the investor's total out-of-pocket costs in acquiring the policy. However, buying a policy heavy with cash is an inefficient use of the investor's funds, as cash values in a policy earn much lower rates than would most alternatives.

Cash surrender value, as established by the issuing carrier, does not directly affect pricing, but can impact the likelihood that a certain policy is brought to market. Policy sellers are less apt to consider the transaction if the purchase price does not include a significant premium over cash surrender value.

Premiums/Policy Loans

Future premium costs and loans against a policy have significant impact on the price of the life settlement.

Future premiums represent the investment the buyer is willing to make in the policy in addition to the purchase price. It is important for a prospective investor to estimate the increasing premiums required to keep the policy in force until the eventual demise of the insured. The can be accomplished by requesting in force illustrations from the carrier and projecting the minimum premium needed to maintain the policy. Alternatively, many pricing models are available that can derive the premium requirements from a standard in-force illustration.

Policy loans also influence the price by creating an immediate loss for the investor. Most investors will price the policy assuming no loan and then subtract the loan balance to derive a value to be paid to the policy owner.

Policy Size

Industry data indicates that the average life settlement policy face amount is over $1,000,000. Given that certain transaction costs are fixed, it follows that larger policies receive the most interest from the buyers. Fixed transaction costs consist of underwriters' time, legal review, medical underwriting, and collection of medical and policy records. Additionally, costs include escrow fees, back wiring charges, postage costs, and closing interviews. It is very difficult for small policies (low death benefit) to overcome these high fixed transaction costs.

Policy size is also relevant when an investor considers the ongoing maintenance and administrative costs related to a policy. Smaller policies can prove to be uneconomical after transaction costs and ongoing maintenance requirements are considered. Most buyers use management companies to set up a policy, make premium payments, track the insured's stocks, and collect death benefits. These costs can accumulate over time.

Credit Market Factors

The spread between the buyer's expected rate of return and its cost of funds ultimately plays a very significant role in what price is offered for the policy. Life settlement offers are dependent on the return on investment desired by the buyer. As the buyer's risk increases, (due to longer LEs, weaker carrier ratings, regulatory changes, and the like) it must be justified with an opportunity for higher returns.

DISCOUNTED CASH FLOW AND NET PRESENT VALUE

The basics of discounted cash flow analysis are taught in many undergraduate finance courses. Here, a review is in order to establish a basis for explaining the pricing models covered later in the chapter.

Discounted cash flow is a method for valuing an asset utilizing the concept of *time value of money*. Future payments and the eventual return to the investor are estimated and discounted to assign a *net present value*, which is the difference between the present value of the future cash outflow and the present value of future cash inflows.

The discount rate used is usually a designated cost of capital, and generally recognizes an estimate of the riskiness or uncertainty of the future payments.

The net present value can be expressed as:

$$NPV = C_t/(1 + d)^t$$

t is the time period of the particular cash flow
d is the discount rate
C_t is the net cash flow at time t

A potential investment, with five-year duration has an immediate cash outflow of \$40,000 and additional cash outflows of \$5,000 for each of the five years. The investment will pay \$100,000 at year five. The discount rate is established at 10 percent.

The present value is calculated for each year as:

Net Present Value Example Calculation:

Year (t) $0 \geq$	$-\$40,000 / (1.10)^0$	$=$	$-\$40,000$
Year (t) $1 \geq$	$-\$5,000 / (1.10)^1$	$=$	$-\$5,500$
Year (t) $2 \geq$	$-\$5,000 / (1.10)^2$	$=$	$-\$6,050$
Year (t) $3 \geq$	$-\$5,000 / (1.10)^3$	$=$	$-\$6,655$
Year (t) $4 \geq$	$-\$5,000 / (1.10)^4$	$=$	$-\$7,320$
Year (t) $5 \geq$	$\$95,000 / (1.10)^5$	$=$	$\$81,896$
	Net Present Value	$=$	$\$16,371$

With a positive net present value of more than \$16,300, the investment appears to have merit. Of course, the calculation is performed in isolation, and no consideration is give to the opportunity costs of selecting this particular option over other opportunities.

LIFE SETTLEMENT PRICING MODELS

Investors generally use one of three methods, all of which involve a present value calculation, to determine the price offered for a policy. All have strengths and weaknesses, but any serious entrant to the settlement marketplace should have an understanding of all three.

Deterministic Pricing Model

The simplest of the three options, the deterministic model was widely implemented during the earliest years of the viatical settlement industry, when insureds' life expectancies were shorter and more predictable.

The deterministic approach to pricing is a "point in time" model that is easily implemented. While there are many variables that could impact the ultimate performance of the policy that is purchased, a deterministic model sets each variable at an expected value and assumes that reality will reflect these assumptions.

The deterministic model calculates a return based on a potential price paid for a policy and the receipt of the net death benefit at a specific point in time. It accomplishes this by assuming payment of death benefit at the insured's life expectancy. The key assumptions made in a deterministic model are the premium payments made over time, the projected life expectancy of the insured, and the discount rate for determining the present value of the cash flows. See Exhibit 10.1.

At the insured's five-year life expectancy, the investor's expected rate of return is 14.98 percent if $385,000 is paid for the policy. Generally speaking,

EXHIBIT 10.1 Deterministic Pricing Example

Face Value/Net Death Benefit:	$1,200,000
Life Expectancy:	Five Years
Purchase Price:	$385,000
Annual Premium:	$55,000
Discount Rate	12%

Assumptions: Premium paid annually at beginning of year, net death benefit paid once at end of year.

Year	Purchase Price	Premium	Discount Rate	Internal Rate of Return (IRR)
1	$385,000	$55,000	12%	172.73%
2	NA	$55,000	12%	59.01%
3	NA	$55,000	12%	32.78%
4	NA	$55,000	12%	21.35%
5	NA	$55,000	12%	14.98%
6	NA	$55,000	12%	10.94%
7	NA	$55,000	12%	8.16%
8	NA	$55,000	12%	6.13%
9	NA	$55,000	12%	4.59%
10	NA	$55,000	12%	3.28%

if the firm's minimum internal rate of return (IRR)—or hurdle rate—is less than 14.98 percent (here, it's stated as 12 percent), and all other acquisition criteria are met, the policy should be purchased.

Additional data can be added to the model, such as monthly maintenance costs, daily cash compounding, and policy fees. The most important and constant characteristic, however, is that assumptions are fixed and the dates are projected to be time-certain.

Because the deterministic pricing model is static, most analysts will conduct a sensitivity analysis to stress test various scenarios surrounding the policy purchase. The most common technique is to assume a range of mortality dates (10 percent to 20 percent longer and shorter) to evaluate how the IRR changes. The other most prevalent sensitivity analysis involves adjustments to the future minimum premium payments. Both techniques seek to offset the deterministic model's greatest shortcoming, which is a reliance on a single set of assumptions.

Pros:

    Easily implemented.

    Straightforward analysis.

Cons:

    Overly simplistic.

    Depends on accuracy of life expectancy prediction.

    Longer durations in modern life settlement market reward more sophisticated modeling.

Probabilistic Pricing Model

Recognizing that the insured's death might occur at any time in the illustration, not just at the estimated life expectancy, the probabilistic modeling technique improves on the deterministic approach by incorporating mortality rates for each year in the analysis. *The price offered is based on a mortality-weighted cash flow approach* and represents an aggregate of the possible outcomes.

The principal difference from a deterministic model lies in the assumption that during each year there is a certain, measurable probability of death. Thus an expected value can be calculated by showing the expected premium that must be paid and the expected death benefit that would be received.

Mortality estimates are made for groups of people, based on actuarial experience. Groups are generally sorted by gender and age. Adjustments are made to these tables for medical conditions and lifestyle attributes. Most life expectancy underwriting firms then calculate a range of mortality odds, showing a percentage chance of death in any given year. It is this annual probability that feeds the probabilistic pricing model.

By incorporating the annual mortality percentage for each forward year, the investor can calculate the expected annual values of premiums, death benefit, and net benefit (death benefit minus premiums). Those amounts can then be utilized to determine the present values of the net benefit for each year by applying the same discounted cash flow methods described previously.

For example, the illustration in Exhibit 10.2 shows that in Year One, there is an expected mortality rate of 5 percent, which implies a survival rate of 95 percent. The established 5 percent mortality rate yields an *expected* premium payment of $28,500 (95 percent chance of paying $30,000), and an *expected* death benefit of $50,000 (5 percent chance of receiving $1,000,000). The net benefit of $21,500 ($50,000 – $28,500) has a present value of $19,196, as calculated with a 12 percent discount rate.

Each year is adjusted for an increasing mortality percentage, yielding the results shown in Exhibit 10.2.

In this scenario, the aggregate present value of the net benefits is $264,687, and represents the price that the investor would be willing to

EXHIBIT 10.2 Probabilistic Pricing Example

Face Value/Net Death Benefit:	$1,000,000
Annual Premium:	$30,000
Discount Rate:	12%

Year	Mortality Rate Estimate	Premiums (Expected Value)	Death Benefit (Expected Value)	Net Benefit	Present Value of Net Benefit
1	5.0%	($28,500)	$50,000	$21,500	$19,196
2	5.3%	($28,425)	$52,500	$24,075	$19,192
3	5.5%	($28,346)	$55,125	$26,779	$19,061
4	5.8%	($28,264)	$57,881	$29,618	$18,823
5	6.1%	($28,177)	$60,775	$32,599	$18,497
6	6.4%	($28,086)	$63,814	$35,729	$18,101
7	6.7%	($27,990)	$67,005	$39,015	$17,648
8	7.0%	($27,889)	$70,355	$42,466	$17,151
9	7.4%	($27,784)	$73,873	$46,089	$16,620
10	7.8%	($27,673)	$77,566	$49,893	$16,064
11	8.1%	($27,557)	$81,445	$53,888	$15,492
12	29.0%	($21,314)	$289,517	$268,202	$68,841
	100%				$264,687

pay for the policy, given the mortality table and discount rate applied (12 percent). (**Note:** The 29 percent mortality rate for Year 12 is used only for illustrative purposes.)

This method models all of the possible timing scenarios for the investment. While no single year is correct, the aggregate result will be more accurate.

Because of the expected value nature of the probabilistic model, it is most effectively used on groups of policies and is very common tool for pricing portfolios.

Pros:

More rational, realistic assumptions than deterministic model.

Acknowledges range of possible outcomes.

Cons:

Good tool for "aggregate" analysis, but not precise enough for a single policy purchase.

Stochastic Pricing Model

Better than any other pricing methodology, the stochastic model acknowledges that unknown, real world events determine the investor's return and attempts to account for these uncertainties.

A stochastic pricing model integrates the precision of a deterministic model with the realistic and flexible expectations of the probabilistic model. This is usually accomplished via a Monte Carlo simulation, where repeated random sampling is used to derive a set of values.

Generally, several stages of preparation and activity are involved for each Monte Carlo analysis.

1. A domain of possible inputs is defined for *each* unknown variable. For life settlement transactions, these variables typically include the total amount of premium payments, the mortality date of the insured, and the policy's interest crediting rate.
2. Each variable is then expressed by a probability distribution. Due to the uncertainty of the actual input values, these distributions define the possible actual future values of the variables. For example, a life expectancy of eight years may be expressed in terms of annual mortality rates as shown in Exhibit 10.2. (Year 1 = 5 percent, Year 2 = 5.3 percent, and so on).

    The range of possible values for premiums and life expectancy are shown in the probability distributions in Exhibit 10.3.

Premiums

Study File Value	Min Allowed Value	10/90	Expected Value	90/10	Max Allowed Value
$20,000	$15,000	$18,558	$19,999	$21,442	$24,000

Normal Distribution

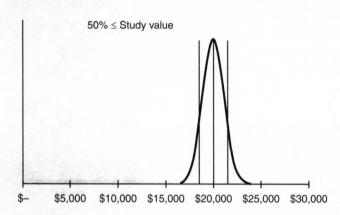

Life Expectancy

Study File Value	Min Allowed Value	10/90	Expected Value	90/10	Max Allowed Value
84	6	33	80	137	260

Gamma Left Distribution

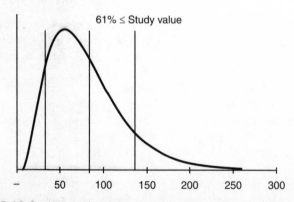

EXHIBIT 10.3   Normal Distribution and Gamma Left Distribution

EXHIBIT 10.4 Simulation Input Values (Abbreviated)

Simulation Number (of 1,000)	Premiums	Mortality (Life Expectancy in Months)
1	$18,501	120
2	$19,778	39
3	$20,646	46
4	$20,754	243
5	$21,571	83
6–995	–	–
996	$19,334	40
997	$19,495	56
998	$22,250	74
999	$18,855	66
1000	$18,795	116

3. The computer then pulls at random a value for each variable from its probability distribution. The first five and last five of the one thousand sample iterations in the sample study are shown in Exhibit 10.4.
4. The model then inserts each random input value into the pricing formula and generates a value for the policy, using the deterministic pricing model's methods. The process is repeated and policy values are calculated for a user-defined number of iterations, often in excess of 1,000. The first five and last five policy values of the one thousand sample iterations in the sample study are shown in Exhibit 10.5.

EXHIBIT 10.5 Simulation Output Values (Abbreviated)

Simulation Number (of 1,000)	Calculated Policy Value
1	$215,725
2	$643,792
3	$586,575
4	$54,350
5	$359,388
6–995	–
996	$635,295
997	$520,233
998	$405,061
999	$461,685
1000	$228,599

Frequency (%)

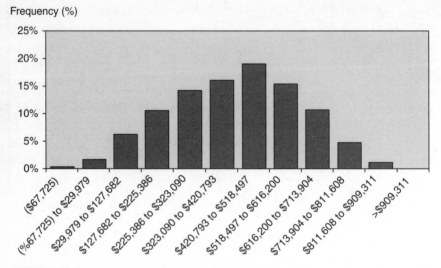

EXHIBIT 10.6   Policy Value Histogram

5. The calculated policy values are then stored in a histogram that shows the likely value of the policy, as well as the range of expected valuations from very high to very low. Here, a plurality of calculations (approximately 19 percent) estimate the policy's value between $420,793 and $518,497. At the extremes, there is a less than 1 percent chance that the policy value will be less than –67,725, and virtually zero probability that the policy's value will exceed $909,311. See Exhibit 10.6.

The information can also be illustrated with a Cumulative Frequency Chart (Exhibit 10.7).

After a satisfactory number of iterations of random variable selection and calculation, the results can be plotted on a chart and the investor can determine with varying degrees of certainty what value the policy may have. Statistical analysis on this data set can reveal much about the likelihood of each outcome.

Stochastic Pricing (Monte Carlo) Policy Value Report

Study Value = $361,074

38.2 percent of simulation results are equal or lower

61.8 percent of simulation results are equal or greater

Minimum Result = ($67,725)

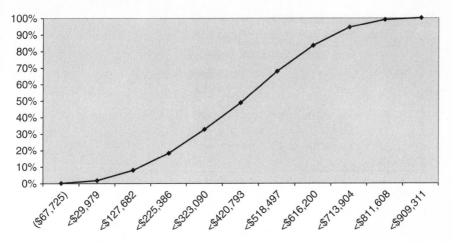

EXHIBIT 10.7 Policy Value Cumulative Frequency Chart

Maximum Result = $909,311
Expected Value = $415,788
Standard Deviation = $194,261
38.2 percent of simulation results are equal or lower
61.8 percent of simulation results are equal or greater
Of 1,000 simulations, 1,000 had numeric values
Of those with numeric values:

05% < $87,086	55% < $455,525
10% < $146,974	60% < $478,614
15% < $200,740	65% < $506,669
20% < $234,310	70% < $528,488
25% < $266,721	75% < $560,568
30% < $300,888	80% < $592,328
35% < $339,837	85% < $626,296
40% < $367,350	90% < $664,117
45% < $394,355	95% < $728,823
50% < $426,623	100% < $909,311

An investor can use his judgment to determine a pricing level that is likely to result in adequate returns. This simulation indicates the policy has a 62 percent chance of achieving a value of $361,000 or more, and an 80 percent chance of $234,300 or more.

Pros:

Combines best attributes of deterministic and probabilistic models.

Accounts for possible volatility in return.

Brings higher confidence levels to settlement investors.

Cons:

Most expensive and complicated model to properly implement.

SUMMARY

Placing the appropriate valuation on a life settlement is particularly complex due to the unique properties of each transaction under consideration, the need to acquire large amounts of information for each potential purchase, and the locked-in, predefined payment inherent in a life insurance policy.

While the short- and long-term objectives, available investment capital, and risk tolerance specific to each investor will play a role in the price ultimately offered for a policy, there is much to gain by applying pricing models designed to yield predictable results.

That said, no financial model is infallible. As the settlement market continues to grow and evolve buyers can expect that pricing methodologies will continue to be reviewed, altered, and ultimately improved.

CHAPTER 11

Using Life Extension-Duration and Life Extension-Convexity to Value Senior Life Settlement Contracts

Charles A. Stone
Professor, Brooklyn College, CUNY, Department of Economics

Anne Zissu
Professor, Citytech, CUNY, Department of Business The Polytechnic Institute
of NYU, Department of Financial Engineering

Investments in senior life settlements are marketed as securities that are uncorrelated with assets traded on other markets such as real estate, commodities, corporate equities, and risky debt. In this chapter we develop a metric that can be used to evaluate the sensitivity of the value of a life settlement contract and portfolios of life settlement contracts with respect to longevity risk. Longevity risk in the context of life settlement contracts is the possibility that a person covered by a life insurance policy lives longer than the purchaser of the policy has forecasted. It is this forecasted life expectancy that is the basis of the valuation of the policy in the secondary market. Forecasts of life expectancy make economic sense only if the policy under consideration is going to be part of a portfolio. As the number of policies that compose a portfolio of life settlement contracts increases, the uncertainty of life expectancy becomes quantifiable. Our summary of longevity risk using duration and convexity can be applied by fund managers to select life settlement contracts that fall within acceptable risk parameters. A fund manager can sort policies by using the life expectancy duration and convexity metrics we develop to select policies that will increase the likelihood that a fund of life settlement contracts attains its target rate of return. Increased accuracy in forecasting the return on a portfolio of life settlement contracts will lead to better pricing and to a more liquid market.

INTRODUCTION

Senior life settlements are financial instruments that are created when the owner of a life insurance policy sells the policy to a purchaser who assumes the premium liability of the policy in return for becoming its beneficiary.[1] The life settlement market allows the owner of the policy—whether an individual or company—to avoid surrendering the policy to the underwriter, letting it lapse or keeping it in force.

Our contribution to the market for life settlements is to offer life settlement providers and investors a useful metric. This tool allows them to understand to what extent the yield on different life settlement contracts will change with respect to deviations in actual longevity of the insured from calculated longevity expectations that are used to price the contracts. We show that the effect that longevity risk has on yield depends on the characteristics of the individual life insurance policies that comprise a life settlement pool. There are more than simple trade-offs between the actual life of the insured, expected life, and price. In other words, not all life settlement contracts lose the same amount of value if the insured lives one year beyond expected life. The values of two life insurance policies that are identical but for the ratio of annual premiums to death benefits (a ratio we call alpha) for two 65-year-old men both of whom have a life expectancy of 5 more years, will revalue differently with respect to extensions in actual life beyond life expectancy.

An excerpt from the October 2, 2006, prospectus for the Franklin Templeton Total Return Fund illustrates the value of a metric such as the one we present here. As information increases the liquidity of the market for traded life policies (the term used in Europe for life settlements), funds such as Templeton will be able to increase the amounts they allocate to this market.

> *Life Settlement Investments. The Franklin Templeton Total Return FDP Fund may invest in life settlements, which are sales to third parties, such as the Fund, of existing life insurance contracts for more than their cash surrender value but less than the net benefits to be paid under the policies. When the Fund acquires such a contract, it pays the policy premiums in return for the expected receipt of the new benefit as the beneficiary under the policy. Investments in these contracts involve certain risks, including liquidity*

risk, credit risk of the insurance company, and inaccurate estimations of life expectancy of the insured individuals (viators). These policies are considered illiquid in that they are bought and sold in a secondary market through life settlement agents. As such, the Fund's investments in life settlement contracts are subject to the Fund's investment restriction relating to illiquid securities. Also, in the event of a bankruptcy of the insurance carrier for a policy, the Fund may receive reduced or no benefits under the contract. The Fund seeks to minimize credit risk by investing in polices issued by a diverse range of highly-rated insurance carriers. Furthermore, the Fund may encounter losses on its investments if there is an inaccurate estimation of life expectancy of viators. The Fund intends to reduce this life expectancy risk by investing only in contracts where life expectancy was reviewed by an experienced actuary, as well as by diversifying its investments across viators* of varying ages and medical profiles.

(FD Series, Inc, Franklin Templeton Total Return FDP Fund, Prospectus October 2, 2006)

In the following section, we offer a broad description of the market for senior life settlement contracts. We describe the general scheme of the market, and then illustrate how life settlement portfolios can be constructed within duration and convexity constraints on longevity.

THE STRUCTURE OF THE LIFE SETTLEMENT MARKET

Life Exchange, Inc. (LFXG.OB) is a publicly traded company that has developed an Internet-based exchange that brings life settlement brokers and life settlement providers together. Life Settlement Exchange makes it possible for

---

*The term "viator" means the person selling the life insurance policy. A predecessor to the life settlement market was the viatical settlement market. A viatical settlement is the sale of a life insurance policy for more than its cash value by a person who has been diagnosed with a terminal illness and has a life expectancy of less than two more years. Originally the market was a source of funds for people who had been diagnosed with HIV or AIDS. Since the introduction of new treatments for these diseases, the ability of experts to accurately predict life expectancy has been severely diminished, and the viatical settlement market has thus become a valuable resource for people with terminal illnesses other than HIV/AIDS, such as heart disease and cancer.

life settlement brokers to elicit bids on life insurance policies from life settlement providers. It also enables life settlement providers to bid in an auction for policies that meet their investment criteria. Life Settlement Exchange is a new company (operational starting in the second quarter of 2007), so it has yet to make an impact on the market for life settlements. Its success or that of another life settlement exchange would add important transparency to the market. An exchange will assure sellers that their policies are being sold in a competitive auction and will attract the best possible price.

In a typical life settlement transaction an individual is advised by his or her financial adviser about the value of selling a life insurance policy to a life settlement provider such as Coventry First, Life Settlement Solutions, or Life Partners Holdings Inc.[2] A state-licensed life settlement broker should work for the owner to solicit bids for the policy from a life settlement provider who must also be licensed in the state of the seller. The broker represents the interests of the seller of the policy. Success as a life settlement provider requires access to the capital markets or a reliable source of institutional capital as well as deep and broad relationships with life settlement brokers and an ability to correctly value policies and service them once they are purchased. A life settlement provider may buy policies on behalf of an institutional investor by using the institution's capital directly. Alternatively, the provider may fund the accumulation of policies on its own balance sheet and then sell them to an entity that funds itself on the capital markets, such as Eastport Financial, LLC, a special purpose vehicle (SPV); Life Settlements Fund Series A, a Saint Vincent and the Grenadines-based investment fund; Pensioenfonds Metalektro, a Dutch pension fund;[3] Loews Corporation, a diversified holding company through its CNA subsidiary; AIG, a multinational-multiline insurance company;[4] and New Stream Capital, LLC, a hedge fund.[5] While it is common to read in the press that hedge funds are significant investors in life settlement contracts and in securities backed by them, the actual investment portfolios of hedge funds are not publicly available. This may change as more hedge funds face lawsuits over their investments in subprime mortgages and their derivatives.

Life settlement companies known as life settlement providers can act as a warehouse for life settlement contracts before selling them to investment funds. They can also act as buying agents for institutional and individual investors. Life Partners Holdings, Inc. is a public company whose shares are traded on the NASDAQ stock market under the symbol LPI.[6] LPI acts as a purchasing agent for its clients and is also the adviser to three life settlement funds. One of these, Life Settlements Fund Series – A, was launched in August 2007.

Life Settlement Solutions, Inc., a private life settlement provider, acts as a conduit between, on the one hand, individuals who are interested in selling policies in the secondary market and, on the other, institutions that have decided to allocate capital to this market. Life Settlement Solutions searches for life settlement policies that meet the investment criteria of its institutional clientele. It screens policies that are offered by a network of life settlement brokers. It may act as a facilitator of the transaction between the individual selling a life insurance policy and an institutional investor or it may purchase the policy for its trading account. Policies may be funded on the money markets or with a loan or investment from the ultimate investor in the life settlement contracts. Once the transaction is closed, Life Settlement Solutions continues to service and manage the policies. Interestingly, one of the sources of capital tapped by Life Settlement Solutions is a bank-sponsored asset-backed commercial-paper program. While the actual performance of the life settlement contracts may be uncorrelated with yields on other asset classes, the capital supporting the industry is not. Market values of life settlement contracts depend on the depth and liquidity of the funding sources available to life settlement providers. If sources of funds supporting the market become relatively expensive, this will have an impact on the pricing of the contracts, just as FNMA's cost of capital influences the yield on mortgages.

The largest life settlement provider is Coventry, but it is a private company, and information on its operations and finances is thus not readily available. Life Partners Holdings estimates that it captured 3 percent of the estimated $5 billion in life settlement contracts that were created in 2006. For the fiscal year ended February 2007, LPI created life settlement contracts in the amount of $151,397,400. Two hundred twenty contracts were settled in 2007.[7]

The size of the current market for life settlements is a fraction of its potential size, and that is in turn a fraction of the size of the overall market for life insurance. The value of outstanding individual life insurance policies at the end of 2006 was $10.056 trillion. According to the American Council of Life Insurers 2007 Fact Book, in 2006 1.6 percent of outstanding individual life insurance policies, worth $140.791 billion, were surrendered, that is, exchanged for their cash value. We do not know what percentage of this amount was surrendered by people over 65 with impaired health. This subgroup might have been able to extract more value by liquidating their policies in the life settlement market. People also let policies lapse. According to the same source, the lapse rate in 2006 for individual life insurance policies was 4.9 percent. Again, it is important to know what percentage of the 4.9 percent was allowed to lapse by senior citizens with impaired health. People who let their policies lapse are another important source of life settlement contracts. The extent to which the potential of the life settlement market can be unlocked will depend on how effective the education efforts of financial planners are. What is certain is that many insured individuals 65 and over are unaware of the value of their policies as life settlement contracts. Life Partners Holdings estimates the current volume of the life settlement market at $2.5 billion (Form 10-KSB, for the fiscal year ended February 28, 2006, Life Partners Holdings, Inc).

Offshore funds offer the greatest insight into the operation of the life settlement market. An offering memorandum is available for these funds. It describes all aspects of the investment policies for the fund, as well as its operations and its targeted yield. We summarize a number of funds to give an overall sense of the investment opportunities that life settlement contracts offer. All of the funds we describe are located in offshore jurisdictions that do not impose any income tax on them or withhold tax from the investors. This is important for a life settlement fund because it may realize incomes as death benefits are paid and interest is earned on the proceeds of reinvested death benefits. Life settlement contracts also appreciate as the insured ages. The income of life settlement funds, whether in the form of capital gains or interest, is not taxed when the fund is located in a favorable tax jurisdiction such as the Isle of Man, Saint Vincent and the Grenadines, the Cayman Islands, the Bahamas, or Guernsey.

In 2006, the Financial Accounting Standards Board (FASB) published FSP FTB 85-4-1. The FASB accounting guidance changed the way companies account for their investments in life settlement contracts. Investors can use either the investment method or the fair-value method to account for their positions in life settlement contracts. Prior to FSP FTB 85-4-1, investments in life settlement contracts had to be accounted for according to FASB Technical Bulletin 85-4. This forced investors to expense, on the date of the investment, the difference between the cash-surrender value and the price paid for the policy. This was always negative because the purchase price of a life settlement contract is always higher than its cash-surrender value. Investors were thus forced to take an immediate loss on the investment.

When the investment method is chosen, the investor records the investment at the transaction price and capitalizes all expected costs (predominantly future premiums) associated with an investment in the life settlement contract. When the death benefit is paid, the investor records to earnings the difference between the carrying value of the policy and the death benefit. If the investor becomes aware that the life settlement contract has been impaired, he must write down the policy to its fair value. Impairment could result from an increased longevity risk or an increased credit risk to the insurer. A significant change in the mortality assumptions for the insured or the credit quality of the insurer, to the extent that the expected value of the death benefit will not cover the capitalized costs of carrying the life settlement contract and the undiscounted marginal costs (additional insurance premiums), would impair the contract.

When the fair-value method is chosen, the investor records the initial investment at the transaction price and then revalues the position periodically, writing it either up or down depending on what happens to its fair value. The change in the fair value of the life settlement contract is incorporated into reported earnings.

Closed-end funds may have a final redemption date (when the fund buys back shares), or a date when the fund begins to distribute proceeds to investors. If there is a market in the shares in a fund, investors can sell them. Open-ended funds may charge high redemption fees in the early years before death benefits begin flowing into it at the expected rate. These funds can reach a steady state if they can replenish maturing contracts with new life settlement contracts. In this way they can issue new shares to redeem shares. If investors try to redeem shares before this steady state is reached, the fund will have to borrow or liquidate contracts to fund redemptions. Investors will be charged early redemption fees to offset these costs. It is typical for a fund to quote an expected or targeted yield range in its offering and marketing materials. For example, a fund may market a 7 percent to 12 percent expected annual yield over a 7-year period. Fund managers must work with their investment advisers, who in turn work with a life settlement provider to select those policies that can be expected to satisfy the marketed yield. The marketed yield makes sense only with respect to a date on which the investment can be sold or redeemed. Via Source, a U.S. investment adviser, works with EEA Life Settlement Fund, a Guernsey-based open-ended protected cell company. A cell company is a fund that is divided into separate cells. Each cell owns different assets, has its own liabilities, and is protected from the creditors of other cells. The offering document for the EEA Life Settlement Fund states an 8 percent targeted return. Aurora Defined Benefits Fund is a life settlement fund managed by the Private Client Portfolio, an open-ended multiclass investment fund established in the Cayman Islands. In its prospectus, it sets an objective of 7 percent to 12 percent capital growth per year. The fund seeks to outperform the yield on the 5-year treasury + 200 basis points. Redemption fees for the fund decline 1 percent per year, from 7 percent for redemptions of shares within a year of subscription to 0 percent for redemption after 7 years. It is implicit that the targeted return is for a 7-year horizon. The Utopia TLP Fund, PLC, states in its offering document that it seeks a net return of 9 percent to 12 percent per year. The fund does not distribute any income. All proceeds received by it are accumulated. Shares can be redeemed on a dealing day with one month notice for their net asset value. Fluctuations in returns for all life settlement funds stem from the uncertainty over when death benefits will be received, which date also determines for how long premiums on outstanding policies must be paid. The Utopia TLP Fund manages life-extension risk, or what it calls "over run," by purchasing extended-longevity insurance. The fund bought $15 million in coverage from Albatross Invest SpA for $900,000. The policy pays off when an insured lives two years beyond life expectancy. The Secure Class of the Defined Return Fund uses stop-loss policies to insure against life extension risk beyond a certain threshold. Life settlement funds lock up investor capital through high penalty fees for early redemption and high entry fees. For example, the redemption-fee schedule for this fund if shares are redeemed prior to the 5-year maturity date for the fund (exit charges) are as follows:

- Year 0 – 1 = 8 percent
- Year 1 – 2 = 6.4 percent
- Year 2 – 3 = 4.8 percent
- Year 3 – 4 = 3.2 percent
- Year 4 – 5 = 1.6 percent
- Year 5 and beyond = 0

Investors willing to finance life-expectancy risk that is embedded in illiquid securities can earn yields that are determined by the difference between the value of financing the premium stream to keep a portfolio of life settlement contracts active and the value of the death benefit. A life settlement fund that uses more leverage will be able to increase its yield. Of course, increased leverage always increases the risk of financial distress and the volatility of the yield. If the weighted average life expectancy of the leveraged fund's assets exceeds expectations by a large enough degree, the fund may face difficulties in rolling over liabilities issued in order to finance premiums and be forced to liquidate life settlement contracts. Since the life settlement market is illiquid, a forced sale of policies would almost certainly reduce the value of the fund's assets. Assets in life settlement funds are marked to model not to market.

Larger portfolios show less variation around the expected life of the insured, and the surest way of minimizing the longevity risk of a life settlement portfolio is to increase the number of life settlement contracts in it. Our duration and convexity metrics are not substitutes for the effect of the law of large numbers. The metrics we develop can help investment managers select the most desirable life settlement contracts that will compose the large number. A fund manager who uses "LE-duration" and "LE-convexity" (described later in the section on methodology) as selection criteria will be able to achieve the same degree of longevity risk with fewer life settlement contracts than an investment manager who simply picks policies based on the expected value of the life settlement contract. Two financial managers using the same impaired-mortality table to value life settlement contracts and the same level of leverage will not choose the same life settlement contracts if one of them also includes LE-duration and LE-convexity among the investment criteria.

Life-extension risk, also called longevity risk, is the principal risk that investors in life settlement contracts and portfolios of such contracts must measure and manage in order to capture expected returns. Liquidity risk is also a fundamental risk that investments in life settlement contracts must price and manage. The life expectancy of the insured at the time the policy is sold on the secondary market is typically less than was forecasted on the mortality table used to underwrite the policy.[8] It is this reduction in life expectancy, which is caused by the impairment of the insured's health, that opens up the possibility of a valuable transaction between the buyer (life settlement provider) and the seller of the life insurance policy (the life settler). The reduced life expectancy in turn lowers the expected value of the premiums that will have to be paid to keep the policy active and brings the date of the expected death benefit forward. The life settlement industry is altering the calculations that life insurers must make when evaluating their underwriting decisions and valuing their portfolio of life insurance contracts. Contracts that at one time would have been surrendered are now liquidated in the life settlement market.

The value of a life settlement contract is based on the life expectancy of the settler, which in turn is a function of his/her age and health.[9] The valuation of a life settlement is achieved by discounting the premiums paid over the established settler's life expectancy and the benefit to be received at the time the settler dies. If a settler lives above life expectancy, premiums need to be paid over a longer period, and it takes longer to receive the death benefit. An increase in the longevity of an insured or the extension of the insured's life beyond the time used to value the life settlement contract reduces the value of senior life settlements. Life settlement providers value life settlement contracts by using mortality tables that have been modified to account for various manifestations of impaired health. They use these tables to calculate the life expectancy of the underlying insured and the expected value of premium payments. These tables can also be used to estimate when a portfolio of life settlement contracts will begin to generate a positive cash flow. The estimates of expected life and stream of premium payments are used to calculate the present value of the life settlement contract. We have included an excerpt from the 2005 offering prospectus of the Lansdown Atlantic Life Settlement Fund.[10]

A report issued in 2005 and entitled "The Life Settlements Market: An Actuarial Perspective on Consumer Economic Value" (the Carriers Report) by Deloitte Consulting, LLP, and the University of Connecticut, argues that it is almost always better for the owner of a life insurance policy to keep it in force and liquidate other financial assets to raise capital. While the authors recognize the value of the life settlement market, they show that most life settlement transactions tend to be inefficient for the seller. Hal J. Singer and Eric Stallard (2005) disagree. They argue that the report is based on faulty assumptions and analytical errors. One of the critiques focuses on the discount rate used in the report to find the intrinsic economic value of a life insurance policy. The discount rate used in the report is the risk-free rate. We also believe that this rate is inappropriate. It would make more sense to use a rate that reflects the cost of borrowing against the policy or other assets owned by the policy owner. A person who places a high value on current income relative to future income will use a higher discount rate than an owner of a life insurance policy who places a higher value on the death benefit relative to current income. Clearly an assumption based on the discount rate drives the conclusion of whether to sell a life insurance policy in the secondary market or to keep it in force.

Two Isle of Man investment companies that specialize in funding pools of life settlement contracts are the EPIC Life Settlement Fund and the Lansdown Atlantic Life Settlement Fund, PLC. The latter's fact sheet characterizes the investment objective of the fund as a "total annual return targeted to be between 10 percent and 14 percent, net of charges." The EPIC fund targets a net annual return of 8 percent. We present an excerpt from the Lansdown Fund's offering summary, which describes how the net asset value of the fund is calculated:

The Fund's assets will be valued in accordance with the Articles as follows:

a) The value of any TLP (traded life policy) will be calculated in accordance with what the Directors consider to be the generally accepted valuation principals of the TLP market. At the current time, the Directors have, following actuarial advice, chosen to employ standard actuarial techniques to value the traded life policies. The policies will be valued individually by the Actuaries and the valuation method will commence by placing a value on i) the sum assured paid out on the death of the life assured; and ii) the premiums payable to maintain each policy while the life assured remains alive.

Since both of these values depend upon the unknown length of time for which the life assured will live, an expected value will be estimated using an assumed rate of mortality for the life assured. The mortality assumption will be chosen based on the professional advice of a qualified medical practitioner as to the life expectancy of the life assured. Using this assumption the payments will be projected for each future period and then discounted at an appropriate rate of interest to convert them into present day equivalents.

Having calculated a total value for both sets of projected cash flows, the value of each policy will be equal to i) less ii) representing the expected income from the policy net of the expected costs of owning the policy."

Lansdown Atlantic Life Settlement Fund PLC,
offering document, October 24, 2005.

METHODOLOGY

Stone and Zissu (2006) have developed what they call the *LE-duration* (life-extension duration), the *modified LE-duration* and the *LE-convexity* (life-extension convexity) to address the longevity risk of senior life settlements. In this chapter "LE" stands for "life expectancy." Using the pool information that a life settlement provider would have, we develop the modified LE-duration and the LE-convexity. These metrics provide information on how sensitive the value of the life settlement contract or portfolio is to deviations around life expectancy. The LE-duration measures the percentage change in value of a life settlement given a percentage change in a settler's life from its life expectancy. The modified LE-duration measures the percentage change in value of a life settlement given a change, rather than a percentage change, in a settler's life from its life expectancy. Life settlement providers accumulating life settlement contracts will have information about various parameters in the underlying insurance policies. Investors in life settlement pools and creditors of life settlement funds will demand estimates of expected yields. The answer will depend on the weighted average life expectancy of the insured underlying the life settlement contracts. The risk that this yield will not be realized can be summarized with the LE-duration and LE-convexity metrics. Knowing the modified LE-duration and LE-convexity will allow investors and creditors to better manage their overall portfolios.

The next section summarizes Stone and Zissu's model. We then describe a typical pool of senior life settlements and apply the LE-duration, modified LE-duration and LE-convexity in order to measure the longevity risk of such a pool. Using these measurements, an investor who has the choice among different pools of life settlements will be able to evaluate which is more sensitive to changes in the longevity of the insured above or below original life expectancy. This is the first step to finding consistent prices for pools of life settlement contracts and individual life insurance policies.

LE-DURATION AND LE-CONVEXITY

The valuation of a senior life settlement, $V(sls)$, is obtained by discounting the premium paid at the end of each year, $-P$, and the death benefit B, collected at the time when the life settler dies. For simplicity, a flat yield curve is assumed, with a discount rate of r. The valuation is based on a life expectancy of t years.

$$V(sls) = -P\left[\frac{1}{(1+r)^1} + \frac{1}{(1+r)^2} \cdots + \frac{1}{(1+r)^t}\right] + \frac{B}{(1+r)^t} \qquad (11.1)$$

Equation (11.1) can be rewritten as:

$$V(sls) = -P\left[\frac{1}{r} - \frac{a^t}{r}\right] + Ba^t \quad \text{where } a = \frac{1}{(1+r)}$$

and after rearranging we have:

$$V(sls) = a^t\left[\frac{P}{r} + B\right] - \frac{P}{r} \qquad (11.2)$$

We can now take the first derivative of equation (11.2) relative to changes in t:

$$\frac{dV(sls)}{dt} = \left[\frac{P}{r} + B\right]a^t \ln(a) \qquad (11.3)$$

and, after multiplying the first derivative by t, dividing it by the value of the life settlement, we obtain the LE-duration:

$$LE\text{-}duration = \frac{[ta^t(P + rB)\ln(a)]}{[a^t(P + rB) - P]} \qquad (11.4)$$

The LE-duration is negative, which implies that the longer a life settler lives beyond life expectancy, the more value the senior life settlement contract will lose.

The percentage change in value of a life settlement relative to changes in time, rather than relative to percentage changes in time, the modified LE-duration is obtained by dividing the LE-duration by t:

$$modified \ LE\text{-}duration = \frac{[a^t(P + rB)\ln(a)]}{[a^t(P + rB) - P]} \qquad (11.5)$$

Investors in pools of senior life settlements can evaluate the pool's sensitivity to life extension dt using the modified LE-duration of the pool:

$$[\%\Delta V(SLS)] = \frac{\Delta t[a^t(P + rB)\ln(a)]}{[a^t(P + rB) - P]} \tag{11.6}$$

The percentage change in value of the pool $[\%\Delta V(SLS)]$ given a change in time due to life extension or reduction (Δt) is equal to the pool's modified LE-duration $\frac{[a^t(P+rB)\ln(a)]}{[a^t(P+rB)-P]}$ multiplied by the life extension/reduction Δt.

For example, for a life extension of two years, $\Delta t = 2$, the percentage change in the value of the pool $[\%\Delta V(SLS)]$ will be equal to:

$$[\%\Delta V(SLS)] = 2\frac{[a^t(P + rB)\ln(a)]}{[a^t(P + rB) - P]} \tag{11.7}$$

Convexity of a fixed income security measures the rate at which duration changes with respect to changes in interest rates. As the convexity of a security increases, the range over which duration is accurate relative to changes in yields diminishes. It is possible to correct for the convexity effect on the accuracy of duration by adding the value of the convexity to that of duration. The LE-convexity is obtained by taking the second derivative of the value of senior life settlement with respect to life expectancy and dividing it by the value of the senior life settlement:

LE-convexity:

$$\frac{d^2 V(SLS)}{dt^2} = \frac{\left(\frac{P}{r} + B\right)a^t(\ln(a))^2}{a^t\left(\frac{P}{r} + B\right) - \frac{P}{r}} \tag{11.8}$$

The result is a positive convexity, which means that as a life settler lives longer than life expectancy, the value of the settlement decreases at an increasing rate.

Results

We now describe the variables from Exhibit 11.1 that a life settlement provider or investor would be able to use to evaluate a policy or pool of policies.

Report Date: This is the date at which all the data in Exhibit 11.1 are reported, and it is very important because that is when a settler's life expectancy is reported. If the report date is six months before we look at the data, the life expectancy has to be readjusted.

Face Amount: This represents the amount of the death benefit the beneficiary receives when the life settler dies.

M/F: The life settler is designated with M for male or F for female.

Age: This is the age of the life settler at the time of the report date.

Date of Birth: Date of birth of the life settler.

State: State of residence of the life settler.

Insurance Company Name: Insurance company that issued the policy.

Policy Type: UL (universal life); whole; endow (a whole life insurance policy is designed to mature (endow) when the insured reaches the age of 100); and adjustable life insurance.

Company Rating: Rating of insurance company that issued the policy. This is important information because A.M. Best requires that insurance companies providing life insurance must have Financial Strength Ratings (FSRs) of "B+" or higher, in order for the corresponding life settlements to be included in a pool to be securitized.

Policy Issue Date: Date at which life insurance was issued.

Years in Force: Number of years since the policy was issued.

EXHIBIT 11.1 Description of a Senior Life Settlement

Report Date:	11/29/2006
Face Amount:	10,000,000
M/F:	M
Age:	86
Date of Birth:	9/21/1927
State:	NY
Insurance Company Name:	Prudential
Policy Type:	UL
Company Rating:	A+
Policy Issue Date:	6/30/2006
Years In Force:	2
Policy Loan Outstanding:	0
Current Cash Surrender Value:	30,000
Annual Premium:	500,000
Life Expectancy Years First Report:	4
Life Expectancy Months First Report:	70
LE Provider/Lab:	XYZ

Policy Loan Outstanding: The life settler can borrow against his/her policy, so any amount borrowed and outstanding is reported.

Current Cash Surrender Value: Cash surrender value is also called cash value. It is the accumulated value of the paid-in premiums that exceeds the expenses of paying for the actual policy.

Annual Premium: Amount of premium paid each year to the life insurance company. Once the policy is consigned to the life settlement company, the company will substitute itself to the life settlers in making the premium payments.

Life Expectancy Years First Report: This is the estimated life expectancy, in years, of the life settler. There may be more reports.

Life Expectancy Months First Report: This is the estimated life expectancy, in months, of the life settler, in the first report.

LE Provider/Lab: Lab that provided medical examination and life expectancy.

Exhibit 11.1 is an example of the actual information on a pool of life settlements (we included the parameters relevant for our analysis).

Investment managers buy blocks of senior life settlements from life settlements companies. A typical block may contain between 40 and 60 life settlements, with a total face value of 150 to 200 million dollars. Each life settlement is described as in Exhibit 11.1.

Before analyzing a pool of senior life settlements, we first look at the life settlement from Exhibit 11.1 with the following characteristics:

Face Amount   = $10,000,000
Yearly Premium = $500,000
Life Expectancy = 4

Using equations (11.5) and (11.8) we compute the modified LE-duration (column 2) and the LE-convexity (column 3) for a range of discount rates (column 1) as shown in Exhibit 11.2.

The interpretation of Exhibit 11.2 is as follows: the value of the life settlement from Exhibit 11.1, with a life expectancy of four years, will decrease by 12.43 percent for a discount rate of 5 percent if the life settler lives one year above LE. The value will decrease by twice that percentage if the life settler lives two year above LE. In each case, we have to add back to the new value obtained from the modified LE-duration, the percentage change in value due to convexity. This is due to the curvature of the price/LE curve of a senior life settlement.

EXHIBIT 11.2 LE-Duration and LE-Convexity

r%	modified LE-duration	LE-convexity
0.03	(0.0996732597)	0.00295
0.04	(0.1120340279)	0.00439
0.05	(0.1243863681)	0.00607
0.06	(0.1367343440)	0.00797
0.07	(0.1490820432)	0.01009
0.08	(0.1614335819)	0.01242
0.09	(0.1737931096)	0.01498
0.1	(0.1861648150)	0.01774
0.11	(0.1985529305)	0.02072
0.12	(0.2109617379)	0.02391
0.13	(0.2233955737)	0.02730
0.14	(0.2358588349)	0.03090
0.15	(0.2483559848)	0.03471

The percentage change in value due to the LE-convexity is computed as follows:

$$[\%\Delta V(SLS)due\ to\ LE\text{-}conv] = \frac{1}{2}\frac{\left[\frac{P}{r}+B\right]a^t(\ln(a))^2}{a^t\left(\frac{P}{r}+B\right)-\frac{P}{r}}(\Delta t)^2 \qquad (11.9)$$

In Exhibit 11.3 we calculate the initial value of the senior life settlement over a range of discount rates using equation (11.1). This is shown in column 2. Still using equation (11.1) we calculate the value of the senior life settlement for a shift by two years above the initial life expectancy of four years. This is shown in column 3. Finally, in column 4, rather than using equation (11.1), we use the modified LE-duration, from equation (11.5), and the LE-convexity, from equation (11.8), to compute the value of the senior life settlement that lives two years above LE.

We graph column 2, 3, and 4 in Exhibit 11.4. We can observe that the downward shift (leftward) in the price/LE curve of the life settlement due to the increase in life by two years above the life settler's LE, is the same whether computed with equation (11.1), column 3, or with the combination of equations (11.5) and (11.8), column 4. Columns 3 and 4 exactly overlap in Exhibit 11.3.

In Exhibit 11.5 we analyze a pool of 13 senior life settlements with different face amounts, annual premiums, and life expectancies, for a total of $82,000,000 in face value and a yield of 5 percent. Fund managers target a yield and then select life settlement contracts that are expected to realize this yield.

EXHIBIT 11.3 Value of Contract at LE and LE + 2 Years

r	Value at LE	Value for LE + 2	New V with LE-Duration + LE-Convexity
0.03	7,026,321.278	5,666,246.845	5,667,050.794
0.04	6,733,094.298	5,282,076.829	5,283,594.115
0.05	6454049.496	4924307.933	4926795.019
0.06	6188383.826	4590943.241	4594664.795
0.07	5935346.492	4280152.408	4285375.322
0.08	5694235.108	3990256.437	3997245.022
0.09	5464392.172	3719713.974	3728726.141
0.1	5245201.83	3467108.951	3478393.223
0.11	5036086.897	3231139.434	3244932.654
0.12	4836506.111	3010607.55	3027133.177
0.13	4645951.614	2804410.38	2823877.264
0.14	4463946.621	2611531.719	2634133.283
0.15	4290043.275	2431034.612	2456948.368

The weighted average modified LE-duration (wa-modified-LE-duration), is obtained by multiplying each life settlement's duration by its corresponding value, dividing it by the value of the entire pool, and summing up the results for each of the n life settlements (13 in our example), as shown in equation (11.10):

$$\text{wa-modified-LE-duration} = \sum_{i=1}^{n} \frac{V(sls)_i}{V(SLS)} (modified\ LE\text{-}duration)_i$$

$$(11.10)$$

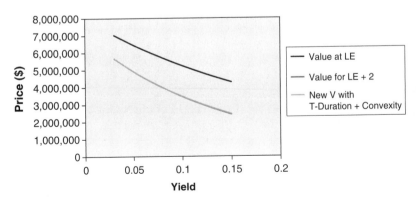

EXHIBIT 11.4 Price/Yield Life Settlement Curve

The weighted average LE-convexity (wa-LE-convexity), is obtained by multiplying each life settlement's convexity by its corresponding value, dividing it by the value of the entire pool, and summing up the results for each of the n life settlements (13 in our example), as shown in equation (11.11):

$$\text{wa-LE-convexity} = \sum_{i=1}^{n} \frac{V(sls)_i}{V(SLS)} (LE\text{-}convexity)_i \qquad (11.11)$$

We find that the wa-modified-LE-duration for our pool of 13 life settlements is equal to -0.11484, and that the wa-LE-convexity is equal to 0.00560.

The total initial value of our pool corresponds to $53,552,671.03$, and for a life extension of two years above LE, the new value of the pool is obtained as follows:

$$Value\ at\ LE + 2 = \$53,552,671.03[1 - 0.11484(2)$$
$$+ (.5)(0.00560)(2)2] = \$41,852,541.76$$

And it corresponds to the sum of the results in column 9 in Exhibit 11.5.

In Exhibit 11.6 we graph columns 4, 5, and 9 from Exhibit 11.5. We can observe that the change in value of each of the 13 life settlements in the pool, due to the increase in life by two years above the life settler's LE, is exactly the same whether computed with equation (11.1), column 5, or with the combination of equations (11.5) and (11.8), column 9. Columns 5 and 9 exactly overlap when graphed in Exhibit 11.6. The value of the 13 life settlements for initial LE (column 4), is the top curve.

It is common parlance in the life settlement industry when describing a life settlement, to refer to the premium (P) and the face value (B) as a ratio $\left(\frac{P}{B}\right)$. For example, a life settlement with an annual premium of $60,000 and a face value (death benefit B) of $1 million can be referred to as 6 percent life settlement. We call the ratio $\frac{P}{B} = \alpha$.

In Exhibit 11.7, we compute the modified LE-durations across a range of α and LE, where α corresponds to the ratio of annual premium, P, to face value, B, $\left(\frac{P}{B}\right)$. The modified LE-duration is obtained by replacing $\frac{P}{B} = \alpha$ in equation (11.5) as follows:

$$\text{Modified LE-duration} = \frac{[a^t B(\alpha + r)\ln(a)]}{a^t B(a + r) - \alpha B} \qquad (11.12)$$

EXHIBIT 11.5 Value of Life Settlement Pool

Face Amount	Annual Premium	LE	Value at LE	Value for LE + 2	%dV for LE+2	LE-Convexity	(1/2)Conv(dt)^2	New V with T-Duration+ Convexity
10,000,000	500,000.00	4	$6,454,049.50	$4,924,307.93	-0.2370	0.00607	0.0121377626	4,926,795.02
15,000,000	700,000.00	5	$8,722,258.83	$6,609,758.57	-0.2422	0.00620	0.0124027242	6,613,193.12
5,000,000	200,000.00	2	$4,163,265.31	$3,404,322.27	-0.1823	0.00467	0.0093352162	3,405,556.18
2,000,000	50,000.00	7	$1,132,043.99	$933,826.75	-0.1751	0.00448	0.0089665921	934,149.01
1,000,000	75,000.00	5	$458,815.42	$276,703.33	-0.3969	0.01016	0.0203259132	276,999.41
3,000,000	150,000.00	6	$1,477,292.38	$1,061,036.17	-0.2818	0.00721	0.0144292432	1,061,712.93
6,000,000	200,000.00	3	$4,638,375.99	$3,835,261.66	-0.1731	0.00443	0.0088666733	3,836,567.38
8,000,000	350,000.00	4	$5,340,537.12	$4,193,230.95	-0.2148	0.00550	0.0110012917	4,195,096.26
1,000,000	100,000.00	5	$350,578.50	$132,043.99	-0.6234	0.01596	0.0319215548	132,399.29
4,000,000	200,000.00	8	$1,414,714.90	$911,306.03	-0.3558	0.00911	0.0182222174	912,124.48
10,000,000	450,000.00	3	$7,412,914.37	$5,886,997.16	-0.2058	0.00527	0.0105412296	5,889,478.03
7,000,000	250,000.00	2	$5,884,353.74	$4,872,429.70	-0.1720	0.00440	0.0088064004	4,874,074.91
10,000,000	400,000.00	5	$6,103,471.00	$4,792,263.94	-0.2148	0.00550	0.0110012917	4,794,395.73

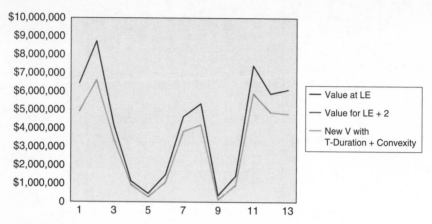

EXHIBIT 11.6   Plots of Value for Life Settlement Pool at LE and LE + 2

Exhibit 11.8 represents the modified LE-durations for a range of life expectancies going from one year to seven years, and for αs ranging from 6 percent to 9 percent. The top curve is for α equal to 6 percent, a smaller premium relative to the bottom curve which corresponds to an α equal to 9 percent. We can observe that life settlements have a modified LE-duration that increases (in absolute value) for higher life expectancies, but the increase in absolute value is greater the higher the ratio of premium to face value, α, is. This means that the higher the premium is, relative to face value, the greater the modified LE-duration is for higher life expectancies.

CONCLUSION

In its "Strategic Capital Resource Report," Emeritus Capital Partners, LLC, describes the structure of its life settlement portfolio. The report outlines the approach it takes to sorting policies in order to achieve an average premium rate of 4 percent per annum (what we call α in this chapter), with an average life expectancy of eight years. The goal is to realize in turn an annualized yield of 11 percent. Many funds sort policies to meet specific targets. The LE-duration and LE-convexity metrics that we have developed can be applied by life settlement companies and investors that are looking to hedge longevity risk by means of insurance products or derivatives. For example, it is important to know the LE-duration of a life settlement portfolio that will be covered by a longevity-risk guarantee. LE-duration will enable the fund manager to more accurately estimate how much coverage will be

EXHIBIT 11.7 LE-Duration Across LE and α

α/le	1	2	3	4	5	6	7	8	9	10	11	12
2%	−0.07	−0.07	−0.07	−0.08	−0.08	−0.08	−0.08	−0.08	−0.09	−0.09	−0.10	−1.00
3%	−0.08	−0.08	−0.09	−0.09	−0.09	−0.10	−0.10	−0.11	−0.12	−0.13	−0.14	−0.15
4%	−0.09	−0.10	−0.10	−0.11	−0.11	−0.12	−0.13	−0.14	−0.16	−0.18	−0.20	−0.24
5%	−0.10	−0.11	−0.12	−0.12	−0.14	−0.15	−0.17	−0.19	−0.22	−0.26	−0.34	−0.48
6%	−0.11	−0.12	−0.13	−0.15	−0.16	−0.18	−0.21	−0.25	−0.32	−0.44	−0.73	−2.39
7%	−0.13	−0.14	−0.15	−0.17	−0.19	−0.22	−0.27	−0.35	−0.51	−0.98	−21.19	1.03
8%	−0.14	−0.15	−0.17	−0.19	−0.23	−0.28	−0.36	−0.54	−1.08	20.36	0.93	0.46
9%	−0.15	−0.17	−0.19	−0.22	−0.27	−0.35	−0.51	−0.97	−17.95	1.04	0.49	0.32
10%	−0.16	−0.18	−0.21	−0.26	−0.33	−0.46	−0.79	−3.25	1.43	0.57	0.35	0.25

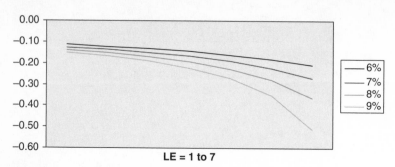

EXHIBIT 11.8 Modified LE-duration

needed and for what ranges of possible life extension. Writing put options on a portfolio of life settlement contracts is a way of managing life extension risk. The contracts would be written to strike if the underlying insured lived X years beyond life expectancy. The writer of the option would have to buy the contracts at the strike price if the death benefit was not paid by a specific expiration date. Knowing the LE-duration and LE-convexity will help in pricing this type of option because the writer of the option would be able to more accurately estimate the effect on the contracts' value for an extension in life beyond life expectancy. LE-convexity could be used to correct for errors in the LE-duration that result from the nonlinear nature of LE-duration. A put option life settlement contract with a relatively high LE-duration will be more costly than a contract with a lower LE-duration. Managers of life settlement funds that plan to use leverage to enhance the returns of the fund can use the LE-duration and LE-convexity measures to manage the amount and maturity of leverage. Once leverage is employed, life extension beyond life expectancy can force a fund manager to liquidate life settlement contracts to make premium payments or rollover obligations in unfavorable conditions.

In March 2007 and December 2007, J.P. Morgan and Goldman Sachs, respectively, introduced tradable indexes on longevity/mortality risk. The J.P. Morgan index is the LifeMetrics Index,[11] while the Goldman Sachs index is called the QxX.LS index.[12] These indices allow managers to hedge positions in longevity risk. QxX.LS is based on a reference population of 46,290 individuals over 65. The reference pool of the index represents the distribution of health impairment of the senior population. These indices enable managers who are long mortality risk to trade with managers who are long longevity risk. A life insurance company is long mortality risk (short longevity risk). A life settlement fund is long longevity risk (short mortality risk). Mortality risk in the context of life insurance contracts is the risk that the actual life of a portfolio of insurance polices is shorter than the expected life. Longevity risk is the risk that the actual life of the portfolio is longer than the expected life. A manager of a life settlement fund that is naturally long longevity risk can take the position in a swap based on the QxX.LS index as a "fixed receiver." This position shortens the fund's exposure to longevity risk. The other side of this swap would offer value to a manager in a life insurance company who would like to shorten its exposure to mortality risk by going long longevity risk. If the life of the assets of the life settlement fund remains outstanding beyond pricing expectations, and the reference pool underlying the QxX.LS index performs as expected, the fund manager will receive a spread from the fixed payer for having taken a long position in mortality risk. This spread would offset to some extent the loss in yield suffered as a result of the extension of the life settlement assets. The fixed receiver, in this example a life insurance company, would receive mortality contingent payments if the rate at which the indexed pool dies is faster than what was forecast. An insurance company could lay off mortality risk during the flu season to life settlement funds for a premium. Trading in longevity and mortality risk will increase the liquidity of the market for life settlement contracts by making the pricing of these contracts more transparent. The LE-duration and LE-convexity metrics that we have discussed in this chapter can be used to estimate the appropriate hedge ratio for an index such as the QxX.LS. If it is not known how sensitive a fund's yield is to changes in the actual life of a fund's assets (LE-duration) or how sensitive this trade-off is (LE-convexity), hedging longevity risk with the indexes we have mentioned is more difficult.

Longevity risk is a real concern to investors in pools of senior life settlements. Using the Stone and Zissu LE-duration and LE-convexity, we have measured the longevity risk both of life settlements both in blocks and individually. Using the LE-duration and LE-convexity metrics, life settlement providers, institutional and individual investors, and hedge fund managers could use LE-duration and α as additional criteria. That way, the life settlement provider can refine pricing and hedging, and more effectively market life settlement contracts. This is a viable alternative to buying blocks of senior life settlements or shares in securitized pools of senior life settlements based on an estimation of expected yield for an estimated holding period.

NOTES

1. The definition of a life settlement contract for the purposes of the Financial Accounting Standards Board FASB Staff Position No. FTB 85-4-1 is: "A life settlement contract for purposes of this FSP is a contract between the owner of

a life insurance policy (the policy owner) and a third-party investor (investor) and has the following characteristics:

  a. The investor does not have an insurable interest (an interest in the survival of the insured, which is required to support the issuance of an insurance policy).

  b. The investor provides consideration to the policy owner of an amount in excess of the current cash surrender value of the life insurance policy.

  c. The contract pays the face value of the life insurance policy to an investor when the insured dies.

2. The Life Insurance Settlement Association (LISA) provides a list of its member companies. This list includes 38 life settlement providers. The list includes 20 members that are "financing entities." Financing entities are sources of capital for life settlement providers.

3. The pension fund will allocate up to 2 percent or EUR 400 million to life settlements. ("Dutch Plans Breathe New Life Into Old Policies; Stable Returns Draw Pension Funds to Growing Market" by Beatrix Payne Crain Communications, April 16, 2007.)

4. "In June 2006, AIG restructured its ownership of life settlement contracts with no effect on the economic substance of these investments. At the same time, it paid $610 million to its former co-investors to acquire all the remaining interests in life settlement contracts held in previously non-consolidated trusts. The life insurers for a small portion of these newly consolidated life settlement contracts include AIG subsidiaries. As a result, amounts related to life insurance issued by AIG subsidiaries are eliminated in consolidation. On December 31, 2006, the carrying value of AIG's life settlement contracts was $1.1 billion, and this amount is included in other invested assets on the consolidated balance sheet. These investments are monitored quarterly for impairment, on a per-contract basis. In 2006, income recognized from life settlement contracts previously held in nonconsolidated trusts was $38 million, and is included in net investment income on the consolidated statement of income." (American International Group, 10-K for the fiscal year ended December 31, 2006.)

5. In "Death Benefits Life Settlements Slowly Emerging As the Next Uncorrelated Hedge Fund Strategy by Managed Account Reports," August 28, 2006, M. Corey Goldman reports that the following hedge funds are active in the life settlement market: Porter Capital, Sagecrest Capital and Ritchie Capital, and Cheyne Capital. A search of free content of HFMweek.com showed that New Stream Capital, LLC, has been investing in the life settlement market.

6. "We believe the overall market for life settlements will increase as more seniors become aware of their option to liquidate an unwanted policy through a life settlement. In light of our experience in the market and our estimates concerning competition and supply and demand for policies, we believe our total business volume for life settlements will be approximately $200 million in face value for fiscal 2008, which is a 37 percent increase over our total business volume of $153 million in fiscal 2007. This amount is 65 percent greater than the

$93 million in total business volume we estimated last year and represents a 76 percent increase over the $87 million of total business volume in fiscal 2006." (Life Partners Holdings, Inc., Form 10-KSB, for the fiscal year ended February 28, 2007).

7. Life Partners Holdings, Inc., Form 10-KSB, for the fiscal year ended: February 28, 2007.

8. "Mortality, morbidity, and casualty expectations incorporate assumptions about many factors, including for example, how a product is distributed, for what purpose the product is purchased, the mix of customers purchasing the products, persistency and lapses, future progress in the fields of health and medicine, and the projected level of used vehicle values. Actual mortality, morbidity, and/or casualty experience will differ from expectations if actual results differ from those assumptions. In addition, continued activity in the viatical, stranger-owned and/or life settlement industry, in which some companies attempt to arbitrage the difference in lapse assumptions used in pricing and actual lapse performance that they can control, could have an adverse impact on the Company's level of persistency and lapses, and thus negatively impact the Company's performance." (Protective Life Insurance Company 10-K, for the fiscal year ended December 31, 2006.)

9. "Central for the calculation of fair value for life settlement contracts is the estimate of mortality rates. Individual mortality rates are typically obtained by multiplying a base mortality curve for the general insured population provided by a professional actuarial organization together with an individual-specific multiplier. Individual-specific multipliers are determined based on data obtained from third-party life expectancy data providers, which examine insured individual's medical conditions, family history, and other factors to arrive at a life expectancy estimate." (Credit Suisse Group, 2006 Form 20-F.)

10. We have included this excerpt with the permission of the fund managers. Lansdown Atlantic Limited, registered office 32 Finch Road, Douglas, Isle of Man, a British Crown Dependency.

11. A full description of the J.P. Morgan LifeMetrics index is given at the company's web site, www.jpmorgan.com/pages/jpmorgan/investbk/solutions/lifemetrics.

12. The Goldman Sachs longevity index, QxX.LS, is described at www.qxx-index.com/.

REFERENCES

A.M. Best. 2005. *Life settlement securitization* (September 1).

Ballotta, Laura, and Steven Haberman. 2006. The fair valuation problem of guaranteed annuity options: The stochastic mortality environment case. *Insurance: Mathematics and Economics* 38 (February): 195–214.

Blake, D., A. J. G. Cairns, and K. Dowd. 2006. Living with mortality: Longevity bonds and other mortality-linked securities. Presented to the Faculty of Actuaries, January 16.

Cairns, A. J.G., D. Blake, and K. Dowd. 2008. Modelling and management of mortality risk: A review forthcoming in the *Scandinavian Actuarial Journal* PDF file.

Cowley, Alex, and J. David Cummins. 2005. Securitization of life insurance assets and liabilities. *Journal of Risk and Insurance* 72 (2) (June): 193–226.

Deloitte Consulting LLP and The University of Connecticut. 2005. The life settlements market: An actuarial perspective or consumer economic value.

Doherty, Neil A., and Hal J. Singer. 2002. The benefits of a secondary market for life insurance policies. *The Wharton Financial Institutions Center* (November 14).

Dowd, Kevin, Andrew J. G. Cairns, and David Blake. 2006. Mortality-dependent financial risk measures. *Insurance: Mathematics and Economics* 38 (3) (June 15): 427–642.

Emeritus Capital Partners LLC. 2005. Strategic Capital Resource Report. Structured settlement portfolios: An assured capital growth resource. *Portfolio Dynamics*.

FASB Staff Position No. FTB 85-4-1. 2006. Accounting for life settlement contracts by third-party investors, Posted March 27.

FD Series, Inc. 2006. Franklin Templeton Total Return FDP Fund. Prospectus. October 2.

Ingraham, Harold G., and Sergio S. Salani. 2004. Life settlements as viable option. *Journal of Financial Service Professionals* (September).

Lansdown Atlantic Life Settlement Fund PLC. 2005. Offering Document. October 24, February.

Lin, Yijia, and Samuel H. Cox. 2005. Securitization of mortality risks in life annuities. *Journal of Risk and Insurance* 72 (2) (June): 227–252.

Milevsky, Moshe A. 2005. The implied longevity yield: A note on developing an index for life annuities. *Journal of Risk and Insurance* 72 (2) (June): 301–320.

Singer, Hal J., and Eric Stallard. 2005. Reply to the life settlements market: An actuarial perspective on consumer economic value. Criterion Economics LLC (November).

Stone, Charles A., and Anne Zissu. 2006. Securitization of senior life settlements: Managing extension risk. *The Journal of Derivatives* (Spring).

CHAPTER 12

Real Options Approach to Life Settlement Valuation

Joseph R. Mason Ph.D
Moyse/Louisiana Bankers Association Chair of Banking, Ourso School
of Business, Louisiana State University, and Senior Fellow, the Wharton School

Hal J. Singer Ph.D
President, Criterion Economics LLC

In April 2006, the American Council of Life Insurers (ACLI) circulated a legislative proposal that would impose a 100 percent excise tax on the proceeds from the sale of a life insurance policy to a third party within five years of the issuance of the policy. The practical effect of such a rule would be to increase the holding period for a life insurance policy from two to five years. Although the proposal has not yet garnered sufficient support in Congress, as of April 2008, the five-year holding period was being considered as "model legislation" by several U.S. states. To measure the costs of the ACLI proposal to policy owners, we introduce the real options framework of financial economics. The option to sell can be modeled using traditional Black-Scholes techniques as a European put option during the holding period and as an American put option after the holding period expires. We calculate that the senior candidates for a life settlement would instantaneously lose between $41 billion and $63 billion in option value if the ACLI's proposal were implemented. Against these costs, one must measure the likely benefits of extending the holding period. Until such a cost-benefit analysis is performed, it would be imprudent to constrain policyholders in such a severe way.

The advent of a robust secondary market in life insurance has created significant welfare benefits for U.S. policyholders. As early as March 2005, Bernstein Research estimated that there was roughly $13 billion of total in-force settlement business—that is, since its inception, life settlement providers had acquired policies with roughly $13 billion in face value (Bernstein Research Call 2005). Bernstein expected the size of the life settlement market to grow more than ten-fold over the next several years. In January 2006, Maple Life predicted that the life settlement industry would buy about $19 billion in life policy death benefits during the course of 2006 (Maple Life 2006). Hence, settlement activity in 2006 alone was greater than the sum of all settlement activity from the industry's inception through 2004 and was expected to grow rapidly in subsequent years.

Before entry of life settlement providers into the secondary market, policy-owners who experienced a sudden change in their liquidity or estate needs were forced to sell or lapse their policies back to the issuing carrier at a nominal fee. By offering additional opportunities to sell a policy, life settlement providers sometimes offer resale values in excess of the annuity value of policyholder premiums, giving policy owners an attractive alternative to lapsing their policy or holding their policy until death. One way to understand those benefits is through the lens of option theory—namely, a robust secondary market provides policy owners financial options that did not previously exist.

In efforts to protect life insurers from competition from life settlement providers, in April 2006, the American Council of Life Insurers (ACLI) advocated a move to extend a moratorium on the sale of life insurance policies to third parties from two to five years. A growing academic literature attempts to quantify those benefits using simple measures of the difference between life settlement values and cash surrender values summed across all policy owners who actually exercised their option to sell their policies in the secondary market (Doherty and Singer 2003a, b, Silverman 2005). Doherty and Singer (2003b) found that life settlement providers improved policy owners' welfare by more than $240 million in 2002. Extending their analysis forward, Singer and Stallard (2005) found that life settlement providers improved policy owners' welfare by more than $686 million in 2004. It has generally been expected that these benefits will increase with the overall growth of the secondary market. Any proposals to limit the size of the secondary market, including longer holding periods for resale as contemplated by the ACLI, will therefore directly limit the benefits to policy owners.

In this chapter, we use the tools of option theory to value the benefits of the secondary market for policy owners who have not yet exercised their options. Any student of finance will recognize that an option can have value well before it is exercised and even if it is not exercised. We use traditional Black-Scholes techniques to value the existing sale option for policy owners as a series of European put options. By seeking a longer holding period, the ACLI proposal effectively seeks to extend the exercise period on the European put, which would destroy a significant amount of option value for consumers if it were adopted.

THE ACLI'S PROPOSAL

On April 11, 2006, the ACLI released a proposed piece of tax legislation that would effectively eliminate all life settlement transactions involving policies that had not reached their fifth-year anniversary. The exact language of the proposal stipulates that the excise tax would be equal to 100 percent of the life settlement value, including premiums, as well as separate payments and fees to the insured. Given this severe penalty, it is reasonable to assume that no policyholder would choose settlement over surrender within the first five years of issuance. Importantly, the excise tax would not apply to secondary market transactions between the policyholder and a specified group of persons or entities, including most importantly an insurance company issuing or reinsuring the life insurance policy (Bernstein Research Call 2005). Hence, under the ACLI's proposal, an insured who wanted to terminate his/her policy within five years of issuance could sell or lapse the policy back to the issuing carrier but could not sell the policy to a third party.

The Cost of the ACLI's Proposal to Policy Owners

The real options framework is extremely helpful in valuing the option created for policy owners by a robust secondary market in life insurance. In this section, we explain the real option framework and apply the framework to the case of life insurance. Like any option, the value decreases with increased mandatory holding periods, as contemplated by the ACLI's proposal. Hence, we calculate that life settlement candidates would instantaneously lose between $41 billion and $63 billion in option value if the ACLI's proposal were implemented.

The Real Options Analysis Framework

In the most general sense, a real option is the right, but not the obligation, to take some action (for example, deferring, expanding, or abandoning) at a predetermined cost (the exercise price), during or at the end of a predetermined period of time (the expiration). In general, all insurance investments reduce exposure to some source of uncertainty (Amram and Kulatilaka 1999). Analysis using the real options approach can value those investments and also check to see whether the value exceeds the cost. The next section uses those real options techniques to value the option to sell life insurance contracts.

The Ability to Resell One's Insurance as a Real Option—Preliminary Financial Concepts

In strict financial terms, a life insurance contract collects periodic payments in return for a payout to some beneficiary upon death of the insured. Because the insured does not receive the payout, the death benefit must be high relative to the stream of periodic payments made throughout the life of the contract. To demonstrate that concept, observe that the typical life insurance contract for a person aged 69 with death benefits of $2 million requires payments of about $40,000 per year in premiums. At that rate, it would take a little over 24 years (at 5.75 percent interest compounded annually) to accumulate an annuity equal to the death benefit. Given that the life expectancy of a 70-year-old male is about 13.5 years and a 70-year-old female is about 16.0 years (U.S. Department of Health and Human Services 2003), at an investment rate of 5.75 percent the expected annuity value of this contract is less than $1 million, while the death benefit is $2 million. Hence, the annuity value does not exceed the death benefit upon the expected death of the policyholder and the arrangement is economical to the insured.

The situation is represented graphically in Exhibit 12.1. Suppose that a 69-year-old policy owner pays annual premium $40,000 per year for death benefit U.S. $2 million. The annual premia comprise a stream of cash payments that is an annuity to the insurance company. The value of that annuity (assuming investment at a 5.75 percent market interest rate) is reflected in Exhibit 12.1 as the annuity value. Now compare the annuity value against three possible outcomes: death, policy surrender, and life settlement.

If the insured dies before the age of roughly 93 years (the year in which the annuity value is equal to the face value of the policy), and if the beneficiary has been paying the premia and experiences no bereavement cost, then the contract will pay off significantly more than the assumed 5.75 percent market return. For example, if the insured dies at age 75, six annual premium payments of 40,000 would have been made on the contract, so that the annuity value of the contract would be worth just over $290,000. Having contributed only $290,000, the beneficiary receives $2 million, which yields a 65.92 percent annual return on the six-year annuity investment of $40,000 per year.

Suppose instead that the policy owner decides to end the policy after maintaining it for four years, when the insured is aged 73. At four years, assuming 5.75 percent discount rate, the annuity value of the $40,000 per year is just over $184,000. The policyholder may end the policy in two ways:

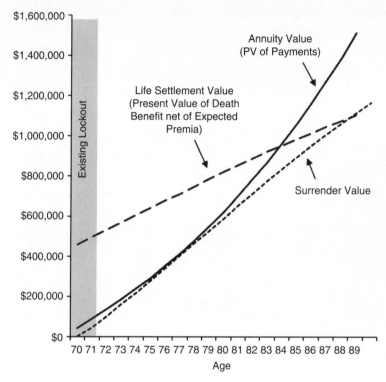

EXHIBIT 12.1 Value of a $2 Million Life Insurance Contract Taken Out at Age 69 with Annual Premia of $40,000

surrender it back to the carrier or sell the policy to a life settlement provider. If the policyholder can presently obtain a payout greater than $184,000 from either the issuing carrier or a third party, and thereby earn more than the discount rate of 5.75 percent on his investment, then he may choose to surrender (to the issuing carrier) or settle the policy (to a third party). If the policyholder cannot presently obtain a payout greater than $184,000, then he will not surrender or settle at this time (even if he is severely liquidity constrained, he could borrow against the death benefit).

How much would the third party pay for the policy? The life settlement value (LSV) is the present value of the death benefit minus premium payments from age 73 minus estimated 20 percent transaction and verification costs (Singer and Stallard 2005) until expected death (85 years of age for a male aged 73). Given those assumptions, the life settlement value is represented as the dashed line in Exhibit 12.1. Exhibit 12.1 shows an

LSV at age 73 of about $568,000. If the policyholder were to obtain the LSV of $568,000 at age 73 after having made payments of $40,000 per year for four years, the policyholder would achieve an annual return of 57.76 percent, more than 10 times the discount rate of 5.75 percent. Now compare the life settlement return to that which the policyholder receives if he sells the policy to the insurer for the surrender value. Computing surrender values using the 2001 schedule of cash surrender values as reported by the American Academy of Actuaries,[1] the policyholder receives $218,000 in return for his four years of annuity payments of $40,000 per year, a 12.8 percent annual return. It is easy to see why the life settlement return of 57.76 percent dominates.

Exhibit 12.1 shows that by the age of about 84, the annuity value is greater than the LSV, so the policyholder would no longer choose the LSV option (because he could borrow against the annuity value). By age 93, the surrender value exceeds the life settlement value, so that the life settlement option is no longer valuable.

In summary, the deviation in value between surrender, the annuity, and the life settlement creates policy equity on behalf of the insured. Over time, that equity erodes as the insured pays into the policy. But while the equity remains outstanding, the ability of the insured to cash out some of that equity can help him meet cash needs arising from temporary health, liquidity, wealth, or market shocks without fully cashing out the policy. Competition among the original insurance company and life settlements in providing that liquidity ensures that the insured will get a good (market) price on the transaction. Hence, the life settlement market enhances efficiency in heretofore illiquid asset markets.

Valuing the Individual Option to Resell One's Insurance

In the previous section, we examined the value of the surrender and settlement decisions at a specific time—that is, we examined the intrinsic value of the option to sell one's policy. In practical terms, at any time before death the policyholder has the right, but not the obligation, to sell the policy for either the present value of the death benefits (net of expected remaining premium payments and transactions costs) or the surrender value—that is, the policyholder holds a put option. Merely possessing that option is valuable, and this section proposes methods to assign a value to that option to better estimate the incremental value of the life settlement market.

The sections that follow use standard options pricing theory [for a primer on financial options, see Hull (2006)] as well as real options theory to better assess the incremental value of the ACLI proposal on the life settlement market. First, the value of the put option is characterized as a series of European put options (options that can be exercised at a specific expiration date in the future) that come into effect sequentially through the life of the policy. Second, the value of the put is characterized more generally as an American put option (options that can be exercised at any time before expiration). The higher exercise price conferred by the life settlements market increases the value of the put option owned by the policy owners. Prohibiting exercise for three years as proposed by the ACLI is therefore estimated to instantaneously reduce consumer value by somewhere between $41 billion and $63 billion in option value.

Valuing the Option to Resell before the Holding Period Expires as a Series of European Puts

According to the Black-Scholes valuation model, the value of a European put on a nondividend-paying stock is estimated by:

$$P = Xe^{-r_f t} N(-d_2) - SN(-d_1)$$

where $d_1 = [\ln(S/X) + r_f T] \div \sigma\sqrt{T} + \frac{1}{2}\sigma\sqrt{T}$; $d_2 = d_1 - \sigma\sqrt{T}$
where X = strike price
S = price of the underlying asset
T = time to maturity
r_f = discount rate
σ = volatility of the underlying asset value

For the present application, allow X to be the settlement value, S and σ to be the market value and volatility of the market value of the annuity made up of the series of premium payments. Assuming that the policyholder could have invested the funds in an S&P 500 index fund, the market volatility of the value of the annuity is $\sigma = 5$ percent.[2] We assume that the discount rate is 5.75.[3]

Consider our 69-year-old who takes out a $2 million insurance policy with annual an premium of $40,000. We assume the policyholder must wait two years before selling the policy to a life settlement provider. What is the option to sell to a life settlement provider (after the mandatory holding period) worth at policy inception? In two years, when the holding period has expired, the life settlement value will be $495,000 and the future value of the annuity two years into the policy will be worth $87,000. Using the

Black-Scholes model, the option value is worth roughly $354,000 at inception (X = $495,000, S = $87,000, and T = 2).

What is the option worth one year into the policy? One year into the policy, when the policyholder is 70 and the holding period is reduced to one year, the life settlement value two years into the policy will be $495,000 and the future value of the annuity two years into the contract will still be worth $87,000. Using the Black-Scholes model, the option value is worth roughly $380,000 one year into the policy (X = $495,000, S = $87,000, and T = 1).

What is the option worth two years into the policy? At this point, the holding period has expired and thus the appropriate option valuation tool is the American put option, which is explained below.

Valuing the Option to Resell after the Holding Period Expires as an American Put

In contrast to the European option, standard American options offer the right, but not the obligation, to exercise the option at any time before expiration. The value of an American put is equal to the difference between the current life settlement value and the current future value of the annuity whenever the life settlement value exceeds the annuity value. When the life settlement value is less than the annuity value, the American put is worth zero.

Continuing our example above, consider the same policyholder who took out at age 69 a $2 million insurance policy with annual premium of $40,000. What is the option to sell the policy to a life settlement provider two years into the policy worth? The life settlement value two years into the policy is worth $495,000 and the future value of the annuity two years into the contract is worth $87,000. Hence, the American option is worth roughly $407,000 (equal to $495,000 less $87,000).

What is the option worth three years into the policy? The life settlement value three years into the policy is worth $531,000 and the future value of the annuity three years into the contract is worth $134,000. Hence, the American option is worth roughly $397,000 (equal to $531,000 less $134,000).

What is the option worth four years into the policy? The life settlement value four years into the policy is worth $568,000 and the future value of the annuity four years into the contract is worth $184,000. Hence, the American option is worth roughly $383,000 (equal to $568,000 less $184,000).

What is the option worth five years into the policy? The life settlement value five years into the policy is worth $604,000 and the future value of the annuity four years into the contract is worth $237,000. Hence, the American option is worth roughly $367,000 (equal to $604,000 less 237,000).

The Decline in the Option Value of a Representative Policy Caused by a Mandatory Five-Year Holding Period

While the total option values estimated above are instructive, they serve only to illustrate that the options held by a policy owner are valuable through the life of the contract. They do not, in themselves, represent the value destruction owing to the proposed increase in the holding period during which the policy cannot be sold to a third party. The cost of extending the holding period from two to five years is easy to measure, however, using the options techniques developed earlier.

Given the fact that 26 states currently have life settlement laws, which largely prevent assignability of one's policy before the second year anniversary of the policy, we assume conservatively that policyholders cannot exercise the option to sell for the first two years of the policy's life. (In reality, policyholders who reside in states without such settlement laws would suffer an even larger loss in option value, as the default rule in those states would be no holding period.) Upon the end of the two-year period, the policyholder is free to exercise at the annuity value (S_0) and strike price (X) available at that date. Hence, at the time the policy is underwritten the policyholder receives a two-year European option on the sale of the policy. We previously used Black-Scholes to value the existing sale option as a series of European options before the holding period expires. We utilize a similar technique here to value the effect of changing the two-year holding period to a five-year period, as proposed by the ACLI.

Exhibit 12.2 presents the results of valuing the various holding periods and their effect on the option value through the expected life of the representative insurance contract examined earlier. In Exhibit 12.2, after the holding period, the option's value follows the path of the American option with the remaining term to expiration. The two-year European put on the option to sell the representative contract examined earlier is valued at just over \$354,000 at inception for the life insurance contract (X = \$495,000, S = \$87,000, and T = 2). Extending the holding period to five years reduces the European put option value at inception to \$216,000 (X = \$604,000, S = \$237,000, and T = 5), a decrease of just over 39 percent of the value of the existing two-year European option. One year into the policy (attained age of 70), the option to sell with a two-year holding period is worth \$380,000 (X = \$495,000, S = \$87,000, and T = 1), while the option with a five-year holding period is worth \$243,000 (X = \$604,000, S = \$237,000, and T = 4). Hence, one year into the policy, the five-year holding period again reduces the option value by nearly 36 percent.

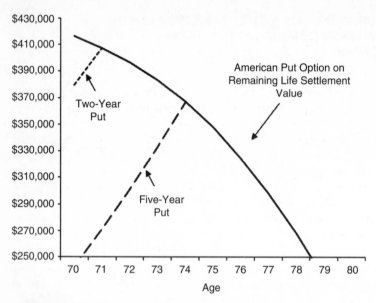

EXHIBIT 12.2   Valuing the Holding Period as a European Put Option

Two years into the policy (attained age of 71), the option to sell with a two-year holding period reverts to the American option, which is worth $407,000 (X = 495,000 and S = $87,000), while the option with a five-year holding period is worth $271,000 (X = $604,000, S = $237,000, and T = 3). Hence, two years into the policy, the five-year holding period again reduces the option value by just over 33 percent. Three years into the policy (attained age of 72), the option to sell with a two-year holding period under the American option is worth $397,000 (X = $531,000 and S = $134,000), while the option with a five-year holding period is worth $301,000 (X = $604,000, S = $237,000, and T = 2). Hence, three years into the policy, the five-year holding period again reduces the option value by just over 24 percent.

Four years into the policy (attained age of 73), the option to sell with a two-year holding period under the American option is worth $383,000 (X = $568,000 and S = $184,000), while the option with a five-year holding period is worth $333,000 (X = $604,000, S = $237,000, and T = 1). Hence, four years into the policy, the five-year holding period again reduces the option value by just over 13 percent. Five years into the policy (attained age of 74), the option to sell with a two-year holding period under the American option is worth $367,000 (X = $604,000 and S = $237,000). The option to sell with a five-year holding period reverts to an American option, which is also worth $410,000 (X = $604,000 and S = $237,000). Hence, five years into the policy, the five-year holding period has no effect on the option value. This would be true for any combination of parameters.

The Decline in the Option Value Summed across All Eligible Policies Caused by a Mandatory Five-Year Holding Period

In this section, we use two independent methods to estimate the cumulative value of assignability rights that would be destroyed by the ACLI's proposal. Under the top-down approach, we begin with industry data on the size of newly issued permanent policies and estimate the number of representative policies—that is, policies with an average $2 million of face value that would be affected by the five-year holding period. Under the bottom-up approach, we begin with survey data from the Survey of Consumer Finances and aggregate up to the industry level.

Top-Down Approach In 2006, individual Americans took out $1.813 trillion in face value of life insurance policies according to the ACLI (2007). Of that $1.813 trillion in face value, direct purchases of permanent life constituted 29 percent of the total face amount issued or $512.4 billion. We assume that the face value of newly issued permanent policies increases annually at the annual growth rate of all individual insurance from 2005 through 2006 (0.9 percent).

According to the most recent Federal Reserve's Survey of Consumer Finances (SCF) (Federal Reserve Board 2004), 31.3 percent of the cumulative face value of all permanent policies issued within the previous five years was held by survey respondents in the target market for a life settlement—that is, respondents who held permanent life insurance policies with combined face value of at least $750,000 and were at least 65 years old.[4] Applying that fraction here, we estimate that $160.4 billion of permanent policies were issued in 2006 to potential candidates for a life settlement (equal to 31.3 percent of $512.4 billion). To estimate the number of policies affected assuming an average face value of $2 million, we divide the estimated face value of newly issued permanent policies in the target market by $2 million. Finally, we multiply the decline in the option value for the representative policy by the estimated number of representative policies that would be affected by the ACLI proposal. Exhibit 12.3 summarizes the results.

As Exhibit 12.3 shows, the cumulative decline in the value of the options for the representative policy is approximately $41.3 billion. Policies issued before 2003 suffer no decline in option value as they are by definition

EXHIBIT 12.3 Cumulative Option Value Destroyed by ACLI Proposal in 2007 (Top-Down Approach)

Policy Age (Year Issued)	Decline in Option Value (A)	Estimated Number of Representative Policies Affected (B)	Value of Decline (U.S.$)
1 (2007)	134,314	80,912	$10,867,592,002
2 (2006)	128,925	80,191	$10,338,628,043
3 (2005)	123,218	80,519	$9,921,382,720
4 (2004)	83,308	82,134	$6,842,420,998
5 (2003)	42,146	78,684	$3,316,202,243
Total			$41,286,226,006

Note: Assumes a personal discount rate of 5.75 percent, which is taken from American Academy of Actuaries Report.

older than five years. In contrast, policies issued in 2007 suffer the greatest decline—an instantaneous loss of approximately $134,314 in option value.

Bottom-Up Approach To calculate the reduction in option value for each policy owner in the SCF database who holds a permanent policy, we estimate the option value under a two-year holding period conditional on an assumed issue age and the value under a five-year holding period conditional on an assumed issue age. For each policy owner who is a potential candidate for a life settlement, these option values are computed using the actual attained age of the policyholder, the face value of the policy, the cash surrender value of the policy, and the annual premium. Recall that the option value is a function of the estimated life settlement value, which depends on the life expectancy of the policyholder. Given the policyholder's age and gender, we estimate life expectancy according to the schedules presented by the Centers for Disease Control and Prevention (Arias 2003). Using the age of the policyholder and the ratio of the cash surrender value to the face value of the policy, we estimate the issue age (and hence the age of the policy) according to the 2001 schedule of cash surrender values as reported by the American Academy of Actuaries.

We recognize that the annual premium data for roughly one-third of our sample is not reliable, either because the premium field is missing or because the ratio of the annual premium to the face value of the policy is unreasonably small.[5] To address this missing data problem, we use standard techniques in statistics of replacing missing or unreliable premium data with the mean of the reliable subset of annual premium. In particular, we calculate the mean of the ratio of the annual premium to the face value for all policies in the SCF database in which that ratio exceeds 1.2 percent. The mean of that subset is 3.086 percent. The cutoff of 1.2 percent is equal to the ratio of annual premium to face value for a 35-year-old who obtains a $2,000,000 whole life policy from State Farm. Because the ratio of annual premium to face value exceeds 1.2 percent for anyone who obtains a policy after age 35, we assume that values of that ratio in the SCF database less than 1.2 percent (including 0 percent) have been miscoded. For each observation in the sample where the ratio of the annual premium to the face value of the policy is less than 1.2 percent, we replace the coded annual premium (which is often equal to zero) with 3.086 percent of the face value of the policy. With an estimate of the issue age and, where necessary, premium level, we can estimate the precise option value under both a two-year and five-year holding period.

For clarity, consider survey respondent 2,689 in the SCF database. The respondent is a male who holds a permanent policy with face value of $2 million. The cash value of the policy is $137,000 and the annual premium to keep the policy in force is $113,000 (equal to 5.65 percent of the face value). Given the age of the policyholder and the cash surrender value as a percentage of the face value (6.85 percent), we infer that the age of the policy is between one and two years based on the schedule of the American Academy of Actuaries. Given the gender (male) and attained age of 79, we estimate that the life expectancy is 8.48 years according to the schedule of Centers for Disease Control and Prevention. We estimate that the life settlement value one year into the future is roughly $468,000 and, given our estimate of the policy's age, the future value one year into the future is roughly $245,000. The option value of selling the policy to a settlement provider with a two-year holding period is roughly $198,000. The option with a five-year holding period is roughly $68. Hence, the destruction in option value caused by a three-year extension to the holding period is $198,000 (equal to $198,000 less $68). The identical exercise is performed for each candidate for a settlement in the SCF database.

Next, we aggregate the SCF database estimates to the scale of the entire U.S. population. According to the ACLI's 2007 Fact Book, the stock of in-force individual life policies (including both term and permanent) in the United States was $10.057 trillion in 2006. In contrast to the flow of new policies, which are separated into permanent and term policies, the Fact Book does not break down the stock of in-force policies by type. The sum of the face value of all term policies in the most recent SCF database (field X4003) is $10.612 billion. The sum of the face value of all permanent

EXHIBIT 12.4 Cumulative Option Value Destroyed by ACLI Proposal in 2007 (Bottom-Up Approach)

Average loss in option value for all life settlement candidates* in the SCF database	$400,915
Cumulative loss in option value for all life settlement candidates* in the SCF database (A)	$123,080,976
Aggregation ratio** (B)	512.82
Cumulative loss in option value for all life settlement candidates in the United States (A × B)	$63,118,386,112

*Life settlement candidate is at least 65 years old and holds a permanent policy with face value of at least $750,000.
**Aggregation ratio is the ratio of the face value of all life insurance policies in the United States to the face value of all life insurance policies in the SCF databases. Losses are based on a personal discount rate of 5.75 percent, which is used in American Academy of Actuaries Report. If we use a personal discount rate of 8 percent, the cumulative loss in option value for all life settlement candidates in the United States is $48.1 billion. Note that computations are based on rounded values.

policies in the SCF database (field X4005) is $9.011 billion. The sum of the face value across all individual policies in the SCF database is $19.624 billion compared to a total stock of in-force policies in the United States of $10.057 trillion. Hence, the estimated losses for the population are equal to the product of roughly $123.1 million of losses in the SCF times the ratio of the sum of the face value of policies in the population ($10.057 trillion) to the sum of the face value of the policies in the sample ($19.624 billion), or $123.1 million times approximately 512.82.

As Exhibit 12.4 shows, the average candidate for a life settlement would instantaneously lose $400,915 in option value if a five-year holding period were imposed. The cumulative losses across all life settlement candidates in the SCF database would be roughly $123.1 million. The maximum damages, which assumes that all policies in the database have aged one year, is $189.7 million. Using the aggregation factor of 512.82 explained above,[6] we estimate that the cumulative losses for all life settlement candidates in the United States would be approximately $63.1 billion.

SUMMARY

Using both the top-down and bottom-up methods, we estimate that the ACLI's proposal would destroy between $41 billion and $63 billion in option value for all U.S. candidates for a life settlement. For policyholders who initiated contracts before the extension of the holding period, such a loss would amount to a taking of property. For policyholders who have not yet initiated contracts before the extension of the holding period, such a loss could be reduced if the premiums were repriced to reflect the loss in option value at the inception of the contract. Hence, insurers should be prepared to compensate new policyholders for the reduced option value of their policies at the inception of new contracts going forward—that is, prices of new life insurance contracts should fall to accommodate the reduced option value if increased holding periods are imposed.

CONCLUSION

The ACLI's proposal presumes incorrectly that very few policyholders reverse their initial decision to obtain life insurance within five years, and the few who do are pursuing illegitimate ends. There is nothing potentially abusive about reacting to such unforeseen changes by reoptimizing one's life insurance coverage. By imposing a five-year moratorium on all life settlements, the ACLI's tax proposal would penalize many insured individuals who are pursuing legitimate ends. From a consumer-welfare perspective, we have demonstrated that insured individuals would suffer tremendous losses under the ACLI's proposed five-year moratorium. The option to sell one's policy to a third party takes on value well in advance of the exercise date. By imposing a five-year moratorium on the exercise of that option, the ACLI's tax proposal destroys much of the option value created by a robust secondary market. Indeed, we estimate that candidates for a life settlement would collectively lose between $41 billion and $63 billion in option value from having to wait an additional three years before they could sell their policies to a life settlement provider.

NOTES

1. Report of the American Academy of Actuaries' Commissioners Standard Ordinary Implications Work Group presented to the National Association of Insurance Commissioners' Life and Health Actuarial Task Force (2002).
2. This value is approximately the average annual returns volatility of the S&P 500 for past three years. Available at http://finance.yahoo.com/q/bc?s=%5EGSPC&t=5y. The 10.5-year duration Vanguard Long-Term U.S. Treasury fund (VUSTX) volatility over the same period is 4.4 percent.
3. Report of the American Academy of Actuaries' Commissioners Standard Ordinary (CSO) Implications Work Group presented to the National Association

of Insurance Commissioners' Life and Health Actuarial Task Force (2002), Appendix A: results for whole life nonforfeiture cash values.

4. The SCF does not report the issue age of the policy. Using the age of the policy-holder and the ratio of the cash surrender value to the face value of the policy from the SCF, we estimate the issue age (and hence the age of the policy) according to the 2001 schedule of cash surrender values as reported by the Report of the American Academy of Actuaries' Commissioners Standard Ordinary Implications Work Group Presented to the National Association of Insurance Commissioners' Life and Health Actuarial Task Force (2002).

5. It is typical for life insurance policies to have zero premium options available, so the zero premium is not necessarily a data problem. Hence, our method of imputing premium produces a conservative estimate of losses.

6. We note that this factor is rounded, and that we use the rounded factor in our computations. The estimates we report throughout are rounded values.

REFERENCES

American Council of Life Insurers. 2007. *Life Insurers Fact Book*.

Amram, M., and N. Kulatilaka. 1999. *Real options: Managing strategic investment in an uncertain world*. Cambridge, MA: Harvard Business School Press.

Arias, E. 2003. United States life tables. Division of Vital Statistics, Centers for Disease Control and Prevention.

Bernstein Research Call. 2005. Life insurance long view—life settlements need not be unsettling. March 4.

Doherty, N., and H. Singer. 2003a. Regulating the secondary market for life insurance policies. *Journal of Insurance Regulation* (21), 63–99.

Doherty, N., and H. Singer. 2003b. The benefits of a secondary market for life insurance. *Real Property, Probate & Trust Journal* (38), 449–478.

Federal Reserve Board. 2004. Survey of Consumer Finances.

Hull, J. 2006. *Options, futures, and other derivatives*. 6th ed. New York: Prentice Hall.

The Economist. 2003. New lease on life: The secondary market in life-insurance policies is good for bonsumers. May 17.

Maple Life Financial, Inc. 2006. *Life Settlement Industry Outlook*.

American Academy of Actuaries' Commissioners Standard Ordinary (CSO) Implications Work Group. 2002. Appendix A: Results for Whole Life Nonforfeiture Cash Values. Report presented to the National Association of Insurance Commissioners' Life and Health Actuarial Task Force.

Silverman, R. 2005. Recognizing life insurance's value. *Wall Street Journal*. May 31.

Singer, H., and E. Stallard. 2005. Reply to The life settlements market: An actuarial perspective on consumer value. November.

U.S. Department of Health and Human Services, Centers for Disease Control and Prevention. 2006. United States life tables 2003. National Vital Statistics Reports (54) April 19.

Risk Explored

CHAPTER 13

Risk Mitigation for Life Settlements

Nemo Perera
Managing Director, Risk Capital Partners

Investors in the secondary market for life insurance are exposed to many complex underlying risks that are unique to the insurance sector. Although some risks can be adequately mitigated using traditional portfolio management principles, others may be more economically managed with risk transfer techniques that utilize both financial and insurance-based risk coverages. As the life settlement market evolves, attracting even greater interest from prospective investors, risk mitigation will have an increased importance in reducing cash flow volatility, thereby enabling institutional participation. As with any type of investing, it is vital that prospective life settlement investors fully understand all the risks and risk mitigation solutions available in today's marketplace.

The most widely used tool for risk mitigation is insurance as it addresses situations where the timing of an incident is uncertain but still predictable. Underwriting risks like those associated with life settlement assets, hinges on the Law of Large Numbers in order to quantify the uncertainty of life, making it more predictable. It would be quite difficult for an actuary to determine the risk of a unique catastrophic event that occurred with little or no predictability. An event is generally only suitable for risk coverage if said event occurs on a relatively frequent basis. Inversely, as a risk occurs less frequently the cost to insure that risk substantially increases making it prohibitively uneconomic for both the insurer and the purchaser of the policy. These last risks are generally better handled with equity capital.

Insurance companies identify and price various types of risks, and generate income from both underwriting and investing. Income produced from underwriting risk is generated when more policy premiums are collected than claims are paid. Like banks that determine the cost of capital to be the rate for which they award their savings account holders, insurance companies measure their "cost of funds" from the rate of claims (ROC). The ROC should be less than the interest rate for the next alternative borrowing source. It is important that the carrier be able to predict effectively when and how many claims are expected to be filed. That said, carriers do include a cushion in their pricing for the risk of parameter misprediction.

The second form of income for carriers is derived from investing the collected premium payments, essentially using their underwriting revenues as a low cost source of capital to make strategic investments in a myriad of theoretically low risk asset classes such as government bonds, U.S. treasuries, corporate bonds, and mortgage-backed securities. Of course, the risk of mortgage-backed securities is now perceived as far higher than in the recent past. The more predictable the carrier's underwriting, the greater the spread on its investments.

Equity or risk capital is an alternate method of risk transference and is defined as the residual value of a business or property beyond any debt incurred. Equity holders not only have an interest in the company's profits but also the associated risks. They are willing to accept the transfer of risk in exchange for some relative return. For example, when an investor values a share in a new company, the price of the stock can be driven by the future expectations of net profits or the company's ability to pay future dividends. From this outlook, the investor can apply an appropriate discount rate and determine the relative stock price. The higher the risk the higher the discount rate. This relative return is analogous to the cost of insurance.

Like insurance, equity can be applied as a risk transfer tool in business enterprises. For a corporation that is financed through debt and equity, the equity participant is the residual owner of the company after debt holders are paid. They are considered to have the last claims to assets of a corporation. Since the equity holder is subordinate to the principal debt holder, the equity is at risk of not receiving any income or returns. The equity holder is essentially providing an insurance layer to protect the debt holders.[1]

Despite the similarities, insurance and equity have quite different vantage points; where equity holders are looking to risk capital for a reasonable return, insurance is looking to minimize risk and create an underwriting and investment profit. The difference can lie in the reasonability of the expected outcome. For less predictable risks, the more likely risk transfer tool is equity. When an insurance company is unable to measure a risk's probability or it cannot achieve the Law of Large Numbers, equity may step in and wager its risk capital in order to initiate the transaction. Further, equity may even backstop future profits, but insurance generally will not. For the

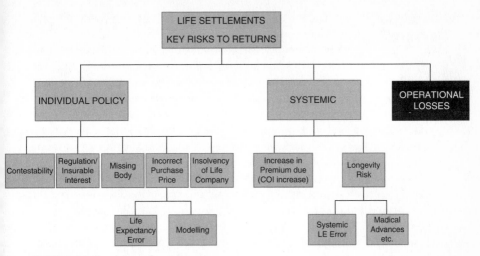

EXHIBIT 13.1   Life Settlements

insurance provided by financial guarantees on mortgage-backed securities, the coverage insures the return of principal, but it does not provide the remaining interest an investor would have received had the loan been paid up to maturity. The interest that is given up is the equity component of the transaction.

As investors seek to generate lucrative returns from the life settlement market, an understanding of risk mitigation and its implementation will become more critical to successful transaction execution. Although rating agency requirements and debt holder covenants will mandate a baseline level of risk transfer protocols to be utilized, it will be the savvy investors who seek to create returns that are greater than those available in "me too" type transactions by deploying sophisticated risk transfer mechanisms that combine equity and bespoke insurance coverages, as a means of unlocking the hidden investment value available in life insurance assets. See Exhibit 13.1.

CONTESTABILITY

In the first two years of a policy's existence, the life insurance company has the right to deny a claim based on fraud, material misstatement, concealment, or other missing details that prevented the accurate underwriting of a case. While the risk of occurrence may be low, the magnitude could be significant depending on the size of the policy in even a medium-sized portfolio. Historically, contest rarely occurs, but it is important to note that these policies were acquired under traditional sales where a person obtains a policy to protect his family's future if he dies and can no longer provide income. With premium financed transactions for senior life insurance policies on the rise, insurance companies may look more closely at a case prior to delivering a death benefit claim since many carriers are concerned about the aggressive tactics that are sometimes deployed in today's life marketplace. This concern could potentially translate into more denied claims, increasing the value of contestability coverage.

Contestability coverage protects funds above the premiums paid into the life insurance policy, as the owner of a contested policy receives the life premiums from the life insurer. Unlike the investors who decide to forgo insurance, a property and casualty insurer is cushioned against loss by insuring a broad book of contestable policies. More important for the investor who purchases coverage, a contestability-insuring company will review the underwriting process, giving investors further comfort that the life policy was legitimately issued. This extra level of scrutiny may be particularly valuable when purchasing policies that were originated through premium-financed programs. Moreover, in transactions that require rating agency approval, the equity required to self-insure against contestation could be too expensive or insufficient for a credit rating.

While we noted previously that a person has no financial incentive to withhold medical data from the settlement provider, a person does have a financial incentive to withhold medical information from the life insurer. This creates a risk that the policy may be rescinded during the contestability period regardless of whether the insured passes. It is best dealt with by assuring that all of the medical records shared with the settlement provider were also shared with the life insurer.

INSURABLE INTEREST RISK

When an individual purchases a life insurance policy he can purchase the policy himself naming his spouse or children as beneficiaries. This arrangement is quite typical and is allowed by state insurance laws. However, with the increased use of trust-owned life insurance, insurable interest laws are attracting more attention. In New York, insurable interest can include family, "related by blood or by law, as substantial interest engendered by love and affection; and in the case of other persons, a lawful and substantial economic interest in the continued life, health, or bodily safety of the person insured."[2] Insurable interest means you, the owner, have an interest in the person's life. Additionally, an entity could have an economic interest in your life, such as a creditor, which would be considered an insurable interest relationship.

While insurable interest is determined at the time of policy issuance, a life insurance company can reexamine insurable interest at any time during the life of the insured. A change of heart by the insurer means the issuing life insurance company rescinds the policy returning only the premiums paid. It is important to distinguish this risk from contestability, as it can still occur beyond the two-year period expiration.

As mentioned earlier, insurable interest is an even greater concern for trust-owned premium finance programs, where program providers seek out legal representation to opine on the program's insurable interest qualification. Although insurable interest is typically an equity risk retained by the purchaser of the life settlement, insurance policies providing insurable interest coverage are now available in some circumstances where it can be determined that insurable interest was not violated based upon specific criteria used to incept the policy. If coverage was offered on all policies without careful examination, it could easily be argued that said coverage did not serve the public's best interest. One could easily imagine the following scenario where a person obtains a policy without the insured's knowledge and then sells the policy to investors who then unknowingly secure insurable interest coverage.

Conversely, insurance coverage for this risk may be viewed as a signal that the program's acquisition protocol, in fact, follows insurable interest rules. Today, only limited insurable interest coverage is available—protection for only the first two to five years of a newly incepted policy. Ideal coverage would provide protection for the life of the policy.

COST OF INSURANCE

Many investors consider the chance of an increase in the cost of insurance (COI) negligible or nonexistent. With people living longer, mortality expense charges would not be expected to increase. To avoid such concerns, guaranteed policies have a fixed premium with no adjustments due to changes in interest rates or increasing costs surrounding mortality. Many people, however, purchase life insurance on a nonguaranteed basis, exposing themselves to risk, but hoping to save money by paying a lesser premium amount necessary to keep the policy in force. Providing such coverage for COI changes would be difficult to price due to the varying policy forms and open-ended exposure to the insuring company. While this risk might be underpriced by life settlement investors, the risk is more economically feasible with equity capital. If it should become available, an insurer will require a spread of policies across a large number of life insurers.

INCORRECT PURCHASE PRICE

The risk of overpaying for a policy can severely impact the returns on a life settlement investment and are typically due to an incorrectly underwritten life expectancy assessment or a modeling error. When underwriting a case file, the significant amount of medical records and health exams collected creates an increased chance for overlooking data. Files could be incomplete or a doctor's file could be missing. However, underwriters will likely protest such a statement, noting that a policy seller is most likely not going to adversely select against the purchaser. The less healthy a person is, the higher the price that his policy can fetch, therefore he is likely to share all of his medical information to achieve the best available price. It would be foolish for a person to hide medical conditions.

The second possible contributing factor to an incorrect price resides in the pricing model. While it is important to do back testing in any model, the basis of the assumptions is the ultimate driver of the economics. A mispricing on an early death will run an investor into reinvestment risk, however, a life living much longer than expected could yield a life settlement investor negative returns. Insurance for this risk would not be plausible as it is open to adverse selection, where the life settlement investor could off-load poorly underwritten cases that were improperly purchased. This kind of risk should be retained by an equity investor who has influence over the risk and return ratio.

MISSING BODY RISK

Missing body risk refers to a situation when a person is presumed dead without physical proof. Some famous examples include Jimmy Hoffa and Amelia Earhart. When an insured life disappears in such cases, the insurance company can delay awarding a death benefit to the heirs pending proof of death. Sometimes the life insurer can delay up to seven years, the typical statute of limitations for such cases. For an investor who owns the policy, this could severely impact returns, as carriers will require ongoing life premiums to continue to keep the policy in force. Once the date of death is determined, the insurer reimburses the premiums overpaid. Some carriers will even apply interest on premiums and/or death benefits; however, this is at a statutory rate that may be lower than a comparable equity rate of return.

While this risk is very remote, its impact could be significant. Depending on the size of the policy and the liquidity constraints, choosing to share this risk with an equity participant or seek insurance coverage depends on the liability constraints set up by the financing structure. For the investor with a small portfolio of lives, it might make sense to make an equity bet. But for structured transactions with large portfolios and financing covenants, using insurance coverage that is readily available in today's marketplace may be prudent.

LIFE INSURANCE COMPANY CREDIT RISK

The risk of insolvency of a life insurance company is considered to be low, as most are investment-grade companies. Also, life insurance provides an additional level of comfort as the policyholders have claims to repayment; in the event of insolvency, they recover ahead of both debt holders and stockholders of the life insurer. Because of the reserve requirements for each policy issued, the substantial insurer capital, and the states' insurance guaranty funds, policyholders have a much better asset recovery rate than in the case of corporate bond defaults.

That being said, certain investors cannot invest in certain credit ratings or require a dual rating; for these people, utilizing credit insurance coverage may make sense. Due to financial covenants, some investors seek the additional credit assurances that if a life carrier is unable to pay its death benefits due to financial constraints (not from contestability or insurable interest claims), there is a financial institution that will step in. With the turmoil in current credit markets this coverage has been structured but not purchased by many investors as the current pricing is considered irrational. When the financial markets return to normalcy, it is assumed that this coverage will be more viable from a pricing point of view. See Exhibit 13.2.

LONGEVITY RISK

Life expectancy risk should be viewed as a systemic risk that the overall life expectancy for a given portfolio increases beyond an expectation point. While some investors are focused on an individual policy falling out of favor, this kind of focused risk attention should not be their concern. If it is, this would suggest a misunderstanding of the attributes of this asset class. Investors should instead worry about an overall change in life expectancy, when the entire portfolio of people live longer than anticipated. If medical advancements were able to cure such diseases as cancer or diabetes, elderly

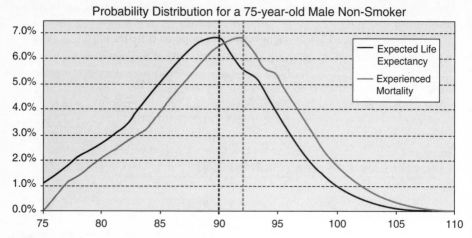

EXHIBIT 13.2   Systemic Mortality Shift

insured individuals would end up living longer than predicted by the medical underwriters and provide life settlement investors with overall diminished returns. Diversification of the settlement portfolio is essential here so as to avoid the debacle of the viatical companies that collapsed on discovery of the protease inhibitors.

The risk transfer tools for covering longevity risk should be a mix between insurance and equity. Since investors price with a heavy emphasis on life expectancy, it does not make sense to remove the original investor and provide a high return at the insured life expectancy, because there is only a 50 percent probability of occurrence based on a normal distribution curve. Based on this kind of pricing, investor equity returns should share in the individual's and portfolio's longevity risk. Hence, coverage claims makes more sense to trigger much beyond life expectancy. That way an investor may still capture the returns he is hoping to earn when acquiring the policy.

Another important fact is that the limit of the claim should not be the full face amount of the policy but rather a percentage amount less. The insuring party must have some form of recovery beyond premiums collected from the coverage buyer.

One way to look at the role of the insurance coverage is not to insure the profits but rather to protect the principal investment. If the equity investor believes that the insured will most likely die before that point, then that is the equity investment he is making. Additionally, the insurance company is looking for an underwriting profit and it wants to recover its exposure. Any profits earned above could be shared with the equity investor. If an insurer were to insure profits, it would extract an equity-like premium not an insurance premium.

Surprisingly some investors nevertheless hope to transfer longevity risk to an insurance counterparty for an insurance premium—akin to finding the holy grail. This desperate search has lead unscrupulous characters to establish sham insurance companies where premiums for life expectancy (LE) coverage have been collected but claims will never be paid—a ponzi scheme.

Although some legitimate insurance carriers do provide coverage for longevity risk, the underwriting criteria is highly restrictive, limiting the number of cases that will qualify. The ideal investor for this coverage maintains a significant portfolio whereby coverage for some portion of the portfolio can be secured while the balance can be managed via diversification and equity. The presence of insurance on some portion of the portfolio should lower the overall volatility thereby increasing value and or decreasing borrowing costs used to maintain premiums.

Other risks that are less common but could still negatively impact a life settlement transaction include:

- **Misstatement of Age/Sex.** A situation where the life insurer discovers a misstatement of age or sex that was used in the calculation of its life insurance benefit.
- **Interest Gap.** An interest shortfall in a life transaction that would result due to a delay in the receipt of the death benefits from the life insurer or because of the difference between the statutory rate of interest paid by the life insurer on the death benefit proceeds versus the loan rate under the structure.
- **Annuity Unwind.** In transactions that use an annuity, where the annuity writer contests the annuity policy resulting in the loss of premiums paid.
- **Supplemental Premium.** Where a life insurer raises monthly term insurance or expense charges or lowers its interest crediting rate, additional premiums may be required (in excess of the original current payment) to keep the life insurance policy in force.
- **Age 105.** If the underlying life reaches age 105, a death benefit may be forfeited leaving the investor without an ability to recoup his investment.
- **Life Settlement Market Disruption.** A change in regulation, legislation, or tax code could potentially eliminate the economics currently associated with the life settlement industry. In this doomsday scenario investors with life settlement portfolios may not be able to achieve their anticipated returns.

These less-than-common risks are easily mitigated with specialty insurance coverages that are offered by well-rated counterparties that not only understand the risks but have priced said risks accordingly.

As the life settlement market continues to attract strong interest from investors, organizers are structuring creative transactions that promise superior returns from an alternative asset class that is mortality-based (not correlated to traditional investments), and secured by the credit worthiness of life insurance carriers. Risk transfer via property casualty coverage is a prudent and proven means of risk mitigation for life settlement transactions. Savvy investors who seek to capture lucrative returns will do so with sophisticated risk transfer mechanisms that combine equity and insurance as a means of unlocking value from life insurance assets. To create this optimal mix, investors must have both a comprehensive understanding of the risks associated with life settlements and access to insurance markets interested in providing risk transfer coverage.

NOTES

1. Nemo Perera and Brian Reeves, "Risk Mitigation for Life Settlements," *The Journal of Structured Finance*, 2006.
2. N.Y. Ins. Law § 3205(a)(1) (McKinney Supp. 2003).

CHAPTER 14

The Risks of a Securitized Portfolio of Senior Life Settlement Contracts

Life Expectancy, Duration, Convexity, and Their Metrics

Charles A. Stone
Professor, Brooklyn College, CUNY, Department of Economics

Anne Zissu
Professor, Citytech, CUNY, Department of Business
The Polytechnic Institute of NYU, Department of Financial Engineering

Projections by the U.S. Census Bureau are that the number of people over the age of 65 will increase by 13.2 million between 2010 and 2020, increasing from 11.4 percent of the population to 14.1 percent. It will be members of this population that face the complex and difficult problem of balancing and managing mortality risk and life extension risk. One class of transactions that has become increasingly popular for senior citizens with impaired health is to liquidate their life insurance polices in the life settlement market to free up cash for living. The secondary market in life insurance is a valuable option that allows people to purchase life insurance and, if needed, liquidate it at its market value to pay for long-term care. The following excerpt for the 10-K filed by Universal American Financial Corp. for the fiscal year ending in 2006 summarizes the source of the growing demand for products that allow individuals to balance longevity and mortality risk.

> *We believe that attractive growth opportunities exist in providing a range of products, particularly health insurance, to the growing senior market. At present, more than 44 million Americans are eligible for Medicare, the Federal program that offers basic hospital and medical insurance to people over 65 years old and certain disabled people under the age of 65. According to the U.S. Census Bureau, more than 2 million Americans turn 65 in the United States each year, and this number is expected to grow as the so-called baby boomers begin to turn 65. In addition, many large employers who traditionally provided medical and prescription drug coverage to their retirees have begun to curtail these benefits. Universal American Financial Corp, 10-K for the fiscal year ended December 31, 2006.*

It is the stock of outstanding life insurance policies that will feed the growth of the future market for life settlements and it is the development of the secondary market in life insurance contracts that will facilitate the execution of transactions and securitization of life settlement pools. Life Partners, Inc. estimates that the value of life insurance policies discounted in the life settlement market in 2008 is $7 billion. (Life Partners Holdings, Inc. Form 10-K for the fiscal year ended February 29, 2008.)

The secondary market for life insurance policies should enhance the value of policies in the primary market. Life insurance companies understand the demand for life insurance is not constant across the life cycle or health conditions. Life insurance companies offer policies that give people options to exchange a life policy for a long-term coverage policy or with market-based preset call options. An important research question that we plan to address in the future is whether it is more efficient to design insurance contracts *ex-ante* that give people the option to liquidate or convert the policy at future dates and presets or to let the secondary market price contracts on the spot when a person decides to liquidate the life insurance policy. Accelerated death benefits are one such option that life insurance companies offer on certain policies. This option was originally designed to give the insureds the right to receive the policy's death benefits prior to death if they have been diagnosed with a terminal illness that has reduced their life expectancy to 24 months or less. This accelerated death benefit option has now been extended to offer benefits to people who are in need of long-term care but not necessarily terminally ill.

For example, in February of 2005, Allianz Life announced a number of riders available with its GenDex-SP^{TM} and GenDex II life insurance polices. Two of these riders are The Optional Long-Term Care Accelerated Death Benefit Rider, which "allows the policyholder to accelerate the payout of the death benefit upon certification of a qualifying chronic illness," and The Terminal Illness Benefit that "offers the option to accelerate the payment of 100 percent of the policy death benefit, up to $1 million—a prepayment charge not to exceed 1 percent will be deducted." (Allianz Life Insurance Company of North America, press release https://www.allianzlife.com/MediaCenter/PressGenDex.aspx.)

Pricing the accelerated death benefit option so that the diagnoses cover more than terminal illnesses and expand coverage outside the limited constraints of a life expectancy of 24 months encroaches at the margin of the value offered by the life settlement market. Life settlements offer a complete liquidation of a policy while accelerated death benefits still only offer partial and constrained liquidation. Of course, if accelerated death benefit options can be priced in the primary market they can also be priced in the secondary market.

In the meantime, the current pool of life insurance policies owned by the over-65-year-old population is so vast that the secondary market in life insurance policies, the life settlement market, has plenty of fodder for growth.

The secondary market in life insurance policies has increased the liquidity of the life insurance policy. Since liquidity has positive value, the development of a secondary market in life policies should increase the value of the life insurance policy. Just as mortgage originators are willing to pay a fee to exchange an illiquid pool of mortgages for a more liquid mortgage-backed security (even during the current disruption of the securitization markets), households will take the increased liquidity of life insurance into their financial planning decisions.

Once the value of protection that life insurance offers to a family should one or both family members responsible for generating income die declines, because the family has accumulated sufficient wealth or the dependent members of the family have become financially independent, then longevity risk will start to weigh heavier in financial decisions than mortality risk. It is when the balance shifts in favor of longevity risk that the option of liquidating a life insurance policy via the life settlement market becomes more interesting.

The recent financial disruption of 2007/2008 sparked by the rapid decline in housing prices and the crash of the subprime mortgage market, enhances the value of financial assets that are uncorrelated with credit and equity markets. The housing crisis has also depleted a source of wealth for a large segment of the U.S. population. Life insurance policies held their value. It would be interesting to know how the stress of the financial disruption of

2008/2009 affects the mortality risk of the population. The performance of life settlement contracts and life settlement funds are uncorrelated with these markets. While life settlement contracts are uncorrelated with the general markets, contract performance is linked to the claims paying ability of the life insurance company that underwrote the policy. Investors mitigate this risk by limiting incents to policies with a minimum claims paying rating and by diversifying across underwriters.

We contribute to the analytics of the market for life settlement contracts to offer insight to fund managers on how they can improve their measurement of the risks embedded in pools of life settlement contracts. With better risk management the market will attract more capital, employ leverage more effectively, and ultimately offer better pricing to people who are interested in selling their life insurance policies. We examine and analyze how changes in longevity impact value and how this risk can be effectively contained by portfolio managers.

Senior life settlements are created when the owner of a life insurance policy sells the policy to an investor who assumes the premium liability of the policy in return for becoming the policy's beneficiary. In general, the investors are life settlement companies. These companies specialize in searching for, valuing, and buying life insurance policies. The distinction of "senior" refers to the age of the settler (the seller of the policy). Currently the market is composed of settlers who are 65 and older. This age is not a fixed constraint. Policies owned by people who are younger than 65 but who have impaired health may also be sold in the secondary market for life insurance. Fund managers buy portfolios of senior life settlements from life settlement companies. The key element that distinguishes portfolios of life settlement contracts from pools of other financial assets that are funded on the capital markets is longevity risk. Longevity risk is the chance that an insured lives longer than the estimate upon which the policy is valued by the life settlement company or by the investor who has purchased a pool of policies. The price that a life settlement company pays for a life settlement contract and the value of the securities issued by the investor to refinance the portfolio in the capital markets are tied to the estimate of the longevity of the pool, that is, how long the policy will be outstanding before a death benefit is recovered. In this chapter we describe a metric we previously developed that can be used to evaluate longevity risk. Our measurement of longevity risk, which is an application of the duration metric used to measure interest rate risk of fixed income securities, can be used by fund managers to select life settlement contracts that fall within acceptable risk parameters. It can also be used by investors who are adding securities backed by life settlement contracts to portfolios of traditional fixed-income securities.

Senior life settlement contracts are financial instruments that transfer a life insurance policy from the insured (the life settler) to a life settlement company, the new beneficiary. The life settlement company purchases the policy at a discount from face from the insured. The purchaser of the policy, the life settlement company, is liable for the premium payments and becomes the beneficiary. Upon the death of the insured the life settlement company receives the death benefit.

The value of a life settlement contract is based on the life expectancy of the settler, which, in turn, is a function of his/her age and health condition. The valuation of a life settlement is achieved by discounting the premia paid over the established settler's life expectancy and the benefit to be received at the time the settler dies. If a settler lives above life expectancy, LE, premia need to be paid over a longer period, and it takes longer to receive the death benefit. An increase in the longevity of an insured or the extension of the insured's life beyond the time used to value the life settlement contract reduces the value of senior life settlements.

EXAMPLE OF A POOL OF SECURITIZED SENIOR LIFE SETTLEMENTS: THE LIFEMARK SECURE INCOME BOND (SIB), SERIES SEK, 5-YEAR TERM/ANNUAL PAYMENT

Following is the description of the Lifemark Secure Income Bond deal (SIB) obtained from http://www.carlkliem.lu/documents/Alternative%20 Investments/Lifemark%20Brochure/Lifemark%20%20-Brochure%20-%20GB%20-%20EUR.pdf.

Asset Allocation

The investment portfolio will have 30 percent held in cash and 70 percent invested in insurance contracts. The cash element is used to pay premiums for contracts and income payments to investors. The asset mix is balanced through maturing contracts.

Contract Selection

The SIB has strict criteria, established by Lifemark S.A., governing the type of insurance contract that can be held within it. There are clearly defined responsibilities for verification and risk.

> **Permitted policy types:** individual term life, noncancelable or converted group policy, variable (flexible) life policy, joint second life insured policy.
>
> **Age of insured:** at least 65 at time of purchase.

Life expectancy: greater than 24 months, less than 94 months.

Internal Rate of Return (IRR): at least 10 percent.

Minimum benefit per insured: $250,000

Maximum benefit per insured: $10 million.

Minimum number of policies in portfolio: 60 for the first $100 million of face value, no limit thereafter.

Rating of issuer: S&P rating at least 'A-' for all issuers.

Weighting of issuer in portfolio: no more than 10 percent to come from any single issuer.

Underwriters expected benefits payable date range: minimum 25 months, maximum 168 months.

Verification of contracts: Meditron Asset Management LLC.

Payment agent for purchasing contracts: Bank of New York.

Payment agent for funding premiums: Bank of New York.

Product Structure

The Lifemark Secure Income Bond is a Euro, Swedish Krona, or British Pound denominated bond that will be listed on the Luxembourg Stock Exchange.

Investment Objective

The investment objective of the SIB is to provide regular fixed-income payments over a five-year term and a full return of capital at maturity. The return of capital is not guaranteed, and it is possible that the investor will get back less than the original investment amount at the end of the term.

Parties Involved

Issuer: Lifemark S.A.

Lifemark is a fast growing company established as one of Europe's largest portfolio investors in American senior life settlement policies. Since establishing its activities in 2006, Lifemark has raised over $750 million in investor funding. Investments in the portfolio of American senior life settlement policies are structured to provide clear investor benefit and understandable levels of risk through proven portfolio building techniques dedicated to delivering results outside correlated equity market performances and benefit from a new asset class product with secured interests in long-term returns. Lifemark S.A. is a Luxembourg Securitization company authorized and regulated by the Commission de Surveillance du Secteur Financier, the financial regulator in Luxembourg.

The Lifemark Secure Income Bond Term Sheet

Product name: The Lifemark Secure Income Bond (SIB).

Issuer: Lifemark S.A.

Customer proposition: The investment objective of the SIB is to provide regular fixed coupon payments over a five-year term and a full return of capital at maturity. The return of capital is not guaranteed and it is possible that the investor will get back less than the original investment amount at the end of the term.

Interest payment frequency: Annually, beginning August 1, 2009.

Term: Five years.

Coupon EURO/SEK: 7 percent annual income, or 1.706 percent quarterly income.

GBP: 7.5 percent annual income or 1.875 percent quarterly income.

Currency: EUR or SEK

Minimum investment: Minimum €6,000, 60,000 SEK, or £4,000 with no maximum.

Nominal: EUR 1, SEK 1, GBP 1.

Issue price: PAR

Redemption price: 100

Collateral: A mix of a portfolio of U.S. senior life insurance contracts issued by institutions 'A-' rated or better and cash.

Charges: All charges included in the terms offered, that is, 100 percent allocation.

Domicile: Luxembourg.

Listing and paying agent: Fortis Banque Luxembourg S.A.

Registrar: Equity Trust Co. (Luxembourg) S.A.

Transfer agent custodian: Société Européenne de Banque S.A. (Lux).

Trustee: The Bank of New York.

Consultant: Investor Luxembourg S.A.

Distributor: Carl Kliem S.A. (institutional settlement) 252, Route d'Arlon, L-1150 Luxembourg, www.carlkliem.lu, Phone: (+352) 45 84 84-254, Craig Griffiths (cgriffiths@bloomberg.net).

Listing: Luxembourg Stock Exchange.

Each contract that is bought undergoes an evaluation from which the expected maturity date can be determined. This might be done twice if there is a decision to buy the contract. The first occasion is to assess the compatibility of the contract with the investment criteria. If the contract then proceeds to purchase, this is verified by an independent third party. The portfolio has been modeled to have a return distribution that is closely aligned with the predictable timing of contracts maturing to create the financial model. No contract can have equivalent benefits lower than $250,000 (approximately €195,000).

Investment Timing

The actuarial model allows six months for the optimum number of contracts to be purchased. This conservative approach has been adopted to create flexibility in the investment process if unforeseen circumstances delay the planned purchase of assets.

Income and Capital Repayment

The SIB has been structured to produce 7 percent income over five years and full capital repayment at maturity.

Five-year term

7 percent annual income or 1.706 percent quarterly income

Its structure means that if there are any residual contracts that have not matured by the SIB maturity date they will be sold. In addition, mechanisms have been put in place to mitigate other risk factors.

Mix of cash and contracts allows payments of income, early redemptions, and premiums to be funded.

The value of a contract increases with time as it nears likely maturity, and there is an established secondhand market in the United States that will buy these contracts.

Predicted Maturity Rates

The actuarial modeling used to provide the financial models for the SIB is based on recognized industry standards. While these are not subject to rapid change, there is a risk that a significant technological or pharmaceutical development could impact on the accuracy of the models and when contracts are likely to mature. This is considered to be a small risk due to the predicted size of the portfolio and the spread of expected maturity dates across the contracts. Furthermore, any such advance is highly unlikely to affect all contracts and would also be difficult to gain regulatory approval for within the five-year term of the SIB.

Valuation of Traded Insurance Contracts

The actuarial models used in the SIB have been stress tested, but there can be no guarantee that they will function as anticipated. This could lead to contracts possibly being mispriced relative to their future sale value if contracts are still current when the bond matures. It is also assumed that the longer a contract is owned by the SIB the greater its market value since it is closer to possible maturity. If the dynamics of the market change this might not be the case and it would therefore be possible for contracts to fall in value. If this were to happen, capital might not be returned in full at the end of the term that involves the sale of residual contracts to generate sufficient cash. Analysis has shown this to be a small risk because of the spread of risk over the large number of issuing companies.

LIFE SETTLEMENT MODELS

In the term sheet of Lifemark S.A.'s Asset Backed Securitization Bond, the investment objective is stated to be a "total annual return targeted to 7 percent (Euro) and 7.5 percent (GBP), net of charges."

Our contribution to the market for life settlements is to offer investors a measurement tool that allows them to understand the effect deviations from the assumed life expectancy will have on investment yield. We show the effect that longevity risk has on yield depends on the characteristics of the individual life insurance policies that compose a life settlement pool.

The key paragraph in the description of the Lifemark S.A. Asset Backed Securitization Bond is the one titled "Investment Objective": The investment objective of the SIB is to provide regular fixed-income payments over a five-year term and a full return of capital at maturity. The return of capital is not guaranteed and it is possible that the investor will get back less than the original investment amount at the end of the term.

It is specified later in the deal that the fixed-income payment objective is 7 percent per year. The main reason the return of capital is not guaranteed is due to the longevity risk, the risk that a settler lives beyond his life expectancy.

Stone and Zissu (2006) have developed what they call the LE-duration (life-extension duration), the modified LE-duration and the LE-convexity (life-extension convexity) to address the longevity risk investors in securitized pools of senior life settlements, or in funds of life settlements, are exposed to. The LE-duration measures the percentage change in value of a life settlement given a percentage change in a settler's life from its life expectancy. The modified LE-duration measures the percentage change in value of a life settlement given a change, rather than a percentage change, in a settler's life from its life expectancy. Investors buying securities backed by a pool of life settlements will have information about various parameters in the underlying insurance policies. Using the pool information that an investor has, we develop the modified LE-duration and the LE-convexity. These metrics provide information on how sensitive the security is to deviation around life expectancy. In this chapter LE stands for "life expectancy."

The next section summarizes Stone and Zissu's model. We then describe a typical pool of senior life settlements and apply the LE-duration, modified LE-duration, and LE-convexity in order to measure the longevity risk of such a pool. Using these measurements an investor who has the choice among different pools of life settlements will be able to evaluate which is more sensitive to changes in settlers' lives above or below original life expectancy. This is the first step to finding consistent prices for pools of life settlement contracts and individual life insurance policies.

STONE AND ZISSU'S MODEL

From *Journal of Derivatives*, 2006.

The valuation of a senior life settlement, $V(sls)$, is obtained by discounting the premium paid at the end of each year, $-P$, and the death benefit B, collected at the time when the life settler dies. For simplicity, a flat yield curve is assumed, with a discount rate of r. The valuation is based on a life expectancy of t years as shown in equation (14.1).

$$V(sls) = -P\left[\frac{1}{(1+r)^1} + \frac{1}{(1+r)^2} \cdots + \frac{1}{(1+r)^t}\right]$$
$$+ \frac{B}{(1+r)^t} \tag{14.1}$$

Equation (14.1) is rewritten as:

$$V(sls) = -P\left[\frac{1}{r} - \frac{a^t}{r}\right] + Ba^t \quad \text{where } a = \frac{1}{(1+r)}$$

and after rearranging it becomes:

$$V(sls) = a^t\left[\frac{P}{r} + B\right] - \frac{P}{r} \tag{14.2}$$

The first derivative of equation (14.2) relative to changes in t is shown in equation (14.3):

$$\frac{dV(sls)}{dt} = \left[\frac{P}{r} + B\right]a^t \ln(a) \tag{14.3}$$

and, after multiplying the first derivative by t, dividing it by the value of the life settlement, the *LE-duration* is obtained in equation (14.4):

$$LE\text{-}duration = \frac{\left[ta^t(P + rB)\ln(a)\right]}{\left[a^t(P + rB) - P\right]} \tag{14.4}$$

The LE-duration is negative, which implies that the longer a life settler lives beyond life expectancy, the more value the senior life settlement contract will lose.

The percentage change in value of a life settlement relative to changes in time, rather than relative to percentage changes in time, the *modified LE-duration* is obtained by dividing the *LE-duration* by t:

$$modified\ LE\text{-}duration = \frac{\left[a^t(P + rB)\ln(a)\right]}{\left[a^t(P + rB) - P\right]} \tag{14.5}$$

Investors in pools of senior life settlements can evaluate the pool's sensitivity to life extension t using the *modified LE-duration* of the pool:

$$[\%\Delta V(SLS)] = \frac{\Delta t\left[a^t(P + rB)\ln(a)\right]}{\left[a^t(P + rB) - P\right]} \tag{14.6}$$

The percentage change in value of the pool [%$\Delta V(SLS)$] given a change in time due to life extension or reduction (Δt) is equal to the pool's *modified duration*

$$LE\text{-}duration \ \frac{\left[a^t(P+rB)\ln(a)\right]}{\left[a^t(P+rB)-P\right]}$$

multiplied by the life extension/reduction Δt.

For example, for a life extension of two years, $\Delta t = 2$, the percentage change in the value of the pool [%$\Delta V(SLS)$] will be equal to:

$$[\%\Delta V(SLS)] = 2\frac{\left[a^t(P+rB)\ln(a)\right]}{\left[a^t(P+rB)-P\right]} \tag{14.7}$$

Convexity of a fixed-income security measures the rate at which duration changes with respect to changes in interest rates. As the convexity of a security increases, the range over which duration is accurate relative to changes in yields diminishes. It is possible to correct for the convexity effect on the accuracy of duration by adding the value of the convexity to that of duration. The *LE-convexity* is obtained by taking the second derivative of the value of senior life settlement with respect to life expectancy and by dividing it by the value of the senior life settlement:

$$LE\text{-}convexity: \ \frac{d^2 V(SLS)}{d\,t^2} = \frac{\left(\frac{P}{r}+B\right)a^t(\ln(a))^2}{a^t\left(\frac{P}{r}+B\right)-\frac{P}{r}} \tag{14.8}$$

The result is a positive convexity, which means that as a life settler lives longer than life expectancy, the value of the settlement decreases at an increasing rate.

The percentage change in value of a senior life settlement due to the *LE-convexity* is computed as follows:

$$[\%\Delta V(SLS)due\ to\ LE\text{-}conv]$$
$$= \frac{1}{2}\frac{\left(\frac{P}{r}+B\right)a^t(\ln(a))^2}{a^t\left(\frac{P}{r}+B\right)-\frac{P}{r}}(\Delta t)^2 \tag{14.9}$$

The weighted average *modified LE-duration (wa-modified-LE-duration)*, is obtained by multiplying each life settlement's duration by its corresponding value, dividing it by the value of the entire pool, and summing up the results for each of the n life settlements (14.13 in our example), as shown in equation (14.10):

$$wa\text{-}modified\text{-}LE\text{-}duration = \sum_{i=1}^{n} \frac{V(sls)_i}{V(SLS)} \; modified \; LE\text{-}duration)_i$$

$$(14.10)$$

The weighted average *LE-convexity*, *wa-LE-convexity*, is obtained by multiplying each life settlement's convexity by its corresponding value, dividing it by the value of the entire pool, and summing up the results for each of the number of life settlements n as shown in equation (14.11):

$$wa\text{-}LE\text{-}convexity = \sum_{i=1}^{n} \frac{V(sls)_i}{V(SLS)} \; (LE\text{-}convexity)_i \qquad (14.11)$$

MACAULAY AND MODIFIED DURATION

Equation (14.12) is the calculation of the Macaulay duration D for a life settlement contract. The present value of each cash flow is multiplied by the time at which it is paid, i, where i runs from year 1 to year t, t being the time the premia stop being paid and when the death benefit is received. The sum of the present values, multiplied by the time at which they are received, is divided by the present value of the life settlement contract, P.

$$\underset{i=1}{\overset{t}{D}} = \left[\sum p(i)/(1+r)^i - tB/(1+r)^t \right] P \qquad (14.12)$$

The modified duration is simply obtained by dividing the Macaulay duration by $(1 + r)$.

We next compute the Macauley duration, the modified duration, and the corresponding change in value of a senior life settlement with the following characteristics:

Face Amount $= \$10,000,000$
Yearly Premium $= \$500,000$
Life Expectancy $= 4$

Investors should be careful when using Macaulay or modified duration as a measure of a pool of senior life settlements' interest rate risk. The

EXHIBIT 14.1 Macaulay vs. Modified Duration

r	Mac Dur	Mod Dur	%chg Price for 100bps
4%	−4.42	−4.25	−4.25%
6%	−4.44	−4.188679245	−4.18%
8%	−4.46	−4.12962963	−4.12%
10%	−4.49	−4.081818182	−4.08%
12%	−4.52	−4.035714286	−4.03%
14%	−4.54	−3.98245614	−3.98%
16%	−4.57	−3.939655172	−3.93%
18%	−4.6	−3.898305085	−3.89%

measurements are only valid for an unchanged LE. As soon as deviations around LE occur, the Macaulay and the modified duration become unreliable, because of the changes in the life settlements projected cash flows.

CONCLUSION

Longevity risk is a real concern to investors in pools of senior life settlements and viaticles. It is common parlance in the life settlement industry when describing a life settlement, to refer to the premium P and the face value B as a ratio $\frac{P}{B}$. For example, a life settlement with annual premium of $40,000 and a face value (death benefit B) of $1 million can be referred to as 4 percent life settlement. We call this ratio α. Using our applications, issuers of securitized pools of senior life settlements, or hedge fund managers, could, instead of buying blocks of senior life settlements, pick each life settlement, with a specific α, to create pools with specific longevity risk in order to meet investors' specific needs.

The need for living benefits has led to the creation of many products with embedded annuities and still more to be engineered. Longevity risk is of great concern to annuity writers. Life expectancy tables are changing rapidly and constantly. Mortality has been declining steadily over time. Securities with longevity risk are very sensitive to changes in life expectancies. With the LE-duration, we are able to measure the sensitivity of these types of securities to changes in life expectancy of annuitants. Insurance companies selling life insurance policies are confronted with the risk of policyholders dying too soon (mortality risk). By investing in pools of securitized senior life settlements, it is possible for insurance companies to reduce mortality risk by adding longevity risk to their portfolios. The portfolio would be immunized against mortality shocks.

REFERENCES

Ballotta, Laura, and Steven Haberman. 2006. The fair valuation problem of guaranteed annuity options: The stochastic mortality environment case. *Insurance: Mathematics and Economics* (February).

Best, A. M. 2005. *Life settlement securitization* (September 1).

Blake, D., A. J. G. Cairns, and K. Dowd. 2006. Living with mortality: Longevity bonds and other mortality-linked securities. Presented to the Faculty of Actuaries, January 16.

Cowley, Alex, and J. David Cummins. 2005. Securitization of life insurance assets and liabilities. *Journal of Risk and Insurance* 72 (2) (June): 193–226.

Doherty, Neil A., and Hal J. Singer. 2002. The benefits of a secondary market for life insurance policies. The Wharton Financial Institutions Center, November 14.

Dowd, Kevin, Andrew J. G. Cairns, and David Blake. 2006. Mortality-dependent financial risk measures. *Insurance: Mathematics and Economics* 38 (3) (June 15): 427–642.

Goldstein, Matthew. 2004. *Dying for 8%—investors beware*. Tavakoli Structured Finance, Inc. August.

Ingraham, Harold G., and Sergio S. Salani. 2004. Life settlements as viable option. *Journal of Financial Service Professionals* (September).

Lin, Yijia, and Samuel H. Cox. 2005. Securitization of mortality risks in life annuities. *Journal of Risk and Insurance* 72 (2) (June): 227–252.

Milevsky, Moshe A. 2005. The implied longevity yield: A note on developing an index for life annuities. *Journal of Risk and Insurance* (72) 2 (June): 301–320.

Richard, Christine. 2004. With $70M bond deal, Wall Street manages to securitize death. *Wall Street Journal*, April 30.

Stone, Charles A., and Anne Zissu. 2006. Securitization of senior life settlements: Managing extension risk. *The Journal of Derivatives*, Spring.

Stone, Charles A., and Anne Zissu. 1996. Risk management—risk measurement. Letter from the Editors, *The Financier* (3) 4 & 5.

Stone, Charles A., Carlos Ortiz, and Anne Zissu. 2008. Securitization of senior life settlements: Managing interest rate risk with a planned duration class. *The Journal of Financial Transformation*, August.

U.S. Department of Health and Human Services, 2007. Long-Term Care Information. Longer lives spur new "death" benefits. *Financial Advisor Magazine*. May 31. www.longtermcare.gov/LTC/Main_Site/Paying_LTC/Private_Programs/Other_Insurance/index.aspx.

CHAPTER 15

Synthetics

New Swaps to Hedge Alpha and Beta Longevity Risks of Life Settlement Pools

Antony R. Mott
Managing Director, Structured Insurance Products, ICAP Capital Markets

Rapid growth. A controversial theme. The promise of high profits uncorrelated to the stock market. These features draw investors and the curious public alike to the life settlement market—an industry where investors pay an insured individual more cash for unwanted life insurance than will the insurance company.

With public attention come regulators. Some of them focus on risks to the insured from intermediaries supposed to serve them. Others focus on the potential threat by the industry to insurance companies' profitability.

Reprinted with permission from the Summer 2007 issue of *The Journal of Structured Finance*, a publication of Institutional Investor Journals, Inc.

Editor's note:

Disclaimer: this material is for your private information and ICAP Capital Markets LLC is not soliciting any action based upon it or making an endorsement, recommendation, solicitation, or sponsorship of or in connection with any security, information, or the data. We do not represent that the information is accurate or complete, and it should not be relied upon as such. Opinions expressed are our current opinions as of the date appearing on this material only. ICAP Capital Markets LLC and its affiliates, officers, directors, partners and employees, including persons involved in the preparation or issuance of this material may, from time to time, have long or short positions in, and buy or sell, any of the commodities, futures, securities, or other instruments and investments mentioned herein, or derivatives (including options) on any of the same.

By contrast, there isn't a whole lot of attention paid to the risks faced by investors. Perhaps that's because those who buy pools of life settlements are professional investors who don't require the same level of protection as the general public. Or maybe it's because certain investment risks peculiar to life settlements are like submerged reefs: If you're unaware *and* lucky, you can sail merrily by. Or perhaps it's because investors must wait four to seven years to know how the investment pans out, and most pools are not yet four years old.

How many investors net the hoped-for 13 percent or 14 percent yields? Some pool owners have reported that cash flows are on target, others report LIBOR-esque returns. And more than one pool has wound up in the distressed market: The fund managers of these pools are kept busy fighting off vulture investors.

Fortunately, once you—the potential investor—know where the risks are, you can choose strategies and risk-transfer products to avoid or manage trouble.

RISKS AFFECTING POOLS OF LIFE SETTLEMENTS

Pools of life settlements are most[1] significantly affected by face-value variance risk and longevity risk, or put simply: Who dies when. Face-value risk arises when the insured individuals underlying a pool of life settlements have policies with differing face values. Face-value variance risk is sometimes called severity risk or event risk.

To illustrate each risk, let's first look at what happens if there is *neither* face-value risk *nor* longevity risk. Exhibit 15.1 shows the most probable cash flows generated by a typical pool of $1 billion worth of life insurance written on 300 or so health-impaired individuals.

Those new to investing in pools of life settlements might be surprised to learn that typical pools, including our example, start as *negative* yield assets. For the first year or two, we expect nearly all the individuals to remain alive and we must pay premiums to keep the policies in force. If we paid $200 million (one-fifth of face value) for our pool, and yearly premiums average 5 percent of face value, then we will pay close to $50 million a year just to maintain the investment—at least for a few years.

Longevity risk leads to excess return or loss when the actual mortality experience of a pool differs from that projected. Usually lumped together, there are actually two types of longevity risk: alpha-longevity risk and beta-longevity risk, with one compounding the other. Alpha-longevity risk arises from information asymmetries between market participants and is akin to

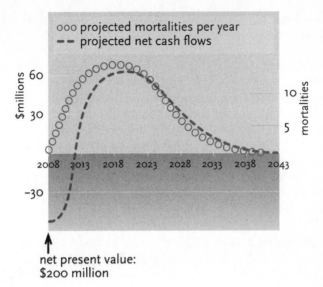

EXHIBIT 15.1   Projected Cash Flows to the Owner of a Pool of Life Settlements (face value $1 billion, 300 unique insured)
Copyright © SwapsMarket.

the alpha technical risk ratio used in stock markets. Beta-longevity risk is the sensitivity of pool returns to changes affecting general population longevity and parallels the beta technical risk ratio used in stock markets.

To contrast one type of longevity risk with the other, consider our pool of life settlements linked to 300 insured individuals each of whom is health impaired. We might expect our pool's 300 health-impaired individuals to live, on average, 8 years, while 300 people drawn at random from the general population might live 11 years.

An example of alpha-longevity risk is the risk that we have miscalculated the degree of health impairment, or maybe a drug is invented that helps manage or cure the specific impairments of the insured individuals linked to the pool, with the result that the insured linked to our pool live 10 not 8 years. An example of beta-longevity risk is the risk of an unexpected increase in longevity of the general population so that the individuals linked to the pool live perhaps 8.1 not 8 years.

Not only is alpha-longevity risk greater than beta-longevity risk, but also the two risks aren't necessarily correlated and there is basis risk between them.

Medical underwriters have the tough job of predicting *life expectancies*. If a medical underwriter tells us that our pool has a life expectancy of 11 years, then approximately half the insured individuals will be living at the start of the 12th year. Relying on these predictions introduces both types of longevity risk.

If our pool's cash flows depended on the lives of 10,000 individuals, we might reasonably expect the smooth and predictable cash flows illustrated in Exhibit 15.1. Yet our pool's cash flows depend on the lives of 300 or so individuals. Exhibit 15.2 illustrates what happens when we add a dose of realism into the modeling.

The degree of randomness of the path is the thing to note here, not the path itself, which is just one of a near infinite number of possibilities modeled using a combination of actual results from similar pools and stochastic techniques.

The only source of variance we've introduced so far comes from a lack of diversity, and the chaotic cash flow projections in Exhibit 15.2 arise even if the medical underwriter does a perfect job and we know for certain the average life expectancy of our pool.

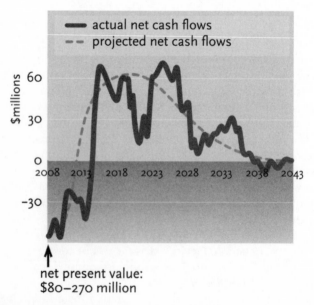

EXHIBIT 15.2   Warning: Actual Results May Vary!
Copyright © SwapsMarket.

Medical underwriters do not generally have enough data to do a perfect job. Systematic under- or overestimation of life expectancies is called *table bias*. For clarity, the next few charts show the effect of table bias on cash flow, and ignore the ever-present and compounding effect of random variance.

Exhibit 15.3 illustrates mean-extension, which is to say that the insured linked to our pool generally live longer than the medical underwriter expects.

Mean-extension nearly halves our net present value (NPV) because we'll receive cash later—and we'll pay premiums longer—than we thought.

Even if the medical underwriter correctly predicts the *average* life estimate, other less-obvious forms of table bias will, if overlooked, lead us to over- or underestimate our pool's NPV.

Exhibit 15.4 shows how NPV is affected when there are fewer early mortalities than expected, acceleration of mortalities in the middle of the pool's life, and fewer mortalities toward the end of the pool's life. The average life expectancy alone fails to warn us that the NPV of our pool is nearer $150 million than $200 million.

To help us better value our pool, the medical underwriter might draw the distribution for us, or include three other statistical measures: standard

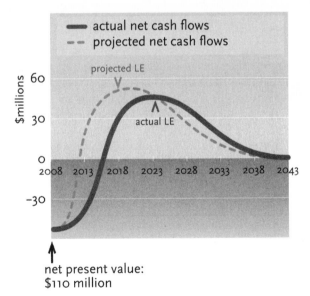

EXHIBIT 15.3 Life Estimates Systematically Understated (longevity extension)
Copyright © SwapsMarket.

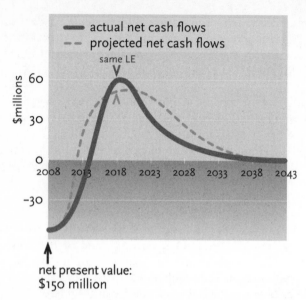

EXHIBIT 15.4 Leptokurtic (pointy looking) Distribution: A Form of Table Bias Not Communicated by the Life Expectancy
Copyright © SwapsMarket.

deviation, kurtosis, and skewness. Whereas standard deviation measures how tightly a distribution is clustered, kurtosis describes the degree of "pointiness" or "flatness" of a distribution, and skewness measures its lopsidedness. Statisticians refer to the shape of the distribution in Exhibit 15.4 as *leptokurtic*, which roughly translates to "thinly bulging."

Exhibit 15.5 illustrates the inverse form of table bias to that of Exhibit 15.4. Without knowing the standard deviation and kurtosis, we don't realize that the NPV of our pool is higher than we think it is. Statisticians refer to the squished-looking distribution in Exhibit 15.5 as *platykurtic*, which means "broadly bulging."

The variance in NPV illustrated by Exhibits 15.3 through 15.5 highlights the potential dangers in the standard industry practice of "simplifying" mortality distributions to a single number: the average. A mortality distribution, like any probability distribution, is a range concept and all but the most basic require more than one statistic for proper description.

To summarize: Before you buy, press your medical underwriter for life expectancy information that includes standard deviation, kurtosis, and skewness, as well as the average.

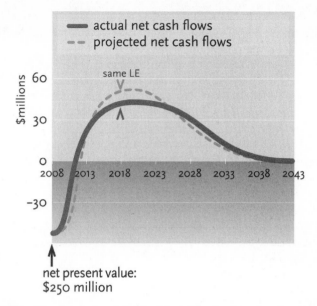

EXHIBIT 15.5 Platykurtic (squished-looking) Distribution: Another Form of Table Bias Not Communicated by the Life Expectancy
Copyright © SwapsMarket.

BUYING STRATEGIES AFFECTED BY ALPHA LONGEVITY RISK

We mentioned previously that alpha longevity risk arises from information asymmetries among market participants. Life settlement investors think they'll make money from insurance companies through the investors' special skills in actuarial science, and some of these investors will make money. Investors new to the market might consider that insurance companies—which on the whole have been profitable for the last hundred years—might also know a thing or two about actuarial science.

1. Insurance companies, intermediaries, and investors make a lot of noise about life settlement buyers *arbitraging* the insurance company's lapse-based pricing model. For certain policy types, lapse rates approach 80 percent, so at first blush, the insurance company's apparent vulnerability appears like a compelling opportunity for investors. Less widely known is that the policies written on seniors—those most likely to wind up as life settlements—can have lapse rates as low as 9 percent, which is a

far cry from 80 percent. If the arbitrage is thinner than you thought, the insurance company needs only to raise premiums a tad to level the playing field or even gain the upper hand.

2. Some investors assume that if the individual is health impaired, the policy must have value. Only if the insured has become *unexpectedly* impaired *after* the policy was issued does this make sense, and aging is not unexpected. If the individual already was health impaired when the policy was issued, then the investor is betting that the insurance company either didn't do its underwriting properly or assumed a high lapse rate.

3. Some investors are looking at "carrier approved" premium-finance origination programs where the insurance company is apparently aware of the high probability that the life insurance policies will be sold as life settlements. Shareholders of insurance companies are unlikely to let management write new business that will destroy shareholder value. Unless insurance companies have higher costs of capital than life settlement investors, an investment in policies that are part of a carrier-endorsed origination program may have high alpha longevity risk—unfavorable to you, the investor.

4. Some investors think that life settlements constitute such a small portion of the insurers' business, that insurers don't care to do much about the problem, and that insurance companies are generally slow to react to a changing marketplace, which creates opportunities for investors.

   Insurance companies have demonstrated both that they can care greatly about small sections of their business and that they are able to react swiftly. In the 1990s, the viatical market (predecessor of today's senior life settlement market) was all but wiped out in part through medical advancements, but mainly through the introduction by insurance companies of the accelerated death benefit, now included in most life policies.

5. Investors value a life settlement based in part on the impairment opinion prepared by one or more medical underwriters. The impairment opinion is in turn based on available medical records, so a major risk to investors is the degree to which medical records do *not* accurately portray the health status of an individual. This is not the risk that medical records may be falsified, but the risk that they may have only limited value. For example, doctors may indicate a condition exists even when the doctor is not too sure. Conservative diagnoses are in line with most doctors' motivation to care for patients (not investors) and avoid a negligence suit later for failing to alert a patient to the possibility of an illness or condition.

6. Medical underwriters can and do make unsystematic and systematic errors. The effects of unsystematic errors are minimized by increasing the number of unique insured underlying the pool. The effects of systematic error, or table bias, can dramatically impact the net present value of the pool and were explained in the previous section.

Many policies do have value as life settlements. Even if you're confident that you're on the right side of alpha longevity risk, bear in mind you have two other non-longevity-related hurdles before you're holding a valuable investment: (1) the intermediaries who represent the insured also know that the policy has value; and (2) only two out of three dollars will get past the intermediaries as invested capital, so your investment has to increase in value by 50 percent just to break even.

The next section looks at existing longevity risk management techniques—insurance and annuities, as well as new derivatives that may provide cheaper, more liquid alternatives to insurance.

HEDGING LONGEVITY RISK

Barring a cure for old age, a worldwide plague, or other global catastrophe, the chance of a small increase in longevity is closer to a certainty than a risk. Beta-longevity risk can therefore be managed simply by increasing the number of unique insured underlying the pool of life settlements.

Alpha-longevity risk is not necessarily reduced through diversification, so one of the few options available to the investor is the purchase of longevity-extension insurance.

Issuers of longevity-extension insurance—otherwise known as a mortality wrap—charge the pool owner an up-front fee roughly equal to 30 percent of the pool's market value. The wrap issuer agrees to purchase any outstanding polices on a future date, for an agreed value, which is usually less than the face value.

The future date is usually the pool's average life expectancy—as determined by the issuer not the pool owner—with a couple of years tacked on for good measure. Some issuers require the owner to prepay all premiums that would fall due before the exercise date. If the average life expectancy of the pool is 10 years, then the pool owner must wait 12 years before exercise. The credit rating of the issuers is sometimes lower than AA, or the issuer may be unrated.

You might wonder why mortality wraps are so expensive. Early pool owners had more information about the insured than the issuer of the wrap, so the owners used the additional information to select insured with a higher likelihood of outliving their life estimates. Also, sellers of policies had more information about their own health than the pool owners. Compounding the problem further was that medical underwriters had little experience forecasting the mortality of people who choose to sell their life insurance to strangers. The result was that the insured tended to outlive their life expectancies, and the wrap issuers lost money. Some issuers refused to pay, blaming the medical underwriters, so the pool owners lost, too. Today's wrap issuers are aware they'll be the targets of adverse selection, and price accordingly.

Another technique is for a pool owner to purchase an annuity to partially offset premium payments. The expected yield on the combined asset may be close to or below LIBOR.

Mortality wraps and annuities have been around for several years, but newly-launched longevity indices are paving the way for derivative transactions because the indices can be used as a reference value against which to settle trades. Most indices were launched by institutions whose customers are affected by longevity risk.

Longevity indices allow derivatives and hedging strategies that settle yearly—sometimes more frequently—rather than pay out once in 10 or 12 years. Some market participants who might wish to make markets in longevity risk would prefer shorter-dated exposure. A series of short-dated derivatives based on these indices could provide an alternative to mortality wraps.

The Credit Suisse Longevity Index^{SM}, released in December 2005, is designed to enable the structuring and settlement of longevity risk transfer instruments such as longevity swaps and structured notes. Credit Suisse expects their index to spur the development of a liquid, tradable market in longevity risk as it provides a standardized measure of the expected average lifetime for general populations based on publicly available U.S. statistics. The index includes both historical and forward values and is released annually.

J.P. Morgan launched its LifeMetrics Index^{SM} in March 2007. An international index designed to benchmark and trade longevity risk, the index is part of a platform aimed at measuring and managing both longevity and mortality exposure. J.P. Morgan expects the index to become the leading industry index used to create securities, derivatives, and other structured products and will enable pension plans to calibrate and hedge the risk associated with the longevity of their beneficiaries. The index incorporates historical and current statistics on mortality rates and life expectancy across genders, ages, and nationalities. Currently the index is available for the United States, England, and Wales.

ICAP markets derivatives that reference vivaDex™ defined-pool longevity indices. Defined-pool longevity indices, first engineered by SwapsMarket^{SM}, reference pensions, annuities, life settlements, and other life-contingent assets or liabilities affected by alpha- and beta-longevity risk. The underlying pools can be an investor's aggregation of life settlements, or can be synthetic pools of insured grouped with similar characteristics like health impairment or cohort (age bracket), for example: "75- to 77-year-old nonsmoking males, table 8–10 impairment." Defined-pool swaps are collateralized with cash margin and expire every year for the expected life of the pool. When strung together, the swaps allow market participants to hedge exposures as short as 2 years and as long as 15 years, as well as enable yield-conversion strategies.

The next section discusses benefits and uses of these new derivatives and gives an example of how a pool-specific swap functions to transfer longevity risk and face-value risk.

BENEFITS AND USES OF LONGEVITY SWAPS

Whether the reference is a generalized index or a specific pool, longevity derivatives may offer increased fungibility over wraps and annuities. Increased fungibility may help broaden the spectrum of users to life markets participants that are exposed to: pools of life settlements, deferred annuities, securities issued to provide regulatory relief, and pension liabilities.

Comparing longevity derivatives, longevity swaps based on a generalized index may have advantages over swaps based on specific pools because swaps based on a generalized index:

- May be more liquid than their pool-specific counterparts, particularly if the correlation of the general-index swap is moderately high across different pension funds, life settlement pools, insurance company assets, and other holders of assets or liabilities affected by longevity risk.
- Are easier to assemble, maintain, and understand; and
- Could become the more efficient of the two types of swap if actuarial science both improves and becomes widely understood by market participants (a wide understanding diminishes alpha-longevity risk).

On the other hand, pool-specific longevity swaps may have some advantages where the aggregations of longevity risk involves only a few hundred individual insured and there is wide variance in face value of the policies. Under these conditions, the pool-specific longevity swap would:

- Better correlate (have a lower basis risk) to the pool's cash flows, because pool-specific swaps take into account face-value variance and impairment.

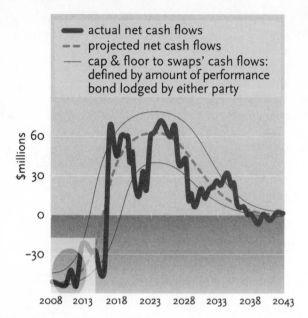

EXHIBIT 15.6   Short-Dated Swaps Allow Actual Cash Flows to Be Swapped
Against Projected Cash Flows
Copyright © SwapsMarket.

- Take account of kurtosis and skew of a pool's mortality distribution, which allows duration and convexity hedging.
- Allow hedging of both alpha-longevity risk and beta-longevity risk.

Exhibits 15.6 and 15.7 illustrate how short-dated pool-specific longevity swaps work.

The "long" swaps party—the one who buys the swap—gains when more people die throughout a six-month period than expected. The "short" swaps party—the one who sells the swap—gains when more people live through a six-month time period than expected. Exhibit 15.8 illustrates the actual cash flows to the long swaps party over a 6.5-year period.

WILL LONGEVITY SWAPS FLY?

Markets have traditionally been slow to take on products designed to transfer longevity risk. Perhaps that's because market participants tend to ignore distant risks and don't think like statisticians. Or it may be because the

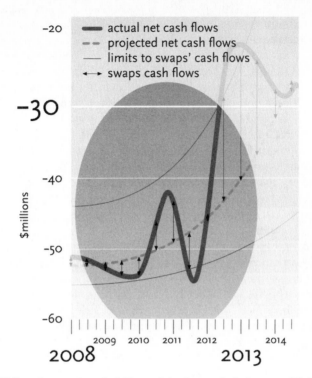

EXHIBIT 15.7   This Is a Detailed View of the Lower-Left Corner of Exhibit 15.6 to Illustrate Actual Hedging Cash Flows Resulting from the Swap
Copyright © SwapsMarket.

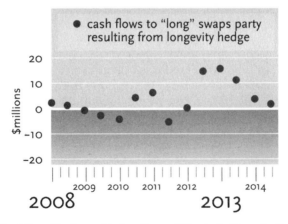

EXHIBIT 15.8   When Used as a Hedge, Swaps Effectively Transfer Face-Value Variance, Alpha-Longevity Risk, and Beta-Longevity Risk
Copyright © SwapsMarket.

incumbent products—which generally use data from homogenized populations as a reference—are geared to work as a beta-longevity hedge, while
market participants might have more exposure to alpha-longevity risk.

The market may not provide enough liquidity if it is one-sided: The
issuer of at least one longevity bond found pension funds willing to hedge
but couldn't find a market for the other side of the trade.

Insurance companies have the opposite alpha-longevity risk to life settlement owners, and the two would appear to be natural counterparties
to longevity swaps. However, insurance companies are in the business of
taking risk not laying it off. Also, the urgency of the pool owner to hedge
alpha-longevity risk may be greater than that of the insurance companies,
some of which view life settlements as a thorn in the side of an otherwise
profitable business. It may take time for insurance companies' profits to be
affected to the point that they'll hedge.

Insurance companies know which of the policies they write are likely to
become life settlements. For these policies specifically, insurance companies
might continue to raise the cost of insurance and lower their lapse-based
assumptions. The life settlement business would suffer, yet the majority of
customers of insurance companies would not be affected.

Insurance companies may start buying back policies from insured who
become unexpectedly health impaired. This move would be analogous to
the introduction of the accelerated death benefit that all but wiped out the
viatical business.

Some potential swap counterparties may not have the resources available to measure how longevity risk could affect their liabilities: What isn't
measured will not be hedged. Other potential users may find alternatives to
swaps; for example, wraps and annuities may become more competitively
priced.

The need to hedge may disappear for one of the counterparties. For
example, some corporate pension funds now offer member annuitants a
lump-sum payout alternative, and if the net present value of the lump sum
is less than the potential liability of the annuity, then the pension fund can
transfer longevity risk directly to the annuitant. Other potential users may
find that longevity risk is dominated by interest rate risk, inflation risk, and
market risk.

Nearly all swaps documentation omits personally identifiable information about the individuals in the pools that underlie the longevity swaps,
and this information is never made available to swaps counterparties. Some
investors argue that identifiable personal information is necessary to make
an informed investment or hedging decision.

Life settlements, along with longevity swaps, are just two products in a
never-ending succession of life insurance innovations (adapted from Doherty

and Singer [2003].)[2] Usually, insurance innovations are designed by insurance companies to help insurance companies and their customers. Whereas life settlements don't always provide an obvious advantage to insurance companies, longevity derivatives do allow the insurance industry to identify, concentrate, and hedge the risks to insurers, perhaps more effectively than the insurers can do themselves.

More and more businesses are actively or passively assuming longevity risk, and the effects are beginning to appear on balance sheets and profit and loss statements. If this trend continues, then there is likely to be an increase both in the need for these types of swap as well as refreshed inventiveness for new types of derivatives that can better manage the transfer of longevity risk.

NOTES

1. Other industry participants believe that the dominant risks are legal, like the risk that an insurance company will refuse to pay a claim, perhaps because the individual from whom the policy was purchased had an intent to sell the policy when it was issued, but the buyer doesn't find out about that until he tries to collect.
2. Neil A. Doherty, and Hal J. Singer, "Regulating the Secondary Market for Life Insurance Policies," *Journal of Insurance Regulation* 21 (2003): 63.

PART Five

Regulation

CHAPTER 16

Life Settlements

Regulatory Framework; Insurance Carrier Reaction and Next Steps for the Marketplace

Boris Ziser
Partner, Stroock & Stroock & Lavan LLP

Joseph Selvidio
Associate, Stroock & Stroock & Lavan LLP

Life insurance is a hedge to a risk. The risk is the death of an individual and the economic hardships that may result. Without life insurance, an untimely death can leave children without the means to pay for college, a spouse without the means to have a comfortable retirement, or a business partner without the money to continue a company created with the deceased. The capital markets refer to this as *mortality risk*.

While protection against mortality risk is an important aspect of financial planning, if an individual has lived long enough to send the children to school, saved enough for the spouse to retire comfortably and sold the interest in the family business, the need for protection against mortality risk declines and may even disappear. In such circumstances, life insurance can be an asset with value that can be unlocked.

One way to unlock the value of a life insurance policy is to sell it to a third party in a transaction called a life settlement. A life settlement occurs when the initial owner of a life insurance policy sells that policy to a third party for an amount greater than its cash surrender value,[1] but for less than its expected death benefit. In a typical transaction, a policy owner works with a broker to find the buyer willing to pay the highest price for the life insurance policy.

In recent years, the life settlement market has become increasingly attractive to senior citizens looking to exchange an unwanted or unneeded life insurance policy for liquidity (that is to say, cash) that can be used during their retirement years.[2] Before the life settlement market existed, individuals who no longer wanted or needed a life insurance policy were left only with the option of allowing their life insurance policies to lapse or surrendering them to the life insurance carrier in exchange for the policy's cash surrender value. With the advent of the life settlement market, a life insurance policy is an alienable asset, like a house, a car or a boat, that can be bought, sold or used as collateral in a financing.[3]

As the life settlement market has grown, lawmakers, market participants, insurance companies and other policymakers have struggled to strike a balance between protecting consumers from fraud and other marketplace abuses, on the one hand, and encouraging market freedoms that will allow the industry to reach its full potential on the other.

This chapter explores regulations and court decisions that have shaped the life settlement market, including the regulatory framework states have enacted or have considered. Also discussed are life insurance carrier reaction to, and participation in, these regulatory efforts and court decisions and how these carriers may view life settlements as this marketplace continues to grow. The chapter concludes with a review of what the consumer (and the regulator) may expect next for the life settlement market in terms of new products and market participants.

REGULATORY FRAMEWORK, MODEL ACTS, COURT DECISIONS, AND SECURITIES LAW ANALYSIS

Insurable Interest and Its Scope

The first regulatory principle to be considered in exploring the life settlement market is the concept of "insurable interest." A person or entity (a policy owner) generally is prohibited from taking out a life insurance policy on the life of any other person (an insured) unless that policy owner has a familial or economic connection with the insured. In other words, a person can only take out a life insurance policy on someone who that person has an interest in keeping alive, like a spouse, a child, or a business partner. The concept of insurable interest dates back at least to medieval England, when courts found that, as a matter of public policy, the insurable interest concept was necessary to prevent individuals from taking out life insurance policies on the lives of others purely to wager on how long the insured would live.[4]

If a policy owner needed to have an insurable interest in an insured for the entire term of a life insurance contract, the life settlement market would not exist. After all, if a policy owner could only sell a life insurance contract to a buyer that also had an insurable interest in the underlying insured,[5] the universe of buyers would be unworkably small. However, nearly 100 years ago the United States Supreme Court held that after a life insurance policy has been issued, the owner of that policy can sell it to a third party buyer, regardless of whether that buyer has an insurable interest in the life of the underlying insured. Insurable interest exists because without it, an individual would have no control over whether someone else (perhaps even an enemy) could take out a life insurance policy on his or her life. This concern does not exist after a policy's issuance because the policy owner makes the decision as to whether to sell the policy.[6] After a life insurance policy has been issued, the policy owner can set it "afloat on the sea of commerce."[7]

Early Regulation and Its Limitations

Although *Grigsby* laid the foundation for a life settlement to exist, a movement toward a marketplace did not begin in earnest until the 1980s, when America's acquired immunodeficiency syndrome (AIDS) epidemic resulted in a significant number of individuals willing to sell their life insurance policies to pay for medical expenses. These transactions, referred to as viatical settlements, involved terminally ill individuals selling their life insurance policies to largely unregulated buyers.[8] Although the statutory definition can be more broad, generally a viatical settlement is a transaction in which the insured has a terminal or chronic illness and is typically expected to live for a period of two years or less. A life settlement is a transaction in which the insured is expected to live longer than two years.[9] This early period of viatical settlements was the Wild West for the industry, and the results were sometimes predictably unfavorable for the consumer. States moved quickly to regulate the transactions, requiring that both parties that acted as the buyers in these transactions (referred to as "life settlement providers") and parties that brokered these transactions (referred to as "life settlement brokers") become licensed with state regulators. States also required life settlement transaction documents to be filed with regulatory bodies and provided state insurance commissioners with jurisdiction to oversee the market.[10]

In many of these early life settlement laws, an individual was prohibited from settling a life insurance policy for a period of two years. Presumably, this two-year prohibition was intended to prevent individuals from taking out a life insurance policy with the sole intent of later entering into a life settlement transaction. The prohibition also prevented individuals from settling a life insurance policy during the policy's contestability period, during which the life insurance carrier has greater discretion to challenge the enforceability of a policy.[11] Life insurance policies settled less than two years after their issuance are sometimes referred to in the industry as "wet ink" policies, meaning that they have been sold before the ink on the underlying life insurance contract has dried.

As the life settlement market matured, market participants avoided the two-year prohibition period in at least two ways. Under a business model known as a beneficial interest, or BI, transfer program, an individual created an irrevocable life insurance trust (referred to as an insurance trust or an ILIT), and the trust then purchased a life insurance policy insuring the life of this individual. The trust named the individual's spouse or one or more members of the individual's family as the trust's beneficiary or beneficiaries. Shortly after the life insurance policy was issued, each beneficiary sold his or her beneficial interest in the ILIT to a third-party buyer. These programs sought to avoid life settlement laws by selling interests in the entity that owned the life insurance policy, rather than selling the policy itself. In this way, a beneficial interest transaction allowed the interest in a policy to be sold before any two-year prohibition on the sale of a policy expired.

Under a business model referred to as an investor-initiated, stranger-initiated, stranger-owned or STOLI transaction, investors structured nonrecourse premium finance programs or other transactions designed to encourage individuals to take out life insurance policies that ultimately would be settled in the secondary market. As with beneficial interest transfer programs, an individual created an insurance trust, and the trust then purchased a life insurance policy on the life of the individual. The trust named the individual's spouse, one or more members of the individual's family, or in some structures even the participating investor (sometimes indirectly) as the trust's beneficiary or beneficiaries. To finance the payment of premiums on the life insurance policy, an investor would provide the insurance trust with a nonrecourse loan secured by the underlying policy or would otherwise fund the premium payment. Unlike beneficial interest transfer programs, the stranger initiated business model was not always intended to allow individuals to sell policies before the end of a two-year prohibition period. Rather, these programs were sometimes structured to make it economically difficult for the insurance trust to do anything but sell the life insurance policy to the premium finance lender or another party, because of high or spiking interest rates, restrictions on selling the policy to a third party, or other structural characteristics. Strongly opposed by life insurance carriers, stranger originated transactions drew the focus of regulators, who viewed these transactions as a way to circumvent state insurable interest laws.

There are situations in which there are legitimate estate and tax planning reasons for creating an insurance trust to serve as owner of a life insurance policy. For example, a high net worth individual may put her life insurance policy in an insurance trust in order to prevent the policy's death benefit from being included in her estate for purposes of calculating estate taxes. Although not addressed definitively in every state, recent trends in court decisions and in legislation support the notion that an insurance trust has an insurable interest in the life of its grantor.

However, as the volume of beneficial interest transfer programs and stranger originated transactions increased, some carriers began to become suspicious of life insurance applications in which the insured was a senior citizen and the applying policy owner was an insurance trust. As part of the application process, some life insurance carriers began requesting copies of the documentation creating the ILITs. Similarly, if an individual applying for life insurance indicated that they intended to finance the premiums for the policy, some life insurance carriers began to require that an insured deliver a personal guaranty or a minimum amount of collateral other than the life insurance policy to secure the loan. Requiring this additional collateral, referred to as the insured's "skin in the game," was viewed as a way to prove that the insured had a legitimate need for life insurance, rather than just a desire to sell the policy to an investor in a settlement.

In addition to the insurance carriers requiring that insureds put skin in the game in premium finance transactions, states issued "STOLI Alerts" informing consumers of the risks associated with stranger originated transactions.[12] Both the National Association of Insurance Commissioners (NAIC) and the National Conference of Insurance Legislators (NCOIL) began to consider amendments to their model acts involving life settlements, and states began looking at new legislation designed to prohibit transactions of the type described above.

Model Acts

To address the regulatory limitations revealed by the increasingly sophisticated life settlement marketplace, both the NAIC and NCOIL endorsed model acts in 2007.

The NAIC endorsed a model act, NAIC Act, that sought to deter STOLI transactions by increasing from two to five years the time period during which an individual is prohibited from settling a life insurance policy (with limited exceptions, one of which generally allows a life settlement after two years if the premiums during the first two years were paid from unencumbered assets, that is, not from the proceeds of a nonrecourse premium finance loan of the type discussed previously). The NAIC's goal in extending this prohibition period was to deter stranger originated transactions by making transactions like the two-year, nonrecourse premium finance programs less economically attractive.

Under the model act endorsed by NCOIL, the NCOIL Act, the period during which a life insurance policy cannot be sold remained at two years. However, the NCOIL Act contained a definition of STOLI designed to identify and prohibit two-year, nonrecourse premium finance programs seemingly designed to allow an investor to obtain a life insurance policy insuring the life of an individual in whom the investor has no insurable interest.[13] The NCOIL Act also expanded the definition of life settlement contract to include the transfer of beneficial interests in a trust. Presumably, the intent of this expanded definition was to prevent beneficial interest transfer programs of the type described previously.

To increase transparency in life settlement transactions, both the NAIC and the NCOIL Acts have required disclosures for providers and brokers involved in these transactions. Among other things, the disclosure provisions of these acts require that each broker participating in a life settlement transaction disclose to the settling policy owner the compensation that it receives in connection with the deal.[14] Under the NAIC Act, no later than the date a life settlement contract is executed, a broker must disclose the amount of the broker's total compensation for the transaction, and the method by which that compensation was calculated.[15] If a portion of a broker's compensation comes from a proposed life settlement offer, the NAIC Act requires disclosure of the amount and the method for calculating this compensation as well.

The NCOIL Act also requires that broker compensation be disclosed no later than the date a life settlement contract is executed.[16] Additionally, the NCOIL Act requires that a settling policy owner receive a reconciliation of the provider's gross purchase price as compared to the net proceeds received by the settling policy owner.

The volume of legislative activity that followed the introduction of the NAIC and NCOIL Acts was significant.[17] Some states that had no life settlement laws, or had laws regulating only viatical settlements, considered legislation based on the NCOIL or the NAIC Acts. Other states with existing life settlement laws considered replacing these laws with legislation based largely on one or the other of those two model acts. A third category of states considered adding a definition of STOLI based on the NCOIL Act into already existing life settlement laws. By July 31, 2008, 31 states had enacted life settlement legislation and state legislators were considering proposed legislation in at least 10 additional states.

Industry Litigation

Another public policy concern stemming from both the beneficial interest transfer and the stranger originated business models was the concept of the prearranged settlement of a life insurance policy. As noted previously, the initial purpose of life insurance as a financial product is to serve as a hedge against mortality risk. If, before a life insurance policy is even issued, the initial policy owner has prearranged the sale of the policy to a third-party investor, this policy is not being purchased as a hedge against mortality risk but as an investment vehicle.

Life insurance carriers and other opponents of prearranged life settlement transactions have argued that these transactions seek to allow individuals to achieve, indirectly, what a state's insurable interest laws otherwise prohibit. Stated otherwise, it has been argued that these transactions are structured solely to allow an investor to take out a life insurance policy on an individual in whom the investor has no insurable interest. Lawmakers and regulators typically have viewed prearranged life settlements as fraudulent. However, enacting effective regulation has proved difficult because in order to prohibit these transactions, a lawmaker or a regulator must determine an individual's subjective intent—specifically, why an individual is taking out a life insurance policy—during the time period that precedes the policy's issuance.

To combat prearranged life settlements, some states have adopted life settlement laws with provisions similar to those contained in the NCOIL Act that define, and then prohibit, these types of arrangements. Life insurance carriers also have sought to combat prearranged transactions by challenging the enforceability of life insurance policies allegedly issued in connection with a prearranged settlement. These claims have been brought on state insurable interest grounds. One life insurance carrier filed suit in federal court alleging that a policy was not enforceable because it was issued in connection with a prearranged settlement, and therefore violated Minnesota's insurable interest laws.[18] The court ruled against the carrier in granting a motion for summary judgment, finding that in order to prove a prearranged life settlement, the alleging party must establish both a willing seller (specifically, the initial policy owner) and a willing buyer (specifically, an investor) prior to the issuance of a policy.

Stalsberg v. New York Life Insurance Company[19] is another example of litigation in which a life insurance carrier filed suit in federal court during a life insurance policy's contestability period. In *Stalsberg*, the carrier alleged that a life insurance policy was unenforceable under Utah's insurable interest laws because the initial policy owner had a prearranged intent to settle the policy before the policy's issuance. This action has since been settled. In a recent complaint entered by AXA Equitable Life Insurance Company in the state of Florida, AXA, the issuer of five life insurance policies, sought not only rescission of the policies, which AXA claimed were fraudulent on various counts, but also to retain the premium payments on the rescinded policies.[20] In the state of New York, Phoenix Life Insurance Company, the issuer of three life insurance policies contested in a complaint by Alice Kramer, along with multiple counterclaims, cross-claims, and other third-party claims, filed a third-party claim alleging a violation of the Racketeer Influenced and Corrupt Organizations Act (RICO), 18 U.S.C. § 1962(c), by the life insurance broker, who allegedly solicited the policy owners to procure life insurance policies as part of a prearranged life settlement transaction.[21] If successful, the RICO allegations could entitle Phoenix to treble damages and to be reimbursed for its costs and attorney's fees relating to the litigation.

The Lobel decision—a summary judgment ruling delivered in the state of New York in connection with an allegedly prearranged life settlement—has generated much discussion in the industry because of its analysis regarding what constitutes a prearranged life settlement.[22] The facts behind the ruling referred to as the Lobel decision are as follows: A retired butcher named Leon Lobel created an insurance trust in order to purchase a policy insuring his life. Mr. Lobel was the named beneficiary of the trust. Six days after taking out the policy, Mr. Lobel sold his beneficial interests in the trust to an investor, and three weeks after these interests were sold, Mr. Lobel died. The investor brought suit against Linda Angel, Mr. Lobel's daughter and the executor of his estate, seeking a declaration that the investor was the rightful beneficiary of the trust. Ms. Angel asserted a counterclaim against the investor, arguing that because there was a prearranged sale before the policy existed, the policy was issued in violation of New York's insurable interest laws. The court denied the investor's motion for summary judgment, reasoning that if every fact Ms. Angel had alleged was true, the court could find that Mr. Lobel had the *intent* to sell the policy before it was issued, in violation of insurable interest laws.

Market participants have debated the Lobel ruling because of its emphasis on Mr. Lobel's subjective intent rather than on whether the objective facts support the conclusion that the sale was prearranged. However, at the very least, NCOIL's efforts to characterize beneficial interest transfers as life settlements, combined with litigation challenging the existence of insurable interest in these transactions (and a willingness of insurance carriers to litigate) has had a chilling effect on this business model.

Securities Law Analysis

The life settlement market has created an entirely new asset class available to the investment community.[23] As an investment, some life settlement structures are subject to federal securities regulation. In order for a life settlement to be subject to federal securities regulation, it must satisfy the characteristics of an investment contract under the Securities Act of 1933 and the Securities and Exchange Act of 1934.[24]

In determining whether a life settlement is an investment contract, courts have applied a three-part test, commonly referred to as the Howie test, which the Supreme Court of the United States adopted in 1946.[25] Applying the Howie test, a life settlement is an investment contract, and as such is subject to federal regulation as a security, if there exists an investment of money in a common enterprise and in which an investor's expectation of profits primarily depends on the efforts of others.[26]

Part one of the Howie test, the existence of an investment of money, is a rarely disputed element of a life settlement. Part two of the test, the existence of a common enterprise, can be satisfied in several ways. First, a common enterprise can exist if multiple investors are grouped together, and each investor has a fractionalized, undivided interest in the same life insurance policy. Courts have referred to this relationship as "horizontal commonality." Other courts have found the existence of a common enterprise where an investor's success is "dependent upon the success of the investment promoter's efforts to secure a return."[27] Courts have referred to this relationship as "vertical commonality." Part three of the Howie test can be satisfied if an investor's chances of receiving a profit from her investment primarily depend on someone else's skill (for example, a fund manager's ability to compile a successful stock portfolio), rather than on external market conditions (for example, a decrease in the market value of a commodity).

In *SEC v. Life Partners, Inc.*, 87 F.3d 536 (D.C. Cir. 1996), the D.C. Circuit Court found that part three of the Howie test was not satisfied unless an investment promoter provided skills on which the investor relied after the investor purchased a life settlement. The Life Partners court reasoned that, under the facts of that case, after a life settlement was purchased, an investor's expectation of receiving a profitable return on the investment did not depend on the investment promoter's skill or efforts (the court explained that the promoter performed only ministerial tasks, like paying premiums and tracking an underlying insured's health status), but rather on how long an underlying insured lived (which was akin to external market forces over which the investment promoter had no control).

Many courts have disagreed with, or drawn distinctions from, the reasoning of the Life Partners decision. For example, in *SEC v. Mutual Benefits Corp.*, a federal court in Florida found that an investment promoter's pre-purchase managerial activities could also satisfy part three of the Howie test. In the words of the Eleventh Circuit, which heard the Mutual Benefits case on appeal, "investment schemes may often involve a combination of both pre- and postpurchase managerial activities, both of which should be taken into account in determining whether Howie's test is satisfied."[28]

Under the facts of the Mutual Benefits decision, an investment promoter was responsible for locating life insurance policies for settlement, bidding on, and negotiating a purchase price for, each of these policies, obtaining life expectancy evaluations and drafting transaction documents for each deal. An investor would identify a preferred term for the investment and the promoter would select a life settlement with an underlying insured that had a life expectancy that, in the promoter's judgment, most closely fit the investor's preferred term.

The Mutual Benefits court found that while the timing of an insured's death is of critical importance, the profitability of an investment under this business model ultimately turned on whether the investment promoter's life expectancy evaluation, and the purchase price based thereon, was correct. In rejecting the "bright line" test adopted in the Life Partners decision, regarding whether a promoter's managerial skills took place before or after an investor's purchase of a life settlement, the Mutual Benefits court explained that courts should use flexibility and discretion in determining whether an investment should be characterized as a security.[29] The Eleventh Circuit subsequently affirmed the Mutual Benefits decision, and the Supreme Court declined to hear the case on further appeal.

A life settlement also will be characterized as a security under federal law if the life insurance contract being settled is a variable policy. A variable life insurance policy is a policy in which any cash surrender value that the policy accrues is invested in a portfolio of securities in an account separate from the assets of the issuing insurance carrier. In 2006, the National Association of Securities Dealers (NASD), a regulatory authority now known as the Financial Industry Regulatory Authority (FINRA), issued a statement (the "Notice to Members") expressly characterizing life settlements that involve variable life insurance policies as securities transactions that are subject to the securities laws.[30] The Notice to Members also sets forth some of the regulatory guidelines that will govern settlements of variable life insurance policies because of their status as securities.

As the Notice to Members explains, under NASD Rule 2310, a firm involved in the settlement of a variable life insurance policy must have a reasonable basis for believing that the transaction is suitable for the policy owner. A suitability analysis involves determining whether a life settlement makes sense for a policy owner in light of that person's financial status, tax status, investment objectives, and other relevant information.[31]

Suitability was the subject of much discussion in the life settlement marketplace in November 2007, when talk show host Larry King filed a lawsuit in connection with certain life settlement transactions in which he participated. Among other things, Mr. King's lawsuit alleged that, in advising him to take out and to subsequently sell certain life insurance policies, the named defendants failed to consider Mr. King's age, his health, or his family status (specifically, the fact that Mr. King had a young wife and minor children). The lawsuit also alleged that these defendants failed to consider the adverse tax consequences that stemmed from the transaction and the fact that Mr. King had other life insurance policies that may have been sold for a higher purchase price.[32]

The Notice to Members also stated that firms facilitating the settlement of variable life insurance policies have an obligation to perform due diligence on the life settlement providers and brokers involved in these transactions to determine what policies and procedures these persons or companies have adopted to protect the personal information of an insured.[33] A due diligence analysis includes determining what, if any, ongoing obligations an insured will have to provide notice of his or her health status after a settlement transaction has been completed. The Notice to Members suggests that firms should also consider developing lists of preferred providers and brokers based on their due diligence findings.

Firms facilitating the settlement of variable life insurance policies also are required to 1) meet the "best execution" obligations of NASD Rule 2320 (which includes finding the best deal for the consumer based on price, speed, and quality of execution, and reliability of the related market participants), and 2) train and supervise their associated persons to comply with applicable FINRA and SEC rules (including rules relating to compensation) when participating in a trade. The Notice to Members expressly states that price alone is not dispositive as to whether this test has been satisfied.

The Notice to Members ends with a broad statement that, in addition to life settlements involving variable policies, "NASD is also concerned about the involvement of NASD members and associated persons in the subsequent marketing and sale of interests in life insurance policies for investment purposes." These remarks have caused some market participants to question whether FINRA will move to characterize both variable and nonvariable life settlements as securities in the future.

NEXT STEPS FOR THE MARKETPLACE

A life settlement can provide benefits to a consumer because the transaction allows the consumer to unlock value from an unwanted or unneeded life insurance policy. A life settlement also can provide benefits to an investor because the transaction allows the investor to access an investment with a rate of return that does not track the performance of the capital markets. For these reasons, as the retiring baby boom generation produces an increasing supply of consumers willing to settle their life insurance policies in the secondary market, investors increasingly have moved to participate in this marketplace. Movement toward the creation of form documentation, best practices, and increased transaction transparency (specifically, transparency in disclosing the compensation agents, brokers, and other intermediaries receive in connection with a given transaction) may further reduce the transaction costs associated with life settlements and encourage investors to become more active in this industry.

In addition to offshore investment funds, which have been active investors for some time, institutional investors have begun to participate in the life settlements marketplace. In 2007, a group of large investment banks formed the Institutional Life Markets Association, Inc. (ILMA), a not-for-profit trade association formed to encourage the development of mortality- and longevity-related financial products, including life settlements and premium finance.[34] In addition to investment banks, there has been some evidence that life insurance carriers also are gaining interest in participating in the life settlement marketplace. For example, in 2007, Transamerica Life Solutions, LLC, was formed to "develop and offer innovative solutions for the life settlement marketplace," and in 2008, the Phoenix Companies, Inc., formed Phoenix Life Solutions, a life settlement provider.

The increasing number of market participants also has encouraged the development of new financial products and business models relating to life settlements. Several institutional investors have begun developing indices that track the lives of pools of individuals. As these indices evolve, these market participants are creating a "synthetic" life settlement market whereby investors buy financial products that deliver returns linked to these indices using derivative products.[35]

A number of exchanges, similar to a commodities exchange, are currently in operation, and more may be on the way. Although the volume traded through these exchanges has been limited, their development is relatively recent and the volume may increase over time. If the exchanges are successful, the nature of the life settlement industry is likely to change in significant ways. Currently, an investor in life settlements must establish a relationship with a life settlement provider, which sources policies for the investor through life settlement brokers. Only regulated states require that a licensed life settlement provider be involved in the transaction. However, even when transactions take place in unregulated states, life settlement providers usually are involved, because they provide access to life settlement brokers and, consequently, policies. If the life settlement exchanges reach their full potential, an investor will be able to purchase life settlements more efficiently, similar to the way in which an investor can currently purchase securities.

Access to investors through the capital markets would be expanded further if a life settlement securitization were to occur. However, several factors have contributed to the delayed arrival of securitizations based solely on settled life insurance policies. The inexact nature of life expectancy determinations has been among the obstacles faced by the rating agencies in attempting to achieve a sufficient comfort level with life expectancy predictions. Consequently, obtaining a rating on a pure life settlement pool (that is, a life settlement pool without the benefit of annuities or other external enhancements) has proved to be difficult. An insurance product that would insure against the longevity risk associated with life expectancy calculations would help give comfort to rating agencies evaluating a proposed life settlement securitization, but to date no such product has been widely accepted by the capital markets. Legal challenges facing a number of major life settlement industry participants also have slowed progress on the road to securitization. Nevertheless, securitization would provide a monetization strategy that has thus far eluded the life settlement industry and many believe that securitization presents the logical progression of the life settlement market.

CONCLUSION

A life settlement is the type of transaction that can provide the consumers of Main Street with the benefits of a secondary market ultimately funded by the capital markets. However, a life settlement is also a complex transaction that involves elements of insurance, tax, privacy, estate planning, consumer protection, and, in some cases, securities laws. As in other asset classes within the capital markets, regulators and market participants are charged with the task of developing public policy that will protect the consumer while allowing the industry to grow. In the meantime, it seems likely that the life settlement markets will continue to grow as they have in recent years—by developing new products, by adapting to new market participants and regulatory principles, and by growing new businesses that find ways to capitalize on the increased convergence between life insurance and the capital markets.

NOTES

1. Black's Law Dictionary defines cash surrender value as "The amount of money payable when an insurance policy having cash value, such as a whole-life

policy, is redeemed before maturity or death." See Black's Law Dictionary 1586 (eighth edition, 2004). To receive its cash surrender value, the policy owner must surrender the life insurance policy to the insurance carrier that issued the policy.

2. According to Conning Research & Consulting, Inc. "Life Settlements: New Challenges to Growth" (2008), approximately $12 billion in face value of United States life insurance was settled in 2007, and for the period from 2008 and 2017, it is estimated that average annual face amount of life settlements will be $21 billion.

3. If an individual retires earlier than expected, or lives longer than expected, a life settlement can also be a way to obtain cash for that individual to maintain his or her quality of life. For this reason, life settlements are sometimes referred to as a hedge against "longevity risk."

4. See *Grigsby v. Russell*, 222 U.S. 149, 156 (1911) (citing Stat. 14 George III., chap. 48).

5. See *Grigsby*, 222 U.S. 149.

6. See *Grigsby*, 222 U.S. at 155-156 ("The law has no universal cynic fear of the temptation opened by a pecuniary benefit accruing upon a death").

7. See *Grigsby*, 56 L. Ed. 133 lawyer's edition counsel headnote (quoting George T. Hughes).

8. The word viatical comes from the Latin word *viaticum,* which translates to "pertaining to a journey." University of Notre Dame, Latin Dictionary and Grammar Aid. Under the Catholic religious tradition, before beginning a dangerous journey, Roman soldiers were given a viaticum—the communion given to a dying person.

9. Despite this general terminology, some states have adopted legislation in which the terms "life settlement" and "viatical settlement" are used interchangeably. Over time, life settlements largely replaced viatical settlements as the preferred business model for market participants.

10. The National Association of Insurance Commissioners adopted its first viatical settlement act in 1993, which was amended in 2000 and in 2007.

11. Although laws vary by state, as a general matter, a life insurance carrier has a period of two years after a life insurance policy has been issued to challenge the policy's enforceability for reasons other than nonpayment of premiums or for certain types of fraud or misrepresentation. See John Alan Appleman, *Appleman on Insurance 2d*, Volume 29, Section 178.03, 2006, 120.

12. For an example, see Utah Insurance Commissioner Bull. 2006-3 (July 10, 2006). Specifically, these alerts explained that an individual can only obtain a finite amount of life insurance over a lifetime, and participating in a stranger-originated transaction could leave an individual without the ability to take out a life insurance policy at a time when he or she legitimately needs it. STOLI alerts also provided consumers with information about potentially adverse tax consequences associated with life settlements.

13. Stranger-Originated Life Insurance or STOLI is a practice or plan to initiate a life insurance policy for the benefit of a third-party investor who, at the time

of policy origination, has no insurable interest in the insured. STOLI practices include, but are not limited to, cases in which life insurance is purchased with resources or guarantees from or through a person, or entity, who, at the time of policy inception, could not lawfully initiate the policy himself or itself, and where, at the time of inception, there is an arrangement or agreement, whether verbal or written, to directly or indirectly transfer the ownership of the policy and/or the policy benefits to a third party. Trusts, which are created to give the appearance of insurable interest and are used to initiate policies for investors, violate insurable interest laws and the prohibition against wagering on life. STOLI arrangements do not include those practices set forth in Section 2L(2) of this Act. See Life Settlements Model Act § 2(Y) (2007).

14. In addition to compensation disclosure, under the NAIC and NCOIL Acts, providers and brokers are required to explain to settling policy owners (referred to as "viators" under the NAIC Act and "owners" under the NCOIL Act): 1) the existence of alternatives to a life settlement contract, 2) the period of time (if any) that a settling policy owner has to rescind the life settlement contract after the policy has been settled, and 3) the broker's fiduciary duty to the settling policy owner.

15. Viatical Settlements Model Act §§ 8(C)(4) & (5) (2007).

16. Life Settlements Model Act §§ 9(C)(4) & (5) (2007).

17. As a general matter, the insurance industry placed its support behind the NAIC Act and its five-year prohibition on the sale of financed policies; and brokers, providers, and institutional investors supported the NCOIL Act and its two-year prohibition.

18. See *Sun Life Assurance Company of Canada v. Paulson*, 2008 U.S. Dist. LEXIS 11719, aff'd, 2008 U.S. Dist. LEXIS 99633. See also *First Penn-Pacific Life Ins. Co. v. Evans*, 2007 U.S. Dist. LEXIS 45112, *aff'd*, 2009 U.S. App. LEXIS 3921.

19. See *Stalsberg v. New York Life Insurance Company*, 2007 WL 2572396 (D.Utah).

20. See *AXA Equitable Life Insurance Co. v. Infinity Financial Group*, complaint docketed, No. 08-80611 (S.D. Fla. June 6, 2008).

21. See *Kramer v. Lockwood Pension Services, Inc.*, answer to complaint docketed, No. 08-02429 (S.D. N.Y. April 9, 2008), answer to amended compliant docketed, No. 08-02429 (S.D.N.Y. May 29, 2008).

22. See *Life Product Clearing LLC v. Angel*, 530 F. Supp. 2d 646 (S.D.N.Y. 2008).

23. Because the return on an investment in a life settlement does not necessarily track general market conditions, life settlements sometimes are referred to as an "uncorrelated" asset class.

24. See *SEC v. Mutual Benefits Corp.*, 323 F.Supp.2d 1337 (S.D. Fla. 2004).

25. See *SEC v. W. J. Howie Co.*, 328 U.S. 293 (1946).

26. *Id.*

27. See *Mutual Benefits*, 323 F.Supp.2d at 14.

28. *Id.* at 15.

29. "Such an approach has the corresponding advantage ... of permitting the SEC and the courts sufficient flexibility to ensure that those who market investments

are not able to escape the coverage of the Securities Acts by creating new instruments that would not be covered by a more determinate definition." See *Id.* at 20 citing *Reves v. Ernst & Young*, 494 U.S. 56, n.2.

30. *Life Settlements*, NASD Notice to Members 06-38 (August 9, 2006).

31. *Id.*

32. See *Larry King v. Alan Meltzer*, CV07-06813 (C.D. Cal), (Compl. docketed 10/22/2007). The life settlement transactions at issue were completed pursuant to a beneficial interest transfer program. The *King* complaint also alleged that the agents participating in these transactions benefited from substantial fees and commissions that were not disclosed to Mr. King at the time of the sale.

33. See generally, NASD Notice to Members 03-71: NASD Reminds Members of Obligations When Selling Non-Conventional Investments (Nov. 2003). The issue of privacy is particularly sensitive in the field of life settlements because a person's confidential information, such as medical history and other medical information, can potentially be disclosed.

34. Founding ILMA members included Bear Sterns & Co., Inc., Credit Suisse, Goldman Sachs & Co., Mizuho International plc, UBS AG, and WestLB AG. In 2008, ILMA membership expanded to include EFG Bank International and J.P. Morgan Chase & Co.

35. The International Swaps and Derivatives Association has considered developing form documentation to be used in connection with mortality- and longevity-related derivative products.

CHAPTER 17

Regulatory Issues and Insurance Company Reaction

George J. Keiser
National Association of Insurance Commissioners,
House of Representatives R-North Dakota

The emergence of viatical settlements in the mid-1900s resulted in a dramatic paradigm shift in the life insurance industry. The cornerstone of the traditional life insurance model had been and remains "insurable interest." The recognition that an insured, suffering a terminal illness, might choose to sell his policy to investors to generate immediate income changed the dynamics of life insurance forever. The insurance industry's subsequent development of cash surrender values for some of its life insurance products is one example. The recognition that life insurance policies might have a cash value on the open market had begun.

Initially, the viatical settlement business model was unregulated with minimal oversight. However, within a relatively short time, legislators and state insurance regulators began to receive feedback from consumers and life insurance companies regarding some of the early viatical industry practices. Constituents complained that they were not adequately informed about the tax implications, the commissions paid to agents or brokers or whether they were receiving the best settlement offer. Additionally, fraudulent practices like "clean sheeting" were being identified.

State policy makers quickly became engaged in the viatical arena and began to create laws to address identified problems in the viatical settlement industry. Transparency, disclosure and marketing began to be regulated through the creation of viatical model legislation developed at the state level.

Insurance companies were concerned about the emerging viatical settlement market because it did alter the traditional actuarial model for life insurance. They recognized that investors purchasing life insurance policies had deep pockets and were not likely to let policies lapse thereby guaranteeing a full settlement. With AIDS as the predominant terminal disease driving the early viatical market, policies that had been issued to relatively young people who were paying lower premiums and who suddenly and unexpectedly developed a short life expectancy created an investment opportunity. With rising medical costs, generally lower incomes, difficulty maintaining employment, and fewer beneficiaries, it could be reasonably anticipated that this population might well have higher lapsation rates on their policies. Instead, by not allowing their policies to lapse but rather selling them to a group of investors, they generated necessary immediate income for living expenses, medical bills, and expendable income.

Eventually, with regulation and oversight, the viatical model became accepted in addressing the needs of terminally ill policyholders. This general acceptance provided policy makers a brief period of tranquility. In the early 2000s, as the viatical settlement market matured, agents, brokers, and investors recognized that life insurance policies of nonterminal, relatively healthy individuals might also be of significant financial value to the insured as well as their beneficiaries. Within a short period, the viatical settlement business model evolved into the life settlement business model we have today.

Once again, legislators and regulators were drawn into the debate. Insurance companies registered concerns regarding potential abuses. Their publicly stated and principal concern revolved around STOLIs or stranger-originated life insurance policies. From a policymaker's, regulator's, and insurance company perspective, STOLIs were a clear violation of the insurable interest principle. There is general consensus within the life insurance and life settlement industries that STOLIs need to be addressed and eliminated through legislation. The moral hazard implications of STOLIs are obvious. Beneficiaries who would pay premiums but have little or no relationship with the insured may not place the same value on maintaining the insured's life. In addition, STOLIs would dramatically alter the underlying principle of why people historically had purchased insurance, and if allowed to continue would clearly erode existing actuarial underwriting models.

The impact on lapsation rates resurfaced during the STOLI debates. Although there are various proprietary underwriting models for life insurance, it is reasonable to assume that those models assume an expected lapsation rate that, in turn, would be factored into the pricing structure. Insurance companies expressed concern that STOLIs would likely reduce lapsation rates and thereby increase the overall costs of life insurance resulting in higher premiums for the consumer.

Although STOLIs were the publicly expressed concern of insurance companies, the impact of life settlements on lapsation rates would seem to be the larger, more important issue. Obviously, an expanding legitimate life settlement industry would result in a more significant reduction in the lapsation rate of life insurance policies.

One of the maxims of representing a constituency, whether elected or appointed, is that the public is always looking for action when problems are identified. Legislators and regulators have a political need to do something. Stranger-originated life insurance provided a near perfect cause for regulators and legislators to become engaged, solve the problem, and demonstrate that they were providing protection to the public. In addition, anything that might cause the cost of premium rates to increase was a concern for policy makers.

However, an interesting thing happened on the way to finding a statutory solution to STOLIs. Everyone, people in the life settlement industry, the life insurance industry, consumer protection groups, regulators, and legislators all strongly opposed STOLIs. However, as rules and statutory solutions were being developed, the discussion frequently extended beyond STOLIs and began to involve and impact life settlements.

Working with the life insurance and life settlement industries, two groups, the National Association of Insurance Commissioners (NAIC) and the National Conference of Insurance Legislators (NCOIL) began to address STOLIs by developing model bills that states could use or modify as each state began addressing the STOLI issue. The two approaches were very different. The NAIC's model used an indirect approach. The focus of the NAIC approach was on transfer of ownership, method of premium financing, and increasing the contestability period for insurance companies from two to five years. The NCOIL model takes a more direct approach. It defines STOLIs, strengthens transparency, makes STOLIs a fraudulent act, and provides a penalty for engaging in the illegal practice.

Prior to considering the NCOIL and NAIC models in greater detail, it is important to recognize that policy development in the life settlement industry is currently extremely dynamic and that the models presented at this time represent a static snapshot of policy statements as they exist today. One would fully expect both models, the NCOIL and NAIC, to evolve in the immediate future.

NAIC MODEL

Transfer of Ownership

The NAIC model requires brokers and providers to disclose to insurance companies any specific plans or transactions to engage in the business of viatical or life settlements during the first five years of a policy. Although well intended, by focusing on the transfer of ownership using a viatical or life settlement, the NAIC model creates a significant loophole that could in effect legalize STOLIs. For instance, what if there is no viatical or life settlement transaction wherein ownership is transferred? Does a trust, in which the insured owns 5 percent or 10 percent or a limited percentage of the trust and investors own a relatively large majority of the trust pass the anti-STOLI test, given that the trust owns the policy from day one? Can limited liability partnerships, limited liability companies, or other business models be used to circumvent the transfer of ownership issue? The NAIC model failed to address the use of trusts, LLCs, LLPs, or other models as they apply to STOLI.

Method of Premium Financing

Traditionally, people purchased insurance using their own money or, in the case of key man policies, the corporation's money. This provided insurance companies with a certain degree of actuarial comfort and for a very long time made a two-year contestability period reasonable. In today's world, there are a variety of reasons that the policy owner might wish to use an alternative financing method to make premium payments. For example, a person with high net worth combined with low liquidity might wish to find a different means of paying premiums. Eventually, recourse and nonrecourse models of financing developed and worked their way into the life insurance market. These alternative methods of financing, especially nonrecourse financing, caused a great deal of actuarial discomfort within the life insurance industry and raised several questions. What are the suitability criteria to determine if either form of financing is appropriate? Are insurance companies allowed to obtain appropriate information from the prospective insured if financing suitability criteria can be identified? Insurance companies expressed concern about recourse financing but more directly about nonrecourse financing as a vehicle that would contribute to the creation of STOLIs.

Contestability Period

Rather than address STOLIs directly, the NAIC model again used an indirect approach. It simply extended the contestability period from the traditional two years to five years. It was generally believed that the extension would decentivize investors wishing to engage in STOLI transactions.

The extension of the contestability period from two to five years also had a significant impact on the legitimate life settlement industry and brought focus to the debate over the policy owners' property rights versus the insurance companies' rights of contestability. For all intents and purposes, the extension transferred ownership back to the insurance company for an additional three years if an owner, for whatever reason, had wanted to sell the policy. The life insurance industry has strongly supported the contestability extension from two to five years. It obviously would have a chilling effect on investors who might be inclined to participate in STOLIs. At the same time, it also reduces the interest of investors to participate in legitimate life settlement transactions.

The effect on investors is obvious. More important from a policy perspective is what is the effect on the policy owner? The extension creates an additional three-year period wherein there will be little interest by investors in purchasing an owner's policy or at best the policy might be sold during that three-year period but at a significant discount in the policy's value. From the owner's perspective, the three-year contestability extension is of dubious value.

The NAIC recognized, in part, the owners' rights by adding to their model six exceptions wherein the five-year contestability period would in effect be waived. The six NAIC exceptions are:

1. The owner or insured is terminally or chronically ill (the traditional viatical model).
2. The owner's spouse dies.
3. The owner divorces his or her spouse.
4. The owner retires from full-time employment.
5. The owner becomes physically or mentally disabled.
6. Bankruptcy.

These exceptions, again well intended, provide a group of options for circumventing anti-STOLI regulations and the mechanism by which the policy was financed. First, the exceptions raise questions regarding timing. Does the two-year contestability period still apply to life settlement transactions if the insured can qualify for one of the exceptions? Second, do they unintentionally legitimize STOLI? It appears that the exceptions in the NAIC model do both. For example, if an individual was approached with a proposition to use premium financing to purchase a policy and subsequently retired six months or one year later, could that individual utilize a life settlement contract or STOLI? Although generally unintended, exceptions to rules frequently create opportunities to circumvent the intent of the rules. One last concern with the exceptions found in the NAIC model is specific to the owner's spouse dying. Although infrequent, there are a large number of cases where family members have been charged and convicted of murder to collect insurance benefits. This exception clearly extends the risk of moral hazard in a new direction. The death of one's spouse would provide the opportunity to access cash available through a life settlement transaction.

Extending the contestability period from two to five years has been strongly supported by the life insurance industry and broadly opposed by the life settlement industry. Although the contestability extension was designed to limit STOLIs, it by itself does not eliminate them. And, as has been argued, the exceptions found in the NAIC model, may in fact increase STOLI-like transactions.

However, the contestability extension would dramatically impact the legitimate life settlement industry. It is arguable whether that was the primary motivation within the life insurance industry. As mentioned earlier, life settlements are changing the life insurance paradigm. Investors are not likely to let purchased policies lapse. The option of receiving a payment greater than the cash value of a policy will lead to changes in the decision process people use when purchasing life insurance.

Other limitations of the current NAIC model are failure to define STOLI and a lack of a penalty clause for people engaging in the practice. The NAIC model also expanded the insurance regulators' role into the securities domain. From a policy perspective, it is imperative that we create a regulatory system that is continuous but which defines a bright line that differentiates insurance regulation and securities regulation thereby preventing dual regulation, unnecessary costs, and potential disagreements between regulators. The negative reaction to the NAIC model expressed by securities regulators seems appropriate. One can only wonder what insurance regulators' reaction would be if security regulators began developing model bills that included insurance products in addition to securities.

The National Conference of Insurance Legislators (NCOIL) took a direct approach in developing its statutory model to control STOLIs. First, the group defined STOLI as follows:

> *Stranger-Originated Life Insurance or STOLI is a practice or plan to initiate a life insurance policy for the benefit of a third-party investor who, at the time of policy origination, has no insurable interest in the insured. STOLI practices include but are not limited to cases in which life insurance is purchased with resources or guarantees from or through a person or entity, who, at the time of policy inception, could not lawfully initiate the policy himself or itself, and where at the time of inception, there is an arrangement or agreement, whether verbal or written, to directly or indirectly transfer the ownership of the policy and/or the policy benefits to a third party. Trusts that are created to give the appearance of insurable interest and are used to initiate policies for investors, violate insurable interest laws and the prohibition against wagering on life. STOLI arrangements do not include those practices set forth in Section 2L(2) of this Act.*

The NCOIL definition of STOLI has several key components that need to be recognized. First, it is limited to the origination period of a policy thereby applying to STOLI directly without interfering with legitimate life settlement transactions. Second, the definition addresses insurable interest by recognizing that a policy "originated for the benefit of a third-party investor, who at the time of the policy origination has no insurable interest in the insured" is by definition a STOLI. Third, STOLI arrangements can be verbal or written, to directly or indirectly transfer ownership . . . to the benefit of a third party. Fourth, the definition directly addresses "trusts that are created to give the appearance of insurable interest." By incorporating trusts in this form, in the STOLI definition, the NCOIL model closes the NAIC model loophole that only defined policies where ownership was transferred as potential STOLIs.

Defining STOLI is a first step in attempting to eliminate the practice. The NCOIL model goes further by making it a violation of the statute "for any Person, Provider, Broker, or any other party related to the business of life settlements to commit a Fraudulent Life Settlement Act." The model then states that a person committing a fraudulent life settlement act is guilty of committing insurance fraud. Making STOLI a fraudulent act brings the regulatory and civil sections of existing state insurance codes into play providing regulators authority to revoke licenses and impose civil penalties when appropriate.

The NCOIL model places a strong emphasis on transparency by requiring appropriate disclosure by the broker to insurance companies and to the policy owner. Brokers are required to disclose all life settlement purchase offers and any affiliation or contractual arrangement the broker has with an entity making an offer and disclosure related to the compensation of the broker. The NAIC model contains the same disclosure requirements.

However, the two models differ significantly on required disclosures to the insurer. The NAIC model requires brokers and providers to disclose to insurance companies any specific plans or transactions to engage in the business of viatical or life settlement during the first five years. Again, note that trust ownership of a policy from its inception would require no notification.

The NCOIL model makes clear that:

- Insurance companies may inquire in the application about the owner's method of financing premiums, including whether the owner intends to pay premiums using financing from a lender that will use the policy as collateral.
- Permits insurance companies to reject the application based on the chosen method of financing premiums.

■ Permits insurers to require certification from brokers, agents, and owners that the applicant has not entered into an agreement to sell the policy at a later date.

Under the NCOIL model, life insurance companies are clearly granted the authority to determine whether they wish to enter into a policy. Providing the required information creates a more level playing field for life insurance companies and their underwriters. It allows companies an informed choice without diminishing the policy owner's rights of ownership.

There are two other important differences between the NAIC and NCOIL models. First, the NAIC model requires a provider and a broker to demonstrate evidence of financial responsibility in the amount of $250,000, whereas the NCOIL model does not include a provision requiring a provider or broker to post bond. The NAIC financial responsibility requirement appears to have a limited negative impact on smaller population states, where the small number of transactions may not warrant the additional cost of the bond. For instance, in North Dakota, some agents and brokers have requested that their licenses be cancelled as a result of the bond requirement.

The second difference between the two models is that the NCOIL model allows the owner to rescind the contract on or before 15 days after it is executed whereas the NAIC model provides a longer recision period.

Where do we go from here? The STOLI debate and the life settlement debate have not ended. It is in the middle innings of a nine-inning game. Exhibit 17.1 summarizes the current status of legislation within the states relative to STOLI/life settlements.

There is certainty that the next legislative cycle will have significantly greater statutory activity directed at STOLIs and life settlements. In addition, NCOIL and the NAIC will actively continue to address policy issues that arise out of the legislative process. Exhibit 17.1 suggests that states are choosing the NCOIL model, the NAIC model, or a blended model, which is frequently the five-year contestability provision from the NAIC model added to the NCOIL model. However, at this point, both model bills are performing as designed in that each state is taking its preferred model and adapting it to its individual policy perspectives.

As the debate goes forward, there are four basic principles that should be considered by all interested parties. First, the principle of insurable interest is a cornerstone of the life insurance industry and must be maintained and protected to ensure the integrity of life insurance underwriting. The life insurance industry and the life settlement industry have a vested interest in guaranteeing the validity of insurable interest is maintained. Without insurable interest, life insurance becomes a security.

EXHIBIT 17.1 Current Status of Legislation within the States Relative to STOLI/life Settlements

State	Bill	Language Source	Current Status
California	SB 124	NCOIL	Set, first hearing. Failed passage in committee, 06/23/008
District of Columbia	B17-0294	NCOIL 2001 Version	Public hearing held on 06/04/08
Illinois	SB 2358 HB 4941	NCOIL NAIC	Senate Floor Amendment No. 2 Re-referred to Rules, 07/01/08 Re-referred to Rules Committee, 05/31/08
Massachusetts	HB 1052 HB 932	NAIC Investor Initiated Life Insurance study bill	House accompanied a study order, 04/09/08 House accompanied a study order, 04/09/08
New York	AB 1169-B SB 8593 AB 7265 SB 8007 SB 7356 AB 10401	NCOIL NCOIL LICONY NY Ins. Dept. proposal NY Ins. Dept. proposal LICONY	Ordered to third reading, 06/24/08 Referred to insurance, 06/18/08 Re-referred to Insurance, 04/04/08 Advanced to third reading, 05/28/08 Referred to Insurance, 03/27/08 Referred to Insurance, 04/28/08
Arizona	SB 2513	NCOIL	Signed by Governor Napolitano, 05/23/08
Connecticut	HB 5512	NCOIL integrating into current law	Signed by Governor Rell, 06/12/08
Hawaii	HB 94	NCOIL	Signed by Governor Lingle, 06/16/08
Indiana	HB 1379	NCOIL	Signed by Governor Daniels, 03/21/08
Iowa	SF 2392	NAIC	Signed by Governor Culver, 05/09/08
Kansas	HB 2110	NCOIL	Approved by Governor Sebelius, 04/21/08

(*Continued*)

EXHIBIT 17.1 (*Continued*)

State	Bill	Language Source	Current Status
Kentucky	HB 348	NCOIL	Signed by the Governor Fletcher, 04/09/08
Maine	LD 2091	NCOIL	Signed by Governor Baldacci, 04/02/08
Nebraska	LB 853	NAIC	Approved by Governor Heineman, 07/18/08
Ohio	HB 404	NAIC with additional provisions	Signed by Governor Strickland, 06/11/08
Oklahoma	SB 190	NAIC	Signed by Governor Henry, 05/19/08
	SB 565	Draft Amends SB 1980	Signed by Governor Henry, 05/23/08
West Virginia	SB 704	NAIC	Approved by Governor Manchin, 03/14/08
Alabama	SB 534	NCOIL	In Senate. Read first time and referred to Banking and Insurance Committee, 03/25/08
	HB 759	NCOIL	In House. In Banking and Insurance Committee, 03/27/08
Georgia	SB 499	NCOIL	House Second Readers, 03/11/08
Hawaii	SB 3246	NCOIL	The committee on CPH deferred the measure, 02/07/08
	SB 3021	NAIC	The committee(s) recommends that the measure be deferred, 03/18/08
	HB 3099	NAIC	Referred to HLT, CPC/JUD, FIN, referral sheet 7, 1/25/08
Iowa	SF 2385	NCOIL	Referred to Commerce, 04/02/08
Louisiana	SB 380	Initially NCOIL. Final version was NAIC. NAIC/NCOIL controls elements of both	Failed to pass committee, 04/30/08
	SB 247		Died in Committee on Insurance, 03/31/08

(*Continued*)

EXHIBIT 17.1 *(Continued)*

State	Bill	Language Source	Current Status
Minnesota	SB 3495 SB 3063 HB 3878	NCOIL NAIC	Referred to Commerce and Labor, 03/06/08 Referred to Commerce and Labor, 03/06/08 Introduction and first reading, referred to Commerce and Labor, 03/06/08
New York	SB 5447 AB 8507	LISA LICONY	Re-referred to Insurance, 04/25/08 Referred to Insurance, 01/09/08
Rhode Island	HB 7442-SUB A SB 2603-SUB A	NCOIL NCOIL	Vetoed by Governor Carcieri on 07/02/08 Vetoed by Governor Carcieri on 07/02/08
Washington	SB 6631 HB 3067	NCOIL	Public hearing held, 01/31/08 Passed to Rules Committee for second reading, 02/06/08
Vermont	HB 819	NAIC	First reading, referred to Commerce Committee, 02/05/08

Second, life settlements provide a legitimate business model that under certain conditions provide a desirable solution for the policyholder. Although it is important to strike a proper balance between the rights of an insurance company and the property rights of the policyholder, the policyholder's rights should be given significant weight provided that the insurable interest provision is met.

Third, transaction transparency must exist. Policy owners, insurance companies, and life settlement companies must be given the authority to obtain the information necessary to make an informed decision as to selling a policy, initiating a policy, or purchasing someone's policy. The policy owner is generally in the weakest position to understand all of the relevant information in making their decision. State policies should be explicit and detailed as to what information is required to be available for the consumer to make an appropriate and informed decision. In contrast, the burden of responsibility for gathering information should fall more to the life insurance companies and life settlement companies. As professionals working in their respective industries, policy makers need only make certain they, life insurance companies, and life settlement companies have the authority necessary to access the information they need to properly underwrite their decisions.

Finally, life settlements may reduce the nonrenewal rate, which could increase costs for insurance companies and in turn drive the cost of policies generally upward. However, there are two alternatives that are equally likely to occur. By eliminating STOLIs and providing adequate transparency, proper underwriting can occur and the impact on premium rates would be minimized. Also, the potential future use of a life settlement contract may add value to the inclusion of life insurance in an individual's overall financial plan and thereby result in a decision to increase the amount of coverage in one's policy, which in turn could dramatically increase premium dollars.

In closing, I would ask you to answer one question. What is the policy or law regarding STOLIs and life settlement in your state of residence (would your answer have been the same without reviewing Exhibit 17.1)? If you, a person interested and engaged in this issue can't answer that question, then what chance does the general public or your legislator have of being informed about these policy questions? Too often, individuals in an industry choose not to be informed or involved in the policy decisions that directly affect them. The assumption is that someone else is going to address it. I'm obviously too busy to be involved. Be careful, the quality of the policy that is developed may be directly proportional to the level of your participation.

CHAPTER 18

Tax Implications

Micah W. Bloomfield
Partner, Stroock & Stroock & Stroock & Lavan LLP

U nder the Internal Revenue Code of 1986, as amended the "Code," U.S. federal taxation of the holders of life insurance policies is something of a mixed bag. Although the Code provides specific guidance regarding a number of issues, with respect to other issues it either doesn't provide guidance or, if it does, it is unclear how that guidance applies in some circumstances.

In this chapter, we discuss both the issues for which the Code provides clear guidance, and those for which it does not, with particular emphasis on those provisions of the Code that may apply to insurance policyholders who do not acquire their policies directly from the insurance company (that is, secondary market purchasers).

But first, some basics.

Life insurance policies are subject to very favorable treatment if the right conditions are met. For example, there is no federal estate tax if the beneficiary of the policy is not the estate of the decedent, and the decedent did not possess incidents of ownership with respect to the policy. See Section 2042 of the Code. To make sure that the insured does not possess incidents of ownership, the policy can be held by a trust that meets certain requirements with respect to its terms and with respect to the identity of the trustees (which is why most life policies are held in a trust). Life policies that are structured so as not to constitute modified endowment contracts (known as MECs), as defined in Section 7702A of the Code, provide another important tax benefit: a holder of a life policy that is not a MEC can borrow from the insurance company using the buildup in the policy's value and not pay a tax on the receipt of that cash.

A particularly important benefit of life insurance is that, in most cases, death proceeds are not subject to income tax, provided that the owner of the policy did not purchase the policy from a prior holder and is not otherwise treated as a transferee for value. See Code Section 101.[1] Even a transferee for value, however, has certain tax benefits. First, even though the policy's value likely is, and its cash surrender value may be, increasing, the transferee for value need not accrue any of that increase as income during the life of the policy. Second, the income it recognizes on receipt of death proceeds from the insurance company is reduced by the amount it paid for the policy, the premiums it paid after acquiring the policy, and any of its interest expense that has been disallowed under Code Section 264(a)(4). See Code Section 101(a)(2).

Not only is the deduction of interest on debt that is attributable to life insurance policies disallowed, in most cases, under Code Section 264, but Code Section 264 also disallows the deduction of premiums paid with respect to insurance policies. These are serious issues for any secondary market purchaser, particularly a purchaser who wants to borrow to purchase life policies. Some possible ways of dealing with the interest deductibility issue are discussed in the following section.

OPEN ISSUES CONCERNING CHARACTER, BASIS, AND SOURCE

Despite the explicit statutory rules dealing with life insurance taxation, there are some fundamental issues that the Code either does not address, or as to which the Code does not provide clear guidance. Among these issues are: 1) the character of any gain on a sale of a life policy (as ordinary income, capital gain, or a mixture of both); 2) the tax basis of a policy in the hands of a holder and whether that basis differs when computing gain on a sale compared to loss on a sale; and 3) the source of income arising from the payment of death proceeds, which is particularly relevant for a foreign holder of a life policy.[2]

Character

Gain that is recognized on the sale of most property that is not inventory is treated as capital gain, and is subject to the favorable treatment (that is, lower tax rates) for individual taxpayers if the property was held for more than a year. See Code Sections 1221 and 1(h).[3] However, in the case of life insurance, various court cases have held that the gain, to the extent of any buildup of cash surrender value in the policy, is taxed as ordinary income.[4] Although the matter is not certain, based on the tax principles that apply with respect to all property, it would seem that any additional gain, over and above the cash surrender value, should be capital gain. However, although some have argued for a similar result for the receipt of death proceeds or surrender of a contract to the insurance company, because such receipt or surrender does not involve a sale or exchange, the transaction should not give rise to a capital gain or loss.[5]

Basis

When determining gain or loss on a sale, it is important to know the taxpayer's basis in the property, since the gain or loss is measured by the difference between the sale proceeds and the tax basis. See Code Section 1001. The Code, as noted previously, provides that even a transferee for value is entitled to reduce his gain from the receipt of death proceeds to the extent of his purchase price plus his premiums. As a matter of parallelism, one would think that premiums should give rise to basis when determining the gain on a sale of a policy. However, Code Section 264(a)(1) disallows a deduction for premiums paid if the taxpayer is directly or indirectly a beneficiary under the policy, and it would seem inconsistent to allow a taxpayer to receive a deduction for his premiums indirectly by adding the amount paid in premium to his basis.

One way to harmonize the statutory provisions would be to allow a basis increase when determining gain but not allow a basis increase when determining loss. The same could apply to interest that is disallowed under Code Section 264: it might be added to basis for determining gain but not loss, although we have found no authority for that result. That the addition of premiums to basis is not inconsistent with Code Section 264 is confirmed by a revenue ruling the IRS issued in 1970, which held that a domestic corporation that purchased life policies on its officers, naming itself as beneficiary, did not have to include the proceeds of a sale in income when it sold the policies to the officers for less than the amount of the premiums. See Rev. Rul. 70-38, 1970-1 CB 11.

It does appear, however, that a loss would be allowed in the unlikely event that the amount received on a sale is less than the cash surrender value. See *Cohen v. Comm'r*, 44 BTA 709 (1941). See also the much criticized case of *Forbes Lithograph Mfg. Co. v. White*, 42 F. 2d 287 (D. Ct. Mass. 1930), which allowed the taxpayer a loss equal to the full difference between the premiums paid and the amount received on surrender of the policy. The IRS is of the view that basis must be reduced for the cost of insurance protection, and that generally the cost of insurance protection can be estimated as the total premiums less the cash surrender value of the policy. See PLR 9443020; ILM 200504001.[6] This was set out explicitly in a revenue ruling, but the ruling has been made obsolete. See Rev. Rul. 55-257, 55-1 CB 428, obsoleted, Rev. Rul. 72-621, 72-2 CB 651. Several court cases have also held that basis is reduced by the cost of insurance protection, but they have done so only in the context of measuring losses. See, for example, *Keystone Consolidated Publishing Co. v. Comm'r*, 26 BTA 1210 (1932), which disagrees with the holding of the Forbes Lithograph case; *London Shoe Co. v. Comm'r*, 80 F. 2d 230 (2d Cir. 1935)(policy surrendered); *Century Wood Preserving Co. v. Comm'r*, 69 F. 2d 967 (3d Cir. 1934)(sale of polices).

Source

Another area of uncertainty is the determination of the source of life policy proceeds on the death of the insured, although the IRS has indicated its view of the matter.[7] The source rule is particularly important for a foreign holder that is not engaged in business in the United States. This is because the United States taxation of a foreign person generally depends on: 1) whether the income is effectively connected to a business the foreign person has in the United States, 2) whether the income is "fixed or determinable annual or periodical" income (known as FDAP), and 3) whether the income is treated as from United States or foreign sources. Unless a tax treaty provides otherwise or the taxpayer is engaged in business in the United States and the income is effectively connected with that business, United States source FDAP is subject to a 30 percent withholding tax.

In Rev. Rul. 2004-75, the IRS determined that withdrawals by a foreign person from the cash values of a life policy issued by a U.S. life insurance company are both FDAP and from U.S. sources, and thus subject to 30 percent withholding tax. It reached its conclusion regarding source by analogy to dividends and interest paid by U.S. corporations. Although contrary arguments can be made, it is likely that proceeds of a life policy (except to the extent excluded from gross income under Code Section 101) would also be treated as FDAP and from U.S. sources, at least if the insured was a citizen or resident of the United States.

The situation differs radically in the case of a sale of a life policy. In that case, it is clear that the income is not FDAP.[8] The gain only would be subject to tax if it is effectively connected with a United States business, whether or not it is from U.S. sources.[9]

STRUCTURES TO DEAL WITH LIMITATION ON INTEREST DEDUCTION

A number of different structures have been created to deal with the interest deduction limitation of Code Section 264. One structure is for a limited partnership or LLC to acquire the life policies, using funds generated through the issuance of preferred partnership interests, not borrowed funds. Amounts equivalent in many respects to interest are allocated to and paid on those partnership interests. If the partnership is obligated to make payments with respect to these interests without regard to the partnership's earnings, the payments likely would be treated as guaranteed payments under Code Section 707. Guaranteed payments are in many respects treated in the same manner as other expenses (unlike allocations of income), and consequently the IRS might have a somewhat better argument that those payments should not be deductible than if the payments were limited to the income of the partnership.

An alternative structure is for a foreign corporation to purchase the life policies. The income of the foreign corporation generally will be included in the income of U.S. stockholders on a current basis, either as Subpart F income of a controlled foreign corporation (a CFC) or as income of a passive foreign investment company (PFIC), although some have made the argument that gain from the sale of a life policy is not Subpart F income and holding the policies does not cause a foreign corporation to be a PFIC.[10] Interest incurred by the foreign corporation to acquire the policies would be disallowed under Code Section 264(a), but no provision of the Code disallows the expense for purposes of determining the foreign corporation's earnings and profits. The income inclusion under Subpart F and the PFIC rules is based on earnings and profits and consequently is reduced by interest expense.

One risk with using a foreign corporation to hold life policies is that payments on the policies generally would be subject to a 30 percent withholding tax on FDAP, as noted above. However, the 30 percent withholding tax may be eliminated under the provisions of various tax treaties, which can apply even when the beneficial owners of the foreign corporation are U.S. citizens or residents. See, for example, the double tax treaties between Ireland and the United States and between Luxembourg and the United States. However, it is important to satisfy the limitations of benefits clause of the relevant treaty.

Another risk is that the foreign corporation may be engaged in a trade or business in the United States. If it is engaged in a trade or business in the United States through a permanent establishment, then even with an applicable treaty, the corporation will be subject to taxation at normal corporate rates and may be subject to a branch profits tax. Careful planning is required to make sure that the activities of the corporation's agents do not give rise to a permanent establishment.

LOAN PROGRAMS: VARIATIONS ON A THEME

Some persons have acquired a significant share of the economics of a life policy either by making loans to the purchasers of the policies or by providing credit support to owners who wish to borrow to pay the premiums on their policies. One benefit of making a loan rather than acquiring ownership of a life policy is that the limitations on the deductibility of interest contained in Code Section 264 do not apply to loans.[11]

Loan programs have their own tax opportunities and risks. For example, a foreign corporation originating loans in the United States may be treated as engaging in a trade or business in the United States, and thus subject to net income and branch profits tax, if any nonministerial activities are conducted in the United States. Loans likely will also be subject to the split dollar regulations contained in Treas. Reg. Section 1.61-22 and 1.7872-15.

The split dollar regulations, finalized in 2003, deal with life policies in which more than one person has an interest. Thus, they can apply to a life policy owned by either an employer or an employee, in which both the employer and the employee have an economic interest. They also apply when one person owns the policy and another person has lent money secured by the policy. The basic thrust of the regulations is to enable the parties to determine in a formalistic manner which of them will be treated as owning the policy (it is generally the person listed as the owner on the policy itself). The other party's payments generally are treated as a loan of money by the nonowner if the nonowner has advanced money to the owner or to the insurance company and a reasonable person would expect to be repaid in full (whether or not repayment is with interest and whether the advance would be treated as a loan under general tax principles). If the payments are not treated as a loan of money, then they are treated as the provision of an economic benefit from the nonowner to the owner. The split dollar regulations by their terms can apply outside of the employer-employee context, and their use of formal ownership rules can occasionally lead to unexpected results.

TAX LEGISLATION AND FUTURE DEVELOPMENTS

Congress has been concerned about the purchase of life insurance by persons or entities with no insurable interest in the insured. In 2006, it added Code Section 6050V, which requires that an information return be filed with the IRS when, among other requirements, a charity has an interest in a life insurance policy. The form to be used to make this information return is Form 8921. Section 6050V expires in September 2008. The legislation also required that the IRS report on the use of charities as beneficiaries of life policies by March 2009. Given the increase in the purchase of life policies in the secondary market, and the expected issuance of reports by the New York State Bar Association and the IRS, it is likely that the proper tax treatment of at least some of the open tax issues will be clarified in the next few years.

NOTES

1. There is an exception from the income exclusion in the case of most employer-owned life insurance. See Code Section 101(j), added by the Pension Protection Act of 2006. It should also be noted that not all policies issued by a life insurance company will qualify for favorable treatment. The policy must satisfy the definition in Code Section 7702, which generally is designed to make sure that the policy is distinct from an investment contract.

2. For good discussions of some of these issues, see "Vulture Capital Tax Manual—A Brief Guide to the Tax Issues Associated with Financial Investments in Life Settlements," 6 *Journal of Taxation of Financial Products*, issue 3, page 37 (2007); unpublished Tax Club article "Life Settlements: Some Thoughts on an Unsettled Subject," James A. Guadiana, February 13, 2008. On December 5, 2008, the Tax Section of the New York State Bar Association issued a report on the taxation of life settlements entitled "Report on Investor-Owned Life Insurance."

3. Similarly, loss on a sale of such property generally is capital loss, which has an unfavorable tax treatment.

4. See Gallun v. Comm'r, 327 F. 2d 809 (7th Cir. 1964) (ordinary income under assignment of income cases, for sale of life policy for cash surrender value); Crocker v. Comm'r, 37 TC 605(1962). Cf. First Nat'l Bank of Kansas City v. Comm'r, 309 F.2d 587 (8th Cir. 1962) (sale of annuity policy); Comm'r v. Phillips, 275 F. 2d 33 (4th Cir. 1959) (endowment policy).

5. Those who make this argument cite Code Section 1234A and TAM 200452033 (which held that 1234A did not apply to the extent amounts received for the surrender of a policy were attributable to ordinary income accretions to the value of the policy). As has been pointed out by a number of commentators, Section 1234A should not apply to a contract that references a person's life, rather than property. See also Code Section 72(e).

6. Arguably supporting a basis increase only to the extent of an increase in cash surrender value is Treas. Reg. Section 1.264(a)-4(d) (capitalizing insurance cost to the extent of cash surrender value increase).

7. See Rev. Rul. 2004-75, 2004-2 CB 109, amplified Rev. Rul. 2004-97, 2004-2 CB 516; ILM 200646001 (Aug. 14, 2006).

8. See Treas. Reg. Sections 1.871-7(b)(1) and 1.1441-2(b) (gains derived from the sale of property generally excluded from FDAP).

9. For the definition of effectively connected income, see Code Section 864 and the regulations thereunder.

10. The argument is that life policies do give rise to income, but not interest, dividends, rents, or royalties, and hence do not give rise on their sale to foreign personal holding company income. See Code Section 954(c).

11. It should be noted, however, that if the loan advances are funded by an annuity on the insured's life, the Code Section 264 limitations can apply with respect to interest on amounts borrowed to fund the annuity.

Ethical Issues

The Ethics of Profiting from Mortality

Professor David Blake
Director, The Pensions Institute, Cass Business School

Dr. Debbie Harrison
Senior Visiting Fellow, The Pensions Institute[1]

Desk Research Sponsored By:
Deutsche Bank
EFG International
Goldman Sachs
The Royal Bank of Scotland

In this chapter, we review the ethical issues surrounding life settlements with reference to our own desk research and to the reports that have been published over the past six years on the U.S. life settlement market; in particular reports from A.M. Best, Bernstein, and Wharton, and also the regular coverage of the market in *Life Settlements Report* (*LSR*).[2]

One of the potential barriers to the growth of the life settlement market is the question of whether it is ethical to profit from betting on when someone will die. Clearly those with a religious or personal objection will not want to do this and, provided investor transparency is achieved (see below), it should be possible for such investors to avoid an inadvertent indirect investment.

Religious objections apart, it must be emphasized that since the eighteenth century, when life insurance began, there has always been a concern about the distinction between insurance and gambling or speculation.

Arguably, the life insurance and annuity industries are based on "gambling on life" through the pooling of mortality and longevity risks. In the case of term life insurance, those who live longer than anticipated cross-subsidize those who die young, while with annuities, the reverse is true. Similar principles apply to general insurance: policyholders whose houses burn down are cross-subsidized by policyholders whose houses do not. However, general insurance does not seem to raise the same ethical concerns as life insurance and annuities, despite the underlying principle of risk pooling being the same.

Mortality projections are a critical feature of a wide range of financial products: life insurance, defined benefit pension plans, annuities (individual and bulk), and equity release plans, among others. It can be argued that pension plan sponsors gain from the early deaths of plan members and pensioners, as do annuity providers. By contrast, providers of term insurance gain when individuals live longer than the age at which their cover ends. These are well-established markets and concerns over "betting on mortality" have generally only arisen in very minor cases, where, for example, a specific religious objection arose to compulsory annuity purchase in the U.K. Furthermore, it can be argued that there is a significant difference between betting on when a named individual will die and transactions linked to the realized mortality experience of large pools of anonymous individuals.

The U.S. life settlement market began when investors identified and responded to a simple problem: the lack of liquidity in life insurance products. They recognized that the surrender values on life policies offered by monopsony life companies are well below the prices that could be offered in a traded market, while still leaving an attractive, albeit not risk-free, profit for the life settlement company. Without this mutual buy-side and sell-side opportunity, it is very unlikely that the life settlement market would ever have got off the ground. The secondary market, therefore, corrects a market inefficiency. Correcting market inefficiencies is not regarded as an ethical issue in other markets, and there is no obvious reason why it should be any different in the case of life settlements, provided the market adheres to recognized standards of best practice (see below). Further, there is the view that secondary market liquidity might actually help the primary market to grow, since prospective policyholders can see that they do not need to be tied to maintaining a long-term policy that is no longer required if their requirements change.

Importantly, the life settlement market is in the vanguard of the new Life Markets—the global markets that are developing to trade mortality- and longevity-linked securities and derivatives. Lessons learned in the life settlement market could well help to speed up and improve the development of the wider Life Markets, which might have positive implications for pension plans and their beneficiaries.

THE FAIR TREATMENT OF POLICYHOLDERS

From the ethical point of view, it can be argued that potential sellers of life policies should understand clearly that a third party will benefit from their death. The most sought-after policies appear to be those owned by older people, who have shorter expected life spans of, say, three to four years. However, these are also the individuals whose dependants might have most to lose when a policy is sold. This suggests that the availability of affordable and genuinely independent advice for such policyholders is an important issue for regulators and investors concerned about the ethics of distress sales. In addition, best practice might highlight the importance of gaining the approval of the beneficiaries of the life policies being sold. We understand that this practice is already well established but *LSR* has reported legal cases where beneficiaries did not appear to have been informed of the transfer of a policy that was held in a trust but which had been taken out under a "stranger-originated life insurance" STOLI arrangement, where seniors are offered a loan or even paid ("premium financing") to take out whole life policies with the intention of selling them to investors.

For a well-regulated market, it is also necessary that policyholders behave reasonably or ethically when they arrange a sale. For this reason, it is important that the concerns about STOLI and premium financing are more widely understood and disseminated to policyholders. Naturally, life insurance companies will be very concerned if individuals taking out a policy are engaging in what they might regard as some kind of deception, where the insured's intention is to sell the policy to an investor as soon as possible. If, in the meantime, policyholders are receiving funding from the investor in order to cover the cost of premiums, they are implicated, albeit perhaps unwittingly, in STOLI arrangements.

STANDARDS OF BEST PRACTICE AMONG INTERMEDIARIES

Almost without exception, the independent research reports on the life settlement market and the fortnightly *LSR* publication raise concerns about poor sales practices, which might imply poor policyholder protection and/or misrepresentation to investors. Currently, STOLI practices are under review by insurers and legislators. *LSR* cites U.S. legal cases where relatives have complained when the proceeds of a policy have been paid to a life settlement company on the death of the policyholder.[3] Such cases are made more complex where the policy is held in a trust and where the trust is established by the investor or a related trustee company.

To avoid such practices, it is becoming more common for insurance companies to ask specifically on the policy application form whether the individual intends to sell the policy. This is a difficult point to contest if the policyholder says he does not intend to sell, as it is possible that such a change of mind genuinely could have been made after the policy came into force. However, where, prior to the policy being taken out, an investor has made money available to the individual to cover the cost of premiums in return for the right to buy the policy at a later date, then premeditation on the part of the policyholder would seem to be evident. These are complex legal issues for the U.S. courts to determine and also will depend on a state-by-state view of the specific legal definition of what constitutes insurable interest.

From the end investor's perspective, the outcome of such litigation (and any future changes in regulation), will be important, as this might affect the return on the policies held in a portfolio if, subsequently, an irregularity in the original purchase emerges and the insurance company contests a claim. Bernstein says this is a critical issue for the market, and, if not addressed, could lead to litigation on the part of investors in life settlement funds, who were led to believe they would achieve higher returns than experienced.

Given the immaturity of the market, it is not yet possible to assess the impact of such cases on the investor's return, as consistent long-term performance data are largely unavailable. The synthetic markets could potentially provide an alternative solution for investors because they make it possible to avoid direct exposure to life insurance policies.[4]

TRANSPARENCY FOR INVESTORS

The maxim "only invest in products you understand" highlights an important aspect of the life settlement market for end investors. While we can see that the label "death bond" does not provide positive promotional copy—particularly in the retail market—nevertheless it is critical that investors understand that the death of policyholders creates their return and that a higher than expected return might be a direct result of early deaths.[5] Therefore, promotional material from the investment manager or insurance company and also any sales practices on the part of intermediaries, must bear this important point in mind. If they do so, this will help to preempt any future claims of ignorance on the part of investors who, with hindsight, might have chosen a different asset class due to ethical concerns.

Equally, it is important that direct investors and also investors in collective funds are able to see process and cost transparency from the origination of the policy—where the rights to the benefits are transferred from the policyholder to the life settlement company or intermediary—through to the point where they invest.

A further critical factor for investors is the reliability of the life expectancy (LE) report on which policy purchases are based. When a policy becomes available, the life settlement company frequently requires two independent medical reports to assess life expectancy in order to determine the purchase price offered. The medical reports contain a summary of pertinent health issues, including the primary disease or condition if relevant, and a prediction of life expectancy. It is important for the life settlement company—and the end investor—to know that reliable and up-to-date mortality tables are used and that the medical examiner's methodology for calculating any adjustments for health conditions is sound. The most common table used by medical practitioners is a version of the 2008 VBT (Valuation Basic Table).

Clearly, longevity risk—known as extension risk in the industry—is a major issue for investors in life settlements and this risk is compounded where the medical reports underestimate life expectancy based on known facts about the policyholder's medical history and also where they use overly optimistic mortality assumptions. An underestimate of one or two years in a portfolio based on insureds with an estimated life expectancy of between 3 and 15 years could significantly alter the potential profits. A.M. Best, in its September 2005 report, analyzed the problem of the potentially systematic underestimation of mortality.[6] The research showed that maturities (deaths) for a portfolio of insureds constructed five years previously were not in keeping with the medical reports provided at the time. In its March 2008 report A.M. Best notes that in recent years medical examiners appear to have been issuing more conservative mortality estimates, although there are still significant variations where medical reports are issued on the same policy and these range from 2 to 24 months.

CLEAR AND CONSISTENT REGULATION

In 1996, following concern over viatical settlements, the U.S. Securities and Exchange Commission (SEC) endeavored to regulate the viatical market under federal securities law. It was unsuccessful, but nevertheless individual states began to introduce their own regulations. This point is important and worth stressing: *at the time of writing, life settlements were not formally classed as securities and the life settlement market was not regulated at the federal level in the United States.*

Some, but not all, states have specific life settlement regulation in place. The National Association of Insurance Commissioners (NAIC), which represents all 50 U.S. states, has issued model regulations for life settlements. According to Bernstein, by 2005, 36 states had implemented some form of regulation, including minimum payout levels as a percentage of the policy's face value. A second feature of life settlement regulation, where it is in place, is that policyholders are required to wait two years after taking out the policy before selling it to a third party.

The licensing of sales agents or brokers is less consistent. In about 15 states, agents with standard life insurance licenses can arrange sales of policies in the secondary market. But the absence of this license extension in other states does not prevent transactions taking place. Furthermore, the agents or brokers might or might not be registered with insurance regulators, depending on the state in which they are based.

It is important to note that the regulation of the market is being reviewed by many states. For example, according to a February 2008 report in *LSR*, Ohio, in a bid to eliminate STOLI practices, has adopted a five-year waiting period before life insurance policies can be settled (sold on) and it has imposed a new requirement for life settlement companies to register with the state insurance department. In the same edition, *LSR* reports that the Indiana State House of Representatives had tried to implement similar legislation, but that this appears to have been stalled, partly due to the opposition of the life settlement companies.

The imposition of a five-year waiting period would make STOLI practices, where they are combined with premium financing, far less attractive. There would be a much greater likelihood that the policyholder might die before the investor acquires the policy and can sell it on, in which case the investor will have paid the premiums but the death benefits would go to the deceased's family.

Wharton points out that most of the consumer concerns over life settlements have arisen in the viatical market and that there have been relatively few incidents where fraudulent practices in the life settlement market have affected policyholders. It also reports that reputable life settlement companies are self-regulating and refers to the proactive work in this area of the Life Settlements Institute (LSI), which is a nonprofit trade group supported by several major institutionally-funded life settlement providers and financiers.[7]

In 2002, the LSI began to build an antifraud database for companies to share information about suspicious or fraudulent activity by policy sellers, brokers, medical practitioners (see below), and other parties to the transaction process. The LSI has argued that life settlements should be classed as securities to ensure that the market complies with the Federal Securities Act of 1933. In its conclusion, the Wharton report (page 38) expresses the concern that life insurance companies might be attempting to obstruct the development of the secondary market in various ways that interfere with the policyholder's rights to assign their policies to a third party:

> *In this paper, we have demonstrated that a competitive secondary market for life insurance policies improves the welfare of both new and existing policyholders. It is therefore in the interests of lawmakers to develop regulations that protect the interests of consumers and investors in the secondary market. Because participation and investment in the secondary market for life insurance policies is pro-competitive, lawmakers should design regulations that encourage, rather than dissuade, such participation or investment.*

As a final point about regulation, according to a report in the *Wall Street Journal*, regulators are concerned that certain brokers buying policies for life settlement companies have "manipulated the bidding process for policies by submitting fictitious bids in exchange for compensation from other players in the market."[8] Such practice could have a very adverse effect on both sellers and buyers of life policies.

We end this section with a list of requirements for a well-regulated market derived from A.M. Best's March 2008 report on the life settlement market, "Life Settlement Securitization":

- Increased clarity and standardization of the general methods for predicting life expectancy of the insured, including the release of data on the performance of medical examiners.
- Transparency in the pricing of life settlements.
- Transparency in the fees earned by intermediaries involved in the transactions.
- Effective data protection safeguards on the part of the life settlement industry with reference to personal details, including the identities, health conditions, and financial status of the original policyholders.
- Effective industry regulation and oversight, including self-policing.
- The establishment of credit rating agency standards for assessing the credit risks associated with life settlement transactions.

CONCLUSION

In the light of the analysis in this chapter, we would argue that best practice in the life settlement market in respect of ethical and regulatory considerations should meet the following standards.

The direct consideration of the ethics of mortality-linked assets as part of the investor's ethical or SRI strategy: Provided that products and processes are transparent, private investors can choose whether to invest in the life settlement market in accordance with their personal views and beliefs. Institutional investors should, however, consider the ethics of the asset class in relation to any socially responsible investment (SRI) strategy that is in place. Given the youthfulness of this asset class, institutional investors might need to review their existing SRI principles to consider if these principles should include provisions relating to life settlements. Disclosure might be an important issue where the institution invests on behalf of private individuals, such as pension plan members or charities, for example.

The fair treatment of policyholders: Transparency is an important issue in relation to policyholders, who must understand that a third party will benefit from their death. The availability of independent advice, which can explain alternative ways of raising capital, is crucial here, particularly if insurance companies develop alternatives to life settlements, such as loans against the policy, repayable on death. Best practice might indicate that policyholders should be required to inform beneficiaries before arranging a sale.

Policyholders should also behave ethically and this requires them to provide accurate information to insurance companies about any STOLI and premium financing arrangements.

The fair treatment of end investors: The regulation of STOLI practices is also relevant for investors, who might suffer if cases are contested and the expected benefits are paid to the deceased's family rather than to the investor's fund. Additionally, transparency in pricing and in the intermediary processes are important safeguards for investors, as is consistency in the assumptions used for life expectancy reports, on which the purchase price of policies are based. In particular, the LE predictions used in pricing policies should be unbiased estimates of true life expectancy and the providers of LE reports should be regularly assessed for the accuracy of their predictions.

Clear and consistent regulation: The analysis made by A.M. Best in its March 2008 report appears to be very thorough and its recommendations appropriate. The company argues for increased clarity and standardization of the methods for predicting life expectancy, including the release of data on the performance of medical examiners; transparency in the pricing of life settlements; transparency in the fees earned by intermediaries; policyholder data protection; effective self-regulation; and the establishment of credit rating agency standards for assessing the credit risks associated with life settlement transactions. To this list, we would add the need for consistent regulation and legislation across all 50 U.S. states, which would enhance market efficiency and improve market reputation.

Synthetic life settlements: For the investor, synthetic life settlements avoid the problems and time involved in building portfolios of physical life policies. This has clear advantages in terms of cost reduction. However, as with physical portfolios, great care is (or should be) taken over the assessment of the LE reports. Synthetics might also permit investors to eliminate exposure to some of the non-longevity risks embodied in policy-based transactions. Such risks include: documentation risk, "portfolio lumpiness," regulatory concerns, administrative burden, crossborder tax risk (for non-U.S. investors), ramp-up risk, insufficient numbers of lives, and carrier credit risks.[9]

The impact of the secondary market on insurers' profitability and pricing: It is too early to predict with any certainty what the impact of the secondary life insurance market will be on the primary market. We note that there might be an adverse impact for certain insurers with a high exposure to the primary market, where the profit margin is eroded due to a reduction in the anticipated percentage of lapses, which currently is about 6 percent annually, although the rate varies by carrier, product type, age, and duration.[10] However, it might be the case that interest in life insurance increases as a result of the development of the secondary market, which creates liquidity for policyholders previously trapped by a monopsony. It is also the case that insurance companies are likely to innovate to compete with life settlement companies by improving surrender values and/or offering alternatives, such as a loan against the policy value, which would be repayable on the policyholder's death. In both cases, consumers would benefit indirectly from the existence of the life settlement market, although we note that if insurance companies improve surrender terms this could reduce the availability of policies for sale in the secondary market.

In addition to the prospect of innovation on the part of insurance companies, a consequence of the very public focus on U.S. whole life insurance policies is that prospective policyholders and their advisors, where applicable, might decide that it would be simpler and, possibly, cheaper to meet protection and investment requirements separately through a combination of term insurance policies and investment plans.

Although the secondary market for life settlements is in its infancy and the synthetic products market is barely out of its swaddling clothes, both might grow very rapidly and therefore it is in the interests of legislators, regulators, and all participants to keep a very close eye on developments and to work toward standard regulation of the market in all U.S. states. If this can be achieved, then ethical issues should cease to be a significant concern and a well-regulated and transparent life settlement market will provide greater liquidity for life insurance policyholders and a welcome new asset class for investors. It will also provide a firm foundation for the development of the wider Life Markets.

NOTES

1. This chapter is drawn from a Pensions Institute report, "And death shall have no dominion: Life settlements and the ethics of profiting from mortality," published in July 2008 (http://pensions-institute.org/DeathShallHaveNoDominion_Final_3July08.pdf).
2. "Life Settlement Securitzation," A.M. Best, March 2008, www.ambest.com/debt/lifesettlement.pdf, hereafter referred to as A.M. Best; Suneet Kamath and Timothy Sledge, "Life Insurance Long View: Life Settlements Need Not Be Unsettling," Bernstein Research Call, March 2005, www.bernsteinresearch.com, hereafter referred to as Bernstein; Neil A. Doherty and Hal J. Singer, "The Benefits of a Secondary Market for Life Insurance Policies," Wharton School, October 2002, www.coventry.com/pdfs/wharton.pdf; Life Settlements Report (www.dealflowmedia.com), hereafter referred to as Wharton.
3. See, for example, *LSR*, February 21, 2008 (www.dealflowmedia.com).
4. Synthetic exposure to policies via a total return swap or a structured note might permit investors to eliminate certain risks inherent in life insurance policies such as carrier credit risk, regulatory risks, and so on. Some dealers apparently have begun to issue transactions linked to the realized longevity of older-age people without reference to policies at all.
5. The description "death bond" appeared in a headline in the *Wall Street Journal* on February 21, 2007. However, understandably, the term is not used by the industry.
6. "Life Settlement Securitization," A.M. Best, September 2005.
7. www.lifesettlementsinstitute.com. Apart from the LSI there is also the Life Insurance Settlement Association, which has a broad-based membership of some 175 companies (www.lisassociation.org).
8. *WSJ*, May 2, 2006.
9. "Portfolio lumpiness" arises when a portfolio consists of a small number of large policies: it can lead to poor portfolio diversification. "Ramp-up risk" occurs during portfolio or fund construction when life settlements (or indeed any asset) are acquired one-by-one over a period of time. The risk is that the investor does not acquire enough policies (assets) to provide a sufficiently diverse pool of exposure, that is, the portfolio does not ramp up enough.
10. Source: Insurance Information Institute (www.iii.org).

Synthetic Longevity Assets—A Primer

Jonathan T. Sadowsky
Managing Director of Finance/Portfolio Manager
Browndorf PEM, LLC

Matthew C. Browndorf, Esq.
Chief Investment Officer Browndorf PEM, LLC

INTRODUCTION

Any investor schooled in the life settlements space is fluent in the inherent specific risks and costs associated with investing in physical policies, such as STOLI (stranger-originated life insurance), rescission, insurable interest, contestability, underwriting fraud, and carrier credit risks to name a few. The advent of synthetics serves to mitigate all of these risks and physical policy costs for the investor in exchange for swap counterparty risk, which is easier to quantify, manage, and hedge, in addition to allowing the investor to target his risk characteristic profile more accurately and efficiently.

In general, a derivative is a financial contract or security whose value is derived from an underlying asset, in this case a life settlement policy. The two main functions of a derivative are for risk transfer, for example in hedging strategies, and to obtain the economics of a physical asset without having to hold said asset, such as in speculation and arbitrage strategies.

Specifically, a synthetic longevity asset is a bilateral financial contract that isolates longevity risk of a specified portfolio of policies and transfers that risk from one party to another. In doing so, synthetic longevity instruments separate the ownership and management of longevity risk from other qualitative aspects of ownership of the physical life settlement asset, such as legal and other policy-specific risks and costs. Such risk transfer mechanisms serve to both increase the efficiency and liquidity of the longevity asset markets as a whole.

TYPES OF SYNTHETICS

There are many ways to obtain longevity risk through synthetics, from swaps to notes to indexes. The beauty of synthetics is the investor is not constrained by the limits of the current physical policy supply in the marketplace, only by the creativity, modeling capacity, and risk appetites of the parties involved. The underlying risk structure can be anything from the mortality of an entire nation, which would reflect the systematic mortality trend of a population (beta or macro longevity risk), to that of an index with 46,000 lives, to a customized portfolio of lives selected by the investor (specific, micro, or alpha longevity risk). The synthetic can be structured such that it emulates the economics and cash flows of a physical portfolio of policies, or as a pure longevity-linked note whereby no cash flows occur until the note's maturity as it is based on the observed mortality experience of the pool over the investment time horizon.

The first main type of synthetic product is the swap, where two counterparties agree to exchange streams of cash flows based on a prearranged set of information or formulas, be they set fixed amounts or variable amounts based on certain conditions, like underlying life insurance policies and maturing lives.

The most basic longevity swap acts like a pass-through instrument where the swap buyer is obligated to pay to the swap seller a predetermined set of premium payments based on the agreed upon underlying portfolio of policies and active lives, and the swap seller pays the buyer the death benefits as they occur. Upfront leverage and built-in premium financing are available depending on investor objectives, market conditions, and the swap counterparty's appetite for offering such products. This product is ideal for those investors who want to replicate the cash flow stream of a physical portfolio and collect income if death benefits outpace premiums in a given period.

For those investors who do not want or need interim cash flows during the life of the investment, they can buy a longevity-linked note whose underlying portfolio acts like an index product decreasing in value as premiums are owed and increasing upon constituent maturities. The initial index value is usually set at par and the final index value at the note's maturity, which usually ranges from one to ten years depending on the investor's objectives, determines the final payout amount.

Hybrid structures are also available such as notes whose returns and cash flows are based on actual mortality experience as opposed to policy cash flow based. These generally pay a fixed amount per mortality, subject to a cap and floor on the number of mortalities, and provide the investor with a smoother return profile. The fixed amount paid per life maturity takes into account the expected mortality models, premiums, financing and death benefit sizes. Other structures such as longevity options and swaptions can also be created.

In addition, unlike physical policies, the return distribution structure can be customized using synthetics depending on the investor's needs, in formats such as total return, fixed coupon, fixed tenor, or principal protection structures.

ADVANTAGES OF SYNTHETICS OVER PHYSICALS

The following table discusses in detail a number of the many advantages synthetics have over investing in physical policies from efficiency of capital deployment to risk mitigation to portfolio construction flexibility and customizable diversification. While this is a pretty comprehensive list, the main theme is that the synthetic product has the ability to target exactly the risks and economics that a longevity investor wants and avoid the ones he doesn't. The ability to tailor the product exactly to the investors' needs and objectives in an efficient manner is the biggest benefit synthetics provide over physicals.

Description	Physicals	Synthetics
Portfolio selection and construction	Purchase of individual policies on the open market: very time consuming, expensive and inefficient. Difficult to construct a portfolio with the exact desired risk characteristics.	Negotiated deal between buyer and seller where lives and all risk characteristics are highly customizable and trade is done quickly and efficiently. Longevity risk and desired cash flows can be targeted and constructed to suit the investor's objectives.
Diversification of lives	Usually 20 to 100 per portfolio but depends on portfolio size and current market supply. The more	Regardless of portfolio size, diversification is highly customizable from 100 to 46,000 lives. Most

(Continued)

(*Continued*)

Description	Physicals	Synthetics
	lives, the harder it is to find and analyze.	portfolios will have about 500 to 1,000 lives depending on risk characteristics desired.
Ramp-up risk for $100 million	Could take 3–9 months. Larger amounts harder to put to work and still get quality assets.	Synthetic deals take days depending on complexity of term sheet. Unlimited scalability and deal size while still obtaining quality assets.
Portfolio lumpiness risk	Can be large as it is dependent on the current supply of policies in the marketplace. Very difficult to build a physical portfolio with equal notionals.	Can be completely mitigated by structuring the synthetics with equal notional amounts per life.
Negative selection risk	Can be large as it is dependent on the current supply of policies in the marketplace.	Small due to huge portfolio diversification available with synthetics on day one.
Carrier credit risk	Physicals are directly exposed to carrier credit risk. Very difficult and expensive to hedge the exact entity and part of the capital structure policy claims fall in.	Synthetic buyers have the option to take on carrier credit risk for higher yields but are not obligated to.
Other nonlongevity risks	Physicals have all the well known risks, including: legal, rescission, insurable interest, contestability, documentation, underwriting fraud, settlement, administrative, regulatory, reputational, tracking, and crossborder tax risks.	Synthetics have swap counterparty risk only, which is more easily quantified, managed, and hedged than physical policy risks. All other policy risks are held by the swap counterparty.
Unwind liquidity	Very low due to large amount of due diligence needed to sell a portfolio of policies. But there are	Very high. As with most derivative instruments, the swap seller will almost always show an unwind

(*Continued*)

Description	Physicals	Synthetics
	numerous sources to go to, which is a positive. A decent size portfolio could take three to six months to find a buyer, which is not ideal if the seller needs to raise capital or stop the negative cash flow due to premiums.	price. The discount to full market value will depend on portfolio construction as they have to replace that risk and will pass that cost along. Due to deal customization, the swap is difficult to assign to another party, thus the original seller is usually the only unwind option.
Premium financing	Currently capital for premium financing is very hard to find and if found is extremely expensive, if not cost prohibitive. Also, due to current market conditions, future death benefits alone are not sufficient collateral, thus requiring additional assets to be pledged.	Premium financing can be built into the synthetic structure. Due to the lower internal cost of capital of the swap counterparties, the premium financing cost is usually lower than traditional hard money sources of funds.
Pricing risk for investors	Due to the illiquid nature of the physical asset and the current lack of mark-to-market rules, investors in funds that only hold physical assets are subject to extreme uncertainty about the true value of their assets.	Like all OTC derivatives, they are required to be marked-to-market at regular intervals (at least monthly) based on the latest models and market information. Swap counterparties valuation models are very sophisticated.
Leverage	Very difficult to obtain leverage in physical policies. Would require lenders accepting these assets as collateral for a loan, which is not common in today's markets.	Upfront leverage is available in the synthetic instrument depending on certain factors including market conditions and swap buyer counterparty risk.

(*Continued*)

(*Continued*)

Description	Physicals	Synthetics
Risk directionality	A physical-only investor can only go short longevity risk (benefitting when constituents mature sooner than expected).	A synthetic investor can go both long and short longevity risk on any portfolio from a customized portfolio to a large index to a nation's mortality.
Policy costs	Large. The operational, servicing, and administrative costs as well as legal and underwriting due diligence are very costly and can eat into returns very quickly and are usually not factored in when buying, so high initial IRRs are not realized.	None. The initial IRR calculated when the swap purchased will come to fruition as long as the realized mortalities equal the expected mortalities.
Policy purchase fees	Brokerage and settlement fees that can get onerous.	None.

UNDERLYING LIVES OF THE SYNTHETIC ASSET

Physical policy purchasers are restricted to the policies sold in the life settlements market, which severely limits their ability to construct a portfolio having the exact risk profiles they desire. The life settlement market is a subset of the insurable population who for whatever reason chose to sell their policies. The insurable population is a subset of the entire population.

Synthetic instruments are flexible in that they can be written with the underlying being an entire nation's population, a large index of policyholders, a customized portfolio of lives, or even "reference lives," people who have given the swap seller permission to underwrite them medically and track their lives without having an actual life insurance policy written on them. The dynamics and risk characteristics of each population subset are very different and need to be analyzed and modeled differently. But the ability of synthetics to target any of the above subsets gives the investor a very powerful tool to target his longevity risk where he has a need or sees value.

This ability to customize the pool of lives is also very valuable to hedgers as they can minimize the basis risk associated with reference pool mismatches. For example, a pension fund that is trying to hedge its longevity risk needs to structure the synthetic hedge to as closely match its constituent's profile as possible. Hedging the possibility of pension liability extension with a swap based on either the mortality of the entire United States population or a pool of only 100 lives doesn't make much sense.

VALUATION OF SYNTHETIC ASSETS

The basic skeleton to valuing a synthetic is exactly the same as valuing the underlying asset, a life settlement policy. For this description, which will be brief because it is covered elsewhere in this book, I will assume we are discussing a synthetic swap that replicates the economics of a physical portfolio of policies. While death itself is a certainty, the mortality rate is anything but. For all synthetic longevity instruments, the foundation of asset valuation is the modeling of the underlying mortality curves and the resulting expected probability of mortality for a life (or portfolio) over time.

With the maturation of life settlements markets, more advanced pricing models have been developed. Most sophisticated investors utilize some version of the Probalistic Pricing Model, which uses different inputs like age, gender, smoking, net worth, impairments and other medical information, policy vintage, and the appropriate mortality table to create an actual expected mortality curve over time. Depending on the age of the insured, the mortality table being used may have to be tweaked to reflect the fact that less life settlement-specific data was used in the older age results. Additional long-term mortality adjustments also need to be made for expected longevity drift over time for that insured's age group as the trend is people are living longer the later they were born as factors such as health and nutrition information and medical advances serve to increase average longevity over time. This adjustment is very subjective as some people think the mortality improvements will seek to reverse due to the reemergence of infection diseases and antibiotic-resistant strains of previously controlled viruses, the increased pollution of the world's air and water supplies, and the recent increase in obesity, especially in the United States as well as the future strains on the Social Security and health care systems as the percentage of elderly increases relative to the total population.

As discussed in Chapter 16, the published life expectancy value is an average of the expected mortality distribution for the insured based on the mathematical probabilities of survival to each possible age, and is of faint usefulness without other information about the mortality curve such as standard deviation, kurtosis, and skewness, which would define the exact shape of the insured's mortality curve. Absent this curve shape information, investors would be prudent to value the asset under different shock scenarios that not only cover a parallel shift of the expected mortality curve but also shape shifts of the curve to account for different standard deviations, kurtosis, and skewness values. For a large diversified portfolio with equal notional amounts per life, the blended mortality curves might mitigate most of the curve shape issue. For the curve shape risk to be minimized, the portfolio needs to be diversified not only by having many lives (at least 350 to minimize the dispersion of the standard deviation of life expectancy probabilities), but also by impairment, geographic region, socioeconomic group, and life expectancy, among others. Synthetic longevity instruments allow an investor to do this very easily and efficiently, unlike in trying to aggregate a physical portfolio. In addition, for a whole portfolio, the more diversification there is among risk characteristic factors, the less expected volatility there will be in expected returns and thus a higher degree of confidence in the models.

Once the underlying mortality curve is defined, two sets of cash flows will be generated based on the calculated probability of mortality curve for each period from today to the policy maturity. The probability of mortality curve, which can also be looked at as a probability of survival curve, will quantify the expected probability the insured will achieve mortality in each time period, or looked at another way, will survive to that point in time. This curve construction theory is similar to the probability of default curves seen in credit default swap models. It is possible for some of the mortality curve to extend past the policy maturity date, which will require an adjustment so that those remaining modeled death benefits don't get missed.

The first set of cash flows will be the expected premium outflows to maturity, or cost of insurance of the policy, and the second will be the expected death benefits received, both of which are proportionally related to the probability of mortality curve. Those cash flows are then discounted back to the present at the investors' required internal rate of return (IRR) to obtain a net present value (NPV) for the asset.

In addition to the valuation of the actual policy cash flows, an additional step must be taken to account for the premium financing built into the swap structure, whose need and cash flows will also be tied to the probability of mortality curve. The cost of financing for premiums will have a surprisingly large impact on the final NPV of the asset, so LIBOR curve modeling will have to be done to estimate future funding rates as most funding sources from swap counterparties tend to be spread over one-month LIBOR (sometimes three-month LIBOR depending on the swap terms).

One further comment about synthetic valuation is the initial calculated IRR upon trade execution will come to fruition if the actual mortalities over the life of the swap equal the expected (modeled) mortalities. There are no hidden costs like physical policies have that are usually not factored in by the purchaser when the initial IRR is calculated. These cause the realized return to be much less than expected. These costs include the legal and underwriting due diligence required when purchasing the policies as well as the annual servicing, administrative, and operations costs. In addition, the risk of rescission or lapse can crush returns if even a small percentage of the portfolio experiences them, which is not a risk present in synthetics.

CONCLUSION

For the sophisticated longevity investor, synthetics represent an opening of the proverbial sea into new avenues from which to obtain customized longevity risk and economics. They also provide the ability to go short as well as long, the flexibility to pick the investment time horizon, and the ability to mitigate the dangerous physical policy-specific risks and costs that are difficult to hedge against, all things not possible in the physical market. Also because there are no hidden costs in synthetics like there are in physicals, there is a higher degree of confidence in the expected returns which is a huge benefit to investors deciding where to deploy capital. Looking forward, innovation in synthetics structures driven by speculators' and hedgers' needs will continue for the foreseeable future and serve to further add efficiency and liquidity to an asset class that is experiencing tremendous growth as a whole.

About the Author

Vishaal B. Bhuyan is the founder and Managing Partner of V.B. Bhuyan & Co. which advises hedge funds, investment banks, and pension funds on the life markets. As an advisor, Vishaal works with institutional investors to develop trading and investment strategies that utilize newly developed structured products tethered to life insurance as well as longevity and mortality risk. Vishaal also publishes *The Wave Report*, a monthly market commentary on the life markets.

Vishaal's views on the life settlement industry have been published or referenced in several industry journals and research reports and he has delivered presentations on the economic context of the life markets at various industry conferences. Furthermore, his views on the life markets, the aging of the West, and pensions have been published by notable economists and investors such as Dr. Marc Faber (The Gloom, Boom, and Doom Report) and in Dr. Nouriel Roubini's RGE Monitor.

Vishaal was born in Norristown, PA, and attended the prestigious University of Pennsylvania where he earned his undergraduate degree in 2005. He got his start briefly working for Mark B. Fisher, president of the largest clearing firm on the New York Mercantile Exchange, who seeded Bhuyan's first venture into the secondary life insurance market, Global Insurance Exchange.

Index